1981

SOUTHERN LITERARY STUDIES

SOUTHERN LITERARY STUDIES

LOUIS D. RUBIN, JR.

Editor

A Season of Dreams: The Fiction of Eudora Welty
ALFRED APPEL, JR.

The Hero with the Private Parts
ANDREW LYTLE

Hunting in the Old South: Original Narratives of the Hunters
CLARENCE GOHDES, EDITOR

Joel Chandler Harris: A Biography
PAUL M. COUSINS

John Crowe Ransom: Critical Essays and a Bibliography
THOMAS DANIEL YOUNG, EDITOR

A Bibliographical Guide to the Study of Southern Literature
LOUIS D. RUBIN, JR., EDITOR

Poe: Journalist and Critic
ROBERT D. JACOBS

Love, Boy: The Letters of Mac Hyman
WILLIAM BLACKBURN, EDITOR

The Complete Works of Kate Chopin
PER SEYERSTED, EDITOR

Kate Chopin: A Critical Biography
PER SEYERSTED

Without Shelter: The Early Career of Ellen Glasgow
J. R. RAPER

Southern Excursions: Essays on Mark Twain and Others
LEWIS LEARY

SOUTHERN EXCURSIONS

SOUTHERN EXCURSIONS

Essays on Mark Twain and Others

§

LEWIS LEARY

LOUISIANA STATE UNIVERSITY PRESS BATON ROUGE

ISBN 0–8071–0938–X
Library of Congress Catalog Card Number 79–154269
Copyright © 1971 by Louisiana State University Press
All rights reserved
Manufactured in the United States of America
Printed by The Vail-Ballou Press, Binghamton, New York
Designed by J. Barney McKee

For George and Thelma

Preface

MOST OF THE following essays were written and published over many years. Though tempted to patch and mend what seem to me now to be occasional infelicities of thought or expression, I have left them much as they were, for it is among my convictions that an older man should almost always allow a younger man to speak without hindrance.

If it seems presumptuous that a person Yankee-born and Yankee-bred, and Irish-named at that, should speak of Southern writers, let me present two perhaps finally unnecessary explanations. First, and most important, I captured a Southern girl many years ago and, professional meetings and war permitting, have been with her ever since, we providing each other with two daughters, Southern-born and both captured in their turn, so that living and working and fathering, my best joys have been Southern, my love and my closest ties.

Beyond that, my exposure to the South has underlined for me the perfectly self-evident truth that its best products— literature, tobacco, and sour mash whiskey—are not produced for local consumption only, but gladden hearts and minds the world over. The instruction and pleasure which I have received from the writers about whom I write are shared by

other readers throughout the United States and across the
world. No one of them is guaranteed Southern solely. Each
extends his voice, or her voice, to cheer or admonish people of
various habitation who are often not at all concerned about
where these writers came from, only about what they have
said.

Like many others, I am not as convinced as several of my
friends are that Mark Twain is genuinely Southern, though
perhaps Samuel Clemens was, from whose brow Mark Twain
sprang full-blown in California when Clemens was almost
thirty. He costumed a later Mark Twain as an old-time
Southern gentleman, immaculate in white, and he spoke as
Mark Twain in a tempo and often in an idiom which we have
been pleased to believe resembled those of the Southwestern
frontier. But he allowed him to live in Hartford in Connecticut, in a house much too elaborately furbelowed for Southern
taste, and there to entertain such a Yankee vandal as Harriet
Beecher Stowe. Mark Twain once confessed having joined a
group of volunteers which intended to attach itself to the
Confederate army but which disbanded when it failed to find
an army to attach itself to. But Mark Twain is not always a
reliable witness in alibi for himself: Samuel Clemens sat out
most of that war among the mining camps and timberlands of
the West. Nor are most of Mark Twain's writings about the
South at all, though Arlin Turner and Louis Rubin, Southern-
born, remind me that his best writings are. Huck Finn in his
Adventures drifts southward amid prayer meetings, log houses,
and plantations, a blood feud, and an honorable, quick-
triggered Southern colonel. "Old Times on the Mississippi"
cannot be too often praised for what it reveals of the menace
and the charm of a great river which flows toward the South.

But each is greatly more than that, transcending place and
time. Mark Twain is prominent on any list of American
writers who are read with interest in Europe, partly, we must
suppose, because he exposes some of the very human venali-

ties of American people, but mostly, I am convinced, because he reveals something of the human condition which overrides nationality. In like manner, students whom I have taught in South America, Europe, Australia, and the Middle East, from Japan, India, and Ghana, have responded to William Faulkner, not because he tells them something of America or the American South, but because he speaks of people not unlike themselves who are driven by impulses, fears, and contradictions not unsimilar to their own. Kate Chopin, if she speaks for women shackled, speaks for all women. She has been translated in France as a link between George Sand and Simone de Beauvoir. Her biography has been written and her *Complete Works* collected by Per Seyersted, a Norwegian. George Arms, Kenneth Eble, Edmund Wilson, and Larzer Ziff, Northern gentlemen all, have led a growing chorus which chants admiration for her courage, insight, and compassion.

Only three of the writers about whom I write are Southern beyond dispute: Sidney Lanier most disastrously of all; William Faulkner, whose place is certified by his attitude toward the Negro; and George Washington Harris. Samuel Clemens and Kate Chopin were both born in Missouri (take that either way), but so were T. S. Eliot and Harry S. Truman. Though sage for many years in Baltimore, H. L. Mencken certainly would have thrown his stein at anyone who did not remember that he was proudly, and with some bravery, German-American with no ties to a Bible-belted Southland. Lafcadio Hearn was a foreigner who wrote more of the West Indies and greatly more of Japan than he did of Louisiana. But each has been designated by someone somewhere at some time as somehow Southern. Because Southern seems to me in large part a state of mind, I have therefore bundled them, however loosely, here together.

That is not to say that there is no such thing as Southern, in stereotype or fact. Nor am I going to bother a reader now as I have bothered friends over the past several years by trying to designate exactly what Southern is. I have long been a student of the subject, and I have done, I think, my home work reasonably well. After that, Frances Gray Patton has been my most admired instructor, partly because her home work is well done also. Among other things, she has taught me that there are three kinds of Southerners: the good people, the nice people, and others, and I have found that pattern to fit the South as snugly as anywhere else. Southerners have pride in family, like my New England relatives, the Adamses, or my New Jersey kin, the Gastons (there were two brothers, I have been told, and one went South, hence Gastonia, the other North, hence me). They have pride of place, like Bostonians or San Franciscans. They have an ingrown sense of position (Have you ever been an Irishman confronting a Massachusetts Brahmin?). They talk a lot, and not always consequentially, like my former neighbors in Westchester County, New York, or in Beirut, Lebanon. Southern girls pay a lot of attention to winning boys, and they cause their fathers to be very fond of them—this I do know. Southern boys drink a lot and sometimes—just sometimes—are not to be completely trusted.

Just as Mark Twain once said that he had never met a man anywhere in the world whose duplicate he had not met on the Mississippi River, so I (a stranger, but student also) can say that I have never met a Southerner whose twin in thought or deed I had not met somewhere else. Concerning Southerners, Mrs. Patton joined by Gertude Stein has taught me that people are people are people. If there is such a thing as Southern, and I think that there is (though you must decide which Southern, and when), then the people of whom I write are part of it, in subject, birth, breeding, or in recognition that the colonel's lady and the Irish girl are beneath veneer very much the same.

I would, if it were necessary, say a special word about William Faulkner, for he seems to me to be at once completely Southern and completely other things besides. And I wish that I had written as well as Mr. Turner and Mr. Rubin have about George Washington Cable, who presents so fine a figure against which to exercise notions of what Southern is or is not. Southern Robert Jacobs has written well of Boston-born Edgar Allan Poe (the last writer of note before Robert Lowell to be born in that city), who was Virginia-bred, but a Baltimorean, I suppose, as much as anything. To list those whom I know or you know to be Southern is to disclose a comforting variety of kinds, attitudes, and voices. As I walked across my campus this afternoon I heard some of those voices, shrill or slurred or deeply resonant. And as I searched for a common denominator, all that I could come up with was the not at all alarming fact that people who through chance or desire were born in or chose to live in the South spoke with a variety of voices, some of which pleased and others of which did not.

I confuse myself when I ask whether they think or write or act Southernly in the same way that other people tell me that people think or write or act New Englandly, Midwesternly, Californianly. And I retreat by supposing that perhaps they do about as much, but certainly no more. May I be excused therefore if I slip out to leave distinctions to those eager for distinction? I can satisfy myself by distinguishing between William Faulkner and Mark Twain, or between William Faulkner and Henry James, but only on grounds other than those on which they have lived or about which they write.

For like any art, literature seems to me unhappy and not at its jubilant best when bound by regional chains. I have been tempted to suppose that those of my friends who insist most strenuously on literature of this, the South, or of any other area-restricted kind, are interested in proving something about literature besides the exhilarating fact that it is literature which is literature which is literature, and which is disclosed not through definition but through exploration. And I am buoyed against their incursions by knowing that literature, when it is good, is tough enough to withstand any handling.

If some of my own explorations—excursions I have called them—have led me to people who are by definition or habitat or argument Southern, that may not have been completely accidental. Converted Southern by the best choice, which is marriage, and I sometimes like to think by disposition also, I have found among Southern friends a large variety of kinds of people who are like other people I have known somewhere else, only more so. For Southerners, if I may now distinguish, seem often more this or more that than many people, more at one end of the spectrum or the other, or more securely in the middle, or moving more swiftly, either way, from one point to another. They are people magnified and articulate, and my sympathy goes out to people who fail to find themselves among the people they write about, and it goes out most particularly to people who write themselves or the writers into enclosures of place.

What I have said here, or later, may not be greatly revealing: talking about literature is less likely to be than is literature itself. If my remarks lead anyone to, or back to, the people whom I have read with pleasure, I shall be pleased, even if his excursion proves mine to have been misdirected. But even without that, my excursions have been fun, and that is one of the things which literature, even writing about it, provides.

LEWIS LEARY

Chapel Hill
October, 1970

Acknowledgments

THESE ESSAYS HAVE appeared in various books and journals
and are reprinted here by permission.

"Mark Twain and the Comic Spirit" is slightly shortened
from Lewis Leary, *Mark Twain*, University of Minnesota
Pamphlets on American Writers, No. 5. Minneapolis: University of Minnesota Press. Copyright © 1960 by the University of Minnesota.

"Mark Twain's Wound: Standing with Reluctant Feet" is
reduced from the introduction to *A Casebook on Mark
Twain's Wound*. New York: Thomas Y. Crowell Company,
1962.

"The Bankruptcy of Mark Twain" appeared in somewhat
different states in the *Carrell*, June, 1968, and as "Mark
Twain among the Malefactors," in *Sense and Sensibility in
Twentieth-Century Writing*, ed. Brom Weber. Carbondale:
Southern Illinois University Press, 1970. Much of the material
in this essay derives from my introduction to and annotations
on *Mark Twain's Correspondence with Henry Huttleston
Rogers* (Berkeley: University of California Press, 1969).

"On Writing about Writers: Especially Mark Twain" appeared in the *Southern Review*, Spring, 1968.

"Tom and Huck: Innocence on Trial" appeared in the *Virginia Quarterly Review*, Summer, 1954.

"The Forlorn Hope of Sidney Lanier" appeared in the *South Atlantic Quarterly*, April, 1947.

"Lafcadio Hearn, 'One of Our Southern Writers' " appeared in *Essays on American Literature in Honor of Jay B. Hubbell*, ed. Clarence Gohdes. Durham, N.C.: Duke University Press, 1967.

"The Awakening of Kate Chopin" is adapted from the introduction to *The Awakening and Other Stories*. Introduction copyright © 1970 by Holt, Rinehart and Winston, Inc. Reprinted by permission of Holt, Rinehart and Winston, Inc.

"Kate Chopin's Other Novel" appeared in the *Southern Literary Journal*, December, 1968.

"H. L. Mencken and the Reluctant Human Race" appeared under the unfortunate title "H. L. Mencken: Changeless Critic in Changing Times" in *The Young Rebel in American Literature*. London, Melbourne, Toronto: Heineman, 1959.

"William Faulkner and the Grace of Comedy" is somewhat altered from the introduction to *Crowell's Handbook on Faulkner*, ed. Dorothy Tuck. New York: Thomas Y. Crowell Company, 1964.

Contents

SOUTHERN EXCURSIONS

1

Mark Twain and the Comic Spirit

MOST AMERICANS REGARD Mark Twain with special affection. They know him as a shaggy man who told stories of boy adventures so like their own or those they would like to have had that they become intimately a part of personal experience. His cheerful irreverence and unhurried pace seem antidotes for attitudes to which they necessarily but unwillingly surrender. His is the image of what they like to think Americans have been or can be: humorously perceptive, undeceived by sham, successful in spite of circumstances because of distinctive personal characteristics.

More often than not they smile approvingly at his portrayal of man as "a museum of diseases, a home of impurities," who "begins as dirt and departs as stench," created for no apparent purpose except the nourishment and entertainment of microbes. The words seem bold and appropriately bitter, iconoclastically vulgar but, for all of that, funny. Evolution failed when man appeared, for his is the only bad heart in all the animal kingdom; only he is capable of malice, vindictiveness; drunkenness; when he is not cruel, he is stupid, like a sheep. It does seem such a pity, commented Mark Twain, that Noah and his companions did not miss their boat. And he tempts

readers toward the compulsive nightmare of our time by
wondering if a device might not be invented which could
exterminate man by withdrawing all oxygen from the air for
two minutes.

They admire Mark Twain's hardheaded exposures of human
venality, but respond also to his unembarrassed sentiment, his
compassion and simple humility. What any man sees in the
human race, he once admitted, "is merely himself in the deep
and private honesty of his own heart." Everything human is
pathetic: "The secret source of Humor itself is not joy but
sorrow. There is no humor in heaven." He would have agreed
with Robert Frost that earth is the right place for love, but
would have added that it is inevitably also the place for stumbling and then forgetting the hurt by recalling or inventing
other, older, and less disreputable times.

No wonder then that Ernest Hemingway found all American literature to begin with Mark Twain. His escape to adventure, to the past, to humor which moves through and beyond
reality, is not unlike Hemingway's escape from thinking
through the simpler pleasures of wine, women, and manly exercise. Not only is Mark Twain's simple declarative style a
parent of Hemingway's style; not only is his boy's-eye view of
the world like Hemingway's view, like Willa Cather's, Sherwood Anderson's, even J. D. Salinger's; the publication of
The Mysterious Stranger in 1916 reveals him mastered by the
same cluster of opinions which produced the retreat to older
times of Henry Adams, as well as the despair of the "lost
generation" of Hemingway and Scott Fitzgerald, and the
wasted land of T. S. Eliot.

It was as difficult to convince people of his time as it is to
convince people of ours that Mark Twain never really existed
except as a character, costumed and carefully rehearsed, cannily
a crowd-pleaser. For in both a literary and psychological sense
the shambling but perceptive humorist remembered as Mark
Twain is a mask, a controlled, drawling, and whimsical voice,

a posturing and flamboyant figure, behind which exists the man, Samuel Langhorne Clemens, who with the help of circumstance and receptive wit created him. Some would explain them, the image and the man, as twins, and Clemens as a man divided, but this is not in any real sense true. The image is partly self-portrait and, indeed, partly self-defense, but shrewdly retouched until the character who is Mark Twain becomes Clemens' most successful achievement, and the voice of Mark Twain speaks in a special literary relation to its creator.

It is probably true that the two became as confused in Clemens' mind as they have in the minds of people who have talked about Mark Twain, but the distinction is radical. Which is which or who did what to whom remains an important critical puzzle. To simplify more than is appropriate, it can be suggested that Mark Twain was a character who inserted himself, sometimes with joyous abandon, into almost everything which Samuel Clemens wrote. He was irrepressible but self-conscious, alert to his responsibilities as diagnostic spokesman for his time and as representative of much which wove itself into the pattern of contemporary notions of success. But failure to remember that Mark Twain was a medium through whom stories were told, and that he was only in an indirect sense their author, is to fall into the attractively baited trap which opens even more invitingly before commentators on such other American writers as Whitman, Thoreau, and Hemingway, whose masks are more subtle and less clearly designated.

Which spoke when cannot always be determined, nor is the distinction in every case important, except that in some of the writings, and many of them the best, the burden of being Mark Twain is discarded and a voice speaks directly, undistorted by comic pose or anger. Either could have admitted, as one of them did, that his books were like water and the books of great geniuses like wine, but it was surely Mark Twain who supplied the twister to remind us that "everyone drinks water." Part of his character was that of a man among littérateurs, a journalist who detested, he said, novels and poetry, but who liked history, biography, curious facts, and strange happenings.

It has not been necessary for Americans to read Mark Twain in order to remember him with affection. Probably more people know of Tom Sawyer's slick method of getting a fence whitewashed than have read the book in which it appears. Hollywood versions of Tom and Huck, of the prince who became a pauper, or of the Yankee from Connecticut who brought American know-how to King Arthur's court have reached millions of viewers, as originally filmed or as adapted for television. A popular comedian has danced and sung his way through a celluloid Camelot. A spectacular Negro boxer has played the runaway slave whose simple loyalty confuses, then converts, Huck Finn. Tom Sawyer has tripped barefooted through a musical comedy, and plans have been considered for a musical adaptation of *Innocents Abroad*. More than one actor has found it profitable to dress and drawl as Mark Twain did, and to hold an audience laughter-bound by retelling some of the tales he told.

Mark Twain's laconic, soft speech, whimsical understatements, and outrageous exaggerations made him a platform favorite and pampered after-dinner speaker for more than forty years, and his witticisms were passed by word of mouth and faithfully recorded in newspapers. He saw to that, for he was in every best sense a showman who kept himself and his books effectively before the public. His heavy shock of hair, once red, but soon an eye-catching white, made him seem larger than he was, an illusion which it pleased him later in life to reinforce by dressing summer and winter in white linen or serge. He learned early how to attract and hold attention, and he used the knowledge well. One way or another, he was the best known and most successfully published author of his generation.

He saw to that also, for—within limits—he was the canny businessman he liked to think himself. His lectures sold his books, and his books helped pack his lectures. As a publisher, he took pride in gauging public taste so well that each book supplied a popular demand. Many were not issued until subscription agents throughout the country had sold in advance enough copies to make them surely profitable. And subscription books in the late nineteenth century were gaudily attractive books, usually handsomely bound and illustrated— the kind almost anyone would be proud to have on his table, particularly when the author had just been or would soon be in town for a lecture.

For these reasons, though not only for these, Mark Twain's books found themselves in a preferred position in thousands of American homes. At the end of the century, he offered a twenty-two-volume Autograph Edition of his works, which found its way into thousands more, and into libraries, even small town and county libraries which could not afford to buy it but received it as a gift when house shelves became crowded or when it was replaced by the new, twenty-five-volume Underwood Edition a few years later. Shortly before Mark Twain's death in 1910 the Author's National Edition began to appear, and then, in the 1920's, the "definitive edition" in thirty-seven volumes. Few authors, perhaps not even Balzac or Dickens, achieved greater shelf space during their lifetime.

Such success has seemed appropriate, for it fit precisely to patterns which Americans have thought peculiarly their own. Mark Twain was a poor boy who by reason of native skill rose to wealth and fame. He was kin to Daniel Boone or Andrew Jackson because he had known the rigors of our frontier. Abraham Lincoln's rise from log cabin to President created a norm of which his career was a verifying variation—indeed, William Dean Howells called him the Lincoln of our literature. He had worked with his hands, like Andrew Carnegie, and then had a large house and servants. These things testified to the validity of what Emerson had said of the divine sufficiency of the individual. Here in truth was the powerful, uneducated, democratic personality for whom Whitman had called. Mark Twain walked with kings and capitalists, but never lost the common touch. In his mansion at Hartford, his residence on Fifth Avenue, or his country place at Stormfield, he still remembered old times and old friends.

This popular image was never completely an accurate likeness, but is sufficiently well drawn to remain attractive. Samuel Langhorne Clemens was born on November 30, 1835, on the Missouri frontier, in a straggling log village called Florida, to which his parents had come from their former home among the hills of Tennessee. His father was a local magistrate and small merchant, originally from Virginia, who had studied law in Kentucky and there met and married auburn-haired Jane Lampton, descended from settlers who had followed Daniel Boone across the mountains. One among thousands of Americans who in the early decades of the nineteenth century moved westward to seek opportunities in newly opened lands, John Marshall Clemens did not prosper in the hamlet in which his third son was born, and so, when Samuel was four years old, moved to Hannibal, a larger town with a population of almost five hundred, on the banks of the Mississippi River.

There, beside this river, Samuel Clemens grew through boyhood much as Tom Sawyer did, fascinated by the life which swarmed over its mile-wide surface or which sought refuge or sustenance on its shores. Through this frontier region passed the picturesque, sometimes mendacious or menacing pilgrims of restlessly expanding America, up or down the river or across it toward the Western plains. Young Samuel must have watched, as any boy might, admiringly, but fearfully also. He saw men maimed or killed in waterfront brawls, Negroes chained like animals for transportation to richer slave markets to the south. He had nightmares and walked in his sleep, and always remembered these things, the rude ways and tremendous talk, and the terror.

Better things were remembered also, like giant rafts and trading scows piled with produce or sweet-smelling timber, coming from or going where a boy could only guess. Gallant river steamers left wake behind in which small boys swimming or in boats could ride excitedly. Below the village lay wooded Holliday Hill, unrivaled for play at Robin Hood or pirate, and near its summit a cave tempting for exploration. Away from its boisterous riverfront, the village was "a heavenly place for a boy," he said, providing immunities and graces which he never forgot: hunting and fishing, a swimming hole, an inevitable graveyard, truant days at Glasscock's Island, and yearnings toward the better freedom of Tom Blankenship, the town drunkard's son, to whom truancy brought no penalties of conscience or recrimination.

But these days were soon over, for when Samuel was twelve years old, his father died, and the boy was apprenticed to local printers, and then—partaking of a tradition which Benjamin Franklin had established a century before—worked as compositor and pressman for his older brother Orion, who managed a not completely successful newspaper in Hannibal. There was room in its pages for humorous features which young Samuel composed, set in type, and printed over the flamboyant signature "W. Spaminodas Adrastas Blab" and for miscellaneous items which he collected for "Our Assistant's Column." He even ventured verse, addressing one poem over the signature of "Rambler" ambiguously to "Miss Katie in H——l." The appropriation of so timeworn a pseudonym seems less indicative of literary consciousness than descriptive of desire. Samuel Clemens was not yet a rambler, though he wanted to be, for—again like Franklin—he chafed under the discipline of a brother, or anyone else.

By the time he was seventeen he was able to think of himself as something more than a local writer. In May, 1852, "The Dandy Frightening the Squatter" appeared in the *Carpet-Bag,* a sportsman's magazine in Boston, signed "S.L.C." Done in the slapstick tradition of native humor

such as was being written or was soon to be written by pseud-
onymous favorites like Sam Slick, Orpheus C. Kerr, and
Artemus Ward, it anticipates much of the later manner of
Mark Twain: it celebrates the laconic shrewdness of the
frontiersman; is told with some of the exaggerated flourishes
of the Western tall tale, seasoned with caricaturing strokes
which may have been learned, even indirectly, from Dickens;
and is laid in Hannibal on the Mississippi River. Comparison
of its tone and language with Nathaniel Hawthorne's *The
Blithedale Romance* or Herman Melville's *Pierre*, which also
appeared in that year, suggests some of the things which, for
better or worse, were happening or about to happen to writing
in the United States.

But wanderlust soon hit young Samuel Clemens, so that he
became in fact a rambler. At eighteen he left little Hannibal
for St. Louis, the largest town in Missouri, where he saved his
wages carefully until he could strike out beyond the limits of
his Western state, to discover whether a young man's fortune
might not be more quickly made in larger cities to the east.
He traveled first, by steamboat and rail, through Chicago and
Buffalo to New York, where he worked briefly as a job printer,
until he moved southward to become a compositor in Philadelphia and later Washington, then again to Philadelphia,
then west to Muscatine, Iowa, to set type for his almost
equally peripatetic brother. Soon he was back in St. Louis,
and then once more, for two years this time, joined his
brother, now in Keokuk, Iowa.

Two years, however, was a long time for a rambler to remain in one place, and his fortune certainly was not being
made. He spent the winter of 1856–57 in Cincinnati, but this
was a way stop, for he had hit on the notion that a young man
almost twenty-two might do well and have fun besides exploring opportunities for riches in South America, along the
lush banks of the Amazon. So it was that in April, 1857—the
date is a turning point—he started down the Mississippi

toward New Orleans, on his first step toward fame. What happened then—his meeting with the veteran steamboat pilot Horace Bixby, his own apprentice pilot days, his four years of life on the Mississippi—has often been told, and never better than by Clemens himself as he later remembered these years and threw about them the color of romance which only made more persuasive the realism of his detail.

But the abortive trip to South America is remembered for other reasons also, for to make it Samuel Clemens entered into a professional engagement of a kind which later would bring him worldwide acclaim. At Keokuk he shaped the first piece of the pattern which would make continued wanderings possible, even profitable, by arranging with the editor of the *Evening Post* that Samuel Clemens, rambler, would supply reports as regularly as possible on what he saw and did on his ramblings. Only three now appeared, probably because Clemens was deep in the more exciting business of learning to pilot a steamboat. Signed "Thomas Jefferson Snodgrass," they were desperately, self-consciously humorous, hardly distinguishable in language or tone from the work of any other journeyman journalist.

Snodgrass was a name always infinitely funny to Clemens. He used it again in writings in California; more than thirty years later in *The American Claimant* he presented two characters, "Zylobalsamum Snodgrass" and "Spinal Meningitis Snodgrass"; and in *Tom Sawyer Abroad* he spoke of the "celebrated author . . . Snodgrass." While steamboating on the Mississippi from 1857 to 1861, a licensed pilot by the spring of 1859, he is said to have contributed letters signed "Quintius Curtius Snodgrass" to the New Orleans *Daily Crescent*, and is said also to have written a burlesque of the pontifical river lore which a retired steamboat captain named Isaiah Sellers printed in a New Orleans paper over the signature of "Mark Twain." A favorite but unverifiable tradition insists that Captain Sellers was so hurt by the ridicule and

Samuel Clemens so conscience-stricken at the wound he had given that a few years later the younger man adopted the old captain's pseudonym—which, as everyone knows, is the leadsman's cry to the pilot when water which is safe, but barely safe, lies ahead.

When in 1861 the Civil War cut across the Mississippi so that river traffic from North to South or South to North was no longer possible, steamboating ceased to be a profitable occupation, and Samuel Clemens was without work. He took only a minor part in the War Between the States: one not very dependable account suggests that he was detailed for river duty; the New Orleans Snodgrass letters suggest that he had some connection with militia drill in that city; and Mark Twain later delighted readers of the *Atlantic Monthly* with a humorous "Private History of a Campaign That Failed," which tells how he and a few companions formed themselves into an irregular company which searched vainly for a unit of the Confederate army to which it might become attached. Whatever his service, it was brief and with the rebellious Southern forces—a circumstance which is supposed to have made the later Northernized Mark Twain extraordinarily circumspect in speaking of it.

In the summer of 1861 Clemens went farther west, with his brother Orion, who had been rewarded for activity in Abraham Lincoln's campaign for the presidency by appointment as secretary of the newly opened Nevada Territory. Orion Clemens, never greatly successful, had little money, but brother Samuel, after profitable years as a river pilot, apparently had his pockets full and provided stage fare for both, traveling himself as unpaid secretary to the new secretary of the territory. The story of their journey across the plains and experiences in Carson City is later recounted in *Roughing It*, in which, as Huck Finn said of him on another occasion, "Mr. Mark Twain . . . he told the truth, mainly." Here we learn of his adventures in staking out timber claims near Lake

Tahoe, only carelessly to leave his campfire unattended so that much of the forest went up in flames. He tells of money invested in silver mines, as he and Orion were caught up in a wild seeking for wealth. Once he was a millionaire for ten days when he found a rich mine, but lost it through carelessness again. Stories of Samuel Clemens in Nevada, variously told by himself or by people who knew him, make up a large share of the public image of Mark Twain. A loose, shambling man, with unruly hair, who lounged about the frontier town in corduroys and shirt sleeves, swapping stories and listening to the way men spoke, he was ready, we are told, to take his chance with the best or worst at poker or in wildcat speculation.

Before he had been in Nevada a year, however, he was back at his old trade as a writer for newspapers, contributing burlesque sketches over the signature of "Josh" to the *Territorial Enterprise* in Virginia City. There he lived freely among friends like fiery Steve Gillis, a printer whose escapades were to keep them both in trouble. The unrestraint of that remarkable frontier paper stimulated Clemens to such journalistic hoaxes as "The Petrified Man" and "The Dutch Nick Massacre," which to his joy were copied as true in Eastern papers. Here he first met Artemus Ward and spent convivial evenings with the popular humorist, who advised him how Mark Twain—for Clemens was now using that name—might extend his reputation. Already known as the Washoe Giant, the wild humorist of the Sage Brush Hills, famed as far as California, Samuel Clemens was ambitious for something more.

But then he ran afoul of an anti-dueling statute when he challenged a rival newspaperman, and he and loyal Steve Gillis beat their way in the spring of 1864 to California, where a range of hills stood between them and Nevada jails. Clemens worked briefly as a reporter on the San Francisco *Call*, but it was "fearful drudgery," he said, "an awful slavery for a lazy man," so he left regular employment to free-lance for the *Golden Era* and Bret Harte's *Californian*. Then he became San Francisco correspondent for his former paper in Virginia City, until he ran headlong against the law again when Steve Gillis was arrested for barroom brawling and released on bail which Clemens supplied. Then when dapper Steve skipped over the mountains back to Nevada, his protector thought it appropriate to leave also.

This time he took flight to the Sierras, where he stayed on Jackass Hill with Steve Gillis' brother Jim, a teller of tales who was to receive later renown as Bret Harte's "Truthful James." Here, at Angel's Camp, he heard old Ross Coon tell of "The Celebrated Jumping Frog of Calaveras County." Clemens wrote it down, this "villainous, backwoods sketch," in just the rhythm of dialect in which Ross Coon told it, and he sent it east to be placed in a book of yarns to which Artemus Ward had asked him to contribute. By fortunate mischance it arrived too late for burial in Ward's collection. Instead, it was pirated by the New York *Evening Post* and became an immediate favorite, copied in newspapers all across the country, even in California to give its author prestige there as an Eastern writer. For all the good it did him—he made nothing from it.

At just this time, in 1865, the Pacific Steamboat Company began regular passenger service between San Francisco and Honolulu, and Clemens took the trip, paying for it with letters to the Sacramento *Union*, thus setting to final form the pattern which four years later was to establish Mark Twain's reputation with *Innocents Abroad*. These Sandwich Island letters are exuberant, and sometimes vulgar. With him traveled an imaginary, completely irrepressible companion named Mr. Brown, whose sweetheart, he boasted, was so elegant that she picked her nose with a fork. When passengers became seasick, "Brown was there, ever kind and thoughtful, passing from one to the other and saying, 'That's all right—

that's all right you know—it'll clean you out like a jog, and then you won't feel so awful and smell so ridiculous.' " It was good for Mark Twain to have someone to hide behind, and good especially for Samuel Clemens who could disguise timidities doubly removed.

Mark Twain liked these lovely Pacific islands: "I would rather smell Honolulu at sunset," he wrote, "than the old Police courtroom in San Francisco." And he liked the islanders, who "always squat on their hams and who knows but they may be the original 'ham sandwiches.' " He liked their customs, especially the "demoralizing *hula hula*," which was forbidden "save at night, with closed doors . . . by permission of the authorities and the payment of ten dollars for the same." Sometimes he became almost lyrical about the beauties of the islands, but when he did, Mr. Brown pulled him up short to remind him that there were also in Honolulu "more 'sentipedes' and scorpions and spiders and mosquitoes and missionaries" than anywhere else in the world.

Clemens had now found the work which suited him best: he could ramble as he pleased and pay his way by being informative and funny, and donning masks which might excuse irresponsibility. In December, 1866, he signed with the *Alta California*, the West's most prominent paper, as its "travelling correspondent . . . not stinted as to place, time or direction," who would circle the globe and write letters as he went. The first step in the journey was to New York, the long way around, by boat, and with the ebullient Mr. Brown beside him. The letters written then are more lively than any he had done before, and without the restraints in concession to taste of his later travel accounts. Here he presents the jovial Captain Wakeman, whose tall tales, profanity, and Biblical lore were to live again in Captain Blakely in *Roughing It* and in Captain Stormfield, who made a voyage to heaven. There is sentimentality in the account of a runaway couple married at sea, and slapstick aplenty in Mr. Brown's further inelegant concern with seasick passengers, but there is compassion also as Mark Twain writes of the misery of cholera in Nicaragua, and anger as he snarls at gouging Floridians.

When he arrives in New York, the letters take on fresh vigor, and reveal much which is sometimes said to be characteristic of an older Mark Twain. The "overgrown metropolis" had changed mightily since he had seen it thirteen years before when he was a "pure and sinless sprout." He looked with indignation now on the squalor of her slums, where the "criminally, sinfully, wickedly poor" lived amid filth and refuse, victims of their "good, kind-hearted, fat, benevolent" neighbors. His social investigations came to climax when he was arrested for disorderly conduct and spent the night in jail, enraged as he talked with tramps, prostitutes, and former soldiers, pawns at the mercy of society's whim. It is not necessary to turn to a later Mark Twain for records of pessimism which damns the whole human race. It is solidly a part of him at thirty. Sin bothered him, even when he was being funny about it.

In New York he saw to the publication of his first book, *The Celebrated Jumping Frog of Calaveras County and Other Sketches*, just as he set out again to continue his wanderings, not around the world, but on an excursion to the Mediterranean and Near East on the steamship *Quaker City*. The letters which he sent back then, to the California paper and also to Horace Greeley's *Tribune* in New York, reached a public ripe for appreciation of his confident assumption that many hallowed shrines of the Old World did not measure up to American standards. And such was public response to what he wrote that, when he returned to New York a few months later, the wild mustang of the Western plains discovered himself a literary lion, sought by magazines, newspapers, lecture audiences, and publishers.

Caught up by currents of popularity, Samuel Clemens from this time forward was swept from one success to another. He had struck his bonanza, not in silver as he had once dreamed, but in selling his jocund alter ego in print and from the platform. He met and, after dogged courtship, married Olivia Langdon, daughter of a wealthy New York industrialist. With money advanced by his future father-in-law, he bought a share in a newspaper in Buffalo. The rambler finally would settle down, not permanently as an editor, for that occupation soon palled, but in a magnificent house which royalties and lecture fees would allow him to build in Hartford. He was through, he said, "with literature and all that bosh."

But when *The Innocents Abroad; or, The New Pilgrim's Progress* appeared in 1869, revised from the *Quaker City* letters (with Mr. Brown's offensive commentary, for example, deleted), reviewers found it "fresh, racy, and sparkling as a glass of champagne." The satire was alert, informed, sophisticated, and sidesplittingly funny. The accent was of Western humor, but the subject, a favorite among men of good will since the Enlightenment of the century before, spoke of the decay of transatlantic institutions and their shoddiness beside the energetic freshness of the New World. Traveling American innocents haggled through native bazaars, delightedly conscious that every language but their own was ridiculous, and unconscious completely of their own outlandishness. Venice was magnificent, though her boatmen were picturesquely absurd, but the Arno at Florence was darkened by blood shed by the Medici on its shores. The Holy Land was hot and dirty, filled with beggars and larcenous dragomans— when confronted by a boatman at Galilee who demanded exorbitant fare, one of the pilgrims remarked, "No wonder Jesus walked." Because he was clever or because he was by nurture one of them, Clemens touched attitudes shared by many of his countrymen, even to admitting preference for copies of masterpieces because they were brighter than the originals.

To many readers *The Innocents Abroad* remains Clemens'

second-best book, finding place in their affection behind *Adventures of Huckleberry Finn* and just ahead of, or side by side with, *Life on the Mississippi*. As if anticipating Henry James, it takes a fresh look at the transatlantic world and the stature of Americans when measured against its requirements. Without James's subtlety, conscious art, or depth of penetration, it discovers faults on both sides so that it becomes a book which cosmopolites and chauvinists can equally admire. The hearty and headlong inelegance of the earlier, more carelessly devised travel letters has been pruned from it, and not only because Mark Twain was surrendering to prudish and Victorian notions of propriety. In submitting to the demands of public taste, Clemens was also learning something of the possibilities of converting a casual colloquialism to art.

Roughing It, in 1871, was also greatly successful, suited, said one commentator, "to the wants of the rich, the poor, the sad, the gay," and a sure recipe for laughter. Again it was a book of traveling, the kind that Mark Twain was always to write best, in which one story after another was strung along a journey overland or on water. Every ingredient was here— the tall tale, the straight-faced shocker, melodrama in adventure, insight into raw life among men unrestrained by convention, folklore and animal lore. The effect was of improvisation, for narrative must flow, Clemens later said, as a stream flows, diverted by every boulder, but proceeding briskly, interestingly, on its course.

Such motion did not characterize *The Gilded Age*, published in 1873, which he wrote in collaboration with his Hartford neighbor, Charles Dudley Warner. For the opening chapters Clemens drew on recollections of frontier life to produce situations not unlike those we associate with *Tobacco Road* or *Li'l Abner*, where backcountry people dream expansively of fortunes they have neither energy nor ability to acquire. Colonel Beriah Sellers is a hill-town Mr. Micawber, but drawn from memory of people, even relatives, whom

Samuel Clemens had known. Some of the river scenes are beautifully realized. And as the locale shifts to Washington and New York, the novel touches with satirical humor on political corruption, the American jury system, and the mania for speculation, so that it became a best seller and gave title to the age which it reviewed. But artistically it was not a success, for the narrative finally collapses under the weight of plot and counterplot, and is not remembered as one of Mark Twain's best.

Given a story to tell, Clemens was almost always able to tell it well. As raconteur he had come to maturity in *Innocents Abroad*. But the invention of stories did not come easily to him. As he approached forty, he felt written out. He collected miscellaneous writings in *Sketches Old and New* and, with an eye on the market, tried to fit further adventures of the popular Colonel Sellers into a new book which failed to go well but which he published many years later, in 1891, as *The American Claimant*. He labored over a boy's story based on his early life in Hannibal, but that did not go well either.

Finally, at the suggestion of a friend, he recalled his years of steamboating and wrote, with hardly any posturing at all, of "Old Times on the Mississippi" in seven installments for the *Atlantic Monthly* in 1875. Eight years later he was to add thirty-nine chapters to make the book called *Life on the Mississippi*, but the added material, arduously compiled, recaptures little of the charm of these earlier portions. In them the viewpoint is consistently that of a boy bound by the spell of the Mississippi who becomes a pilot and learns her secrets. It is a story of an initiation. Seen from the pilothouse, the river loses much of her glamour; beneath her beauty, painted by sun and shaded by clouds, lurked an implacable menace of snags, hidden reefs, and treacherously changing shores. The face of the water was a wonderful book, he said, which he was never to forget, and piloting was a profession Clemens loved more than any he followed again: "a pilot in those days was

the only unfettered and entirely independent human being
that lived on the earth."

On the river he became "personally and familiarly acquainted with about all the different types of human nature
to be found in fiction, biography, or history." He never read
of or met anyone again without "warm personal interest in
him, for the reason that I had known him before—met him
on the river." But for all its attention to remembered detail,
"Old Times on the Mississippi" was not in the strictest sense
realistic. Its narrator seldom looked aside to notice people not
admitted to the pilothouse, like the sharpers, gamblers, and
painted women who plied a profitable trade on Mississippi
steamers, but kept his eyes on the river and his mind on the
discipline she demanded from men who knew her charm but
also her mystery and menace, who were skilled, not only in
finding their own way among her dangers, but in guiding
others safely through. Thus a reminiscent account becomes
more than re-creation of times that are gone and will not return because steamboating, like the whaling of which Melville
wrote in *Moby Dick*, was the product of a way of life which
was past. It speaks of appearance as opposed to reality, of innocence and experience, of man's duty in a world of perils,
and also of a conception of the function of literature.

The Mississippi River appeared triumphantly again in *The
Adventures of Tom Sawyer*, which in 1876 placed Mark Twain
once more at the head of best-seller lists. Probably no more
continuingly popular book has ever appeared in the United
States. On first reading it seems loose and shambling—as
Mark Twain was loose and shambling. Episodes designed "to
pleasantly remind adults of what they once were themselves"
often remain longer in memory than the plot of murder and
pursuit which must have been intended to hold younger readers. But there is artistry in it also, beyond the artistry of the
raconteur who engraved minor realisms about provincial society for all time. Perhaps because he worked long over it,

this first independent novel, published when its author was forty, is better constructed than any he was to write again. And its structure reveals levels of meaning which Mark Twain may not have known were there.[1] Its underlying theme of the excellence of simple innocence, imaginative and irrepressible and superior to adult methods of confronting the world, was one to which Mark Twain would often return.

After several years of miscellaneous publications, which included the popular, now forgotten, *Punch, Brothers, Punch and Other Sketches* in 1878 and a second account of European travel, *A Tramp Abroad*, in 1880, Clemens turned to the theme again in *The Prince and the Pauper*, in 1882, but with less success. The account of Tom Canty's adventures in the court of Edward VI was again addressed to boys and girls, tested by readings of the manuscript to the Clemens children and the children of friends, but it was addressed also to adults as an expression of its author's continuing assurance that, for all its shortcomings, democracy as practiced in the United States was superior to any other manner of living anywhere. It is the kind of melodramatic story which Tom Sawyer might have told, of a poor boy who became heir to a king and of a prince who learned humility through mixing with common men.

"My idea," Clemens told one of his friends, "is to afford a realistic sense of the severity of the laws of that day by inflicting some of their penalties upon the king himself." Poverty which brutalizes and restrictive statutes which force men to thievery are ridiculed, as well as superstition and meaningless ritual. The language of old England, with which Mark Twain had experimented in the surreptitiously printed, mildly ribald *1601, or Conversation as It Was by the Fireside in the Time of the Tudors*, two years before, comes in for a full share of burlesque. When Tom's nose "itcheth cruelly," he asks, "What is the custom and usage of this emergence?" He

[1] See "Tom and Huck: Innocence on Trial," pp. 96–110 below.

fills his pockets with nuts and uses the Royal Seal to crack them. When Henry VIII dies and his funeral is delayed to an appropriate ceremonial time in the future, the boy observes, " 'Tis strange folly. Will he keep?" Hardly any of the kinds of humor which the public had come to expect from Mark Twain, or of sagacious insight into the frailties of man, is left out of *The Prince and the Pauper*.

In spite of this and largely, Clemens thought, because he had changed to a new publisher, inexperienced in selling copies in great number by subscription, *The Prince and the Pauper* did not do as well commercially as Mark Twain's previous books. So Clemens established his own publishing house and launched it in 1885 with another boy's book which he was careful to link in the public mind to his earlier, encouragingly popular account of young life beside the Mississippi by identifying its hero in a subtitle as "Tom Sawyer's comrade." But *Adventures of Huckleberry Finn* made no such immediate impression as its predecessor. At Concord in Massachusetts, still the mecca of genteel New England cultural aspiration, it was banished from the local library as presenting a bad example for youth. Years later, it was blacklisted in Denver, Omaha, and even Brooklyn. When chapters from it appeared in the *Century Magazine*, some readers found it indefensibly coarse, "destitute of a single redeeming quality."

But *Adventures of Huckleberry Finn* has outlived almost every criticism of those who have spoken against it to become a native classic thrust forward exultantly in the face of any who still dare inquire, "Who reads an American book?"—its health endangered only by a smothering swarm of commentators who threaten to maim it with excessive kind attention. Except perhaps for *Moby Dick*, no American book has recently been opened with more tender explicatory care or by critics to whom we are better prepared to listen. The river on which or beside which the action develops is a great brown god to T. S. Eliot; and Lionel Trilling reminds us of the "subtle, implicit moral meaning of the great river" as he translates Emerson to contemporary idiom by explaining that "against the money-god stands the river-god, whose comments are silent," that Huck is "the servant of the river-god," and that Mr. Eliot is right in saying, "The river is within us."

Other commentators call attention to the social criticism, the satire, the savagery in this book of boy adventures; to its language so cleanly direct and simply natural that reasons for Hemingway's admiration for it come to mind; to its structure which is at one time or to one critic great art, at another fumbling improvisation; to the recurrent imagery, so like what E. M. Forster pointed to in writings of Marcel Proust and called repetition by variation. Its mythic quality is explained as reinforced by elements of popular lore and superstition or by parallels with primitive initiation rites. The once familiar three-part division of the blackface minstrel show, a genuinely indigenous art form, has been superimposed on *Adventures of Huckleberry Finn* to reveal instructive similarities. Various interpretations of its theme, some inevitably religious, have been patiently explored. Its endlessness, as if the adventures might have gone on forever, has been persuasively held forth as similar to other distinctively American contrivances which emphasize process rather than product, like the skyscraper, jazz, the comic strip, chewing gum, and *Moby Dick*.

These things are all probably true, if only because attentive readers have discovered them. An encompassing and synthesizing rightness reveals itself now in the casual career of Samuel Clemens, who drifted from one occupation to another, managing by accident of birth and qualities which moralists cannot always hold up for emulation to have been at many right places at exactly the right time. His was indeed a pioneer talent, and sometimes so unused to itself that it postured boisterously, almost always ready to break into laughter if response to what was said proved it ridiculous. Its melancholy, even when invaded by the mockery of burlesque, was related to that of home-starved men who sang sad songs on lonesome prairies or rivers, in forests or mountain camps. Its sentimentality was like theirs, ready to retreat to guffaw when detected. The aggressive playfulness which delighted in hoaxes and practical joking changed in almost classic pattern to anger like that of gods—or of simple men—when the joke is turned against them.

Clemens had known backcountry America and the overland push toward great fortunes in the gold-filled, silver-lined West. He had known, better than he learned to know anything else, her great arterial river through which the lifeblood of middle America had once flowed. And he had known men in these places, of all kinds, and then known riches and the company of well-fed, respectable people whom he also recognized as types known before. He had listened to men talk, boastfully or in anger, had heard their tales and their blandishments, and had learned to speak as they spoke. For his ultimate discovery was linguistic, the creation of a language which was simple, supple, and sustained, in what Richard Chase has called "a joyous exorcism of traditional literary English." No one had ever written like him before. What is more difficult to remember is that no one ever effectively will again because, to say it very simply, his models were not in literature but in life. Even he, when he tried to write something like something he had written before, succeeded only in producing books which were amusing because written in Mark Twain's manner.

Adventures of Huckleberry Finn is the story of a boy who will not accept the kinds of freedom the world is able to offer, and so flees from them, one after another, to become to many readers a symbol of man's inevitable, restless flight. It is instructive to recall that it appeared in the same year that Clemens' friend William Dean Howells presented in *The Rise of Silas Lapham* another simple protagonist who retreated when confronted by perplexities, and a year before Henry James, who approached maturity through avenues almost completely different from those which Clemens followed, revealed in both *The Princess Casamassima* and *The Bostonians* the struggle of honest young provincials forced to reject promises offered by society. Each played variations on a familiar American theme, which Emerson had expressed, which Whitman approached, and Melville also, and which has reappeared often again. It poses what has been called the inescapable dilemma of democracy—to what degree may each single and separate person live as an unencumbered individual and to what extent must he submit to distortions of personality required by society? If Clemens presented it better than most, by endowing it with qualities of myth interwoven with fantasy, realism, satire, and superstition, it was not because his convictions were different. It was because he had mastered a language supple enough to reveal the honest observations of an attractive boy and the ambiguous aspirations of many kinds of men whom he came upon, and also the subtly ominous but compelling spirit which in this book is a river.

Huckleberry Finn's solution of the problem of freedom is direct and unworldly: having tested society, he will have none of it, for civilization finally makes culprits of all men. Huck is a simple boy, with little education and great confidence in omens. One measure of his character is its proneness to deceit which, though not always successful, is instinctive, as if it were a trait shared with other wild things, relating him to nature, in opposition to the tradition-grounded, book-learned imaginative deceptions of Tom Sawyer. The dilatory adventures of Huck and his Negro companion, both natural men enslaved, have even reminded some readers of the more consciously directed explorations in Faulkner's "The Bear" of Ike McCaslin and his part-Negro, part-Indian guide, if only because they suggest more than can easily be explained. American fictions, we are told, are filled with white boys who are influenced by darker companions.

Young Huck had become something of a hero to the inhabitants of the little river village because of his help to Tom Sawyer in tracking down Injun Joe. He had been adopted by the Widow Douglas, washed, dressed in clean clothes, and sent to school. With Tom he shared the incredible wealth of one dollar a day for each of them derived as income from the treasure they had discovered in *The Adventures of Tom Sawyer*. But Huck is not happy. Tom's make-believe is incomprehensible to him. The religion of retribution which Miss Watson, the widow's sister, teaches makes no sense at all. The religion of love which the widow suggests is better, but he will not commit himself. When his scapegrace father returns and carries Huck across the river to a desolate log house, the boy accepts the abduction with relief because, though he fears his father's beatings and drunken rages, he is freed from restraints of tight clothing, school, and regular hours, and from the preaching and the puzzling tangle of ideas which confuse village life. But the bondage of life with his father chafes also, so he steals down the river at night to Jackson Island, where he meets the Negro Jim, Miss Watson's slave, who had run away because his Christian owner was going to sell him.

Thus the first eleven chapters of *Adventures of Huckleberry Finn* tell of adventures on land, with Huck bewildered or miserable or in flight. The next twenty chapters detail adventures on the river or beside the river, in a pattern of withdrawal and return, as Huck and Jim float with their raft toward what they hope will be freedom for both. On the river or its shores many kinds of men are encountered, most of them evil or stupid or mean: cutthroats, murderers, cheats, liars, swindlers, cowards, slave hunters, dupes, and hypocrites of every variety. Even the isolation from society which life on a raft might be thought to afford is violated, for malevolence also intrudes there in grotesque guises. Nor is the movement of the great brown river to be trusted. It carries Jim beyond freedom to capture again by respectable, benevolent people whose conscience is untroubled by human slavery.

The final twelve chapters take place again on land. Tom Sawyer once more appears, filled with romance-bred notions of how Jim might be freed. And Huck joins in the laborious nonsense, for he admires Tom, if he does not understand him —often on the river when confronted with crisis or cleverly, he thought, surmounting difficulties, he wished Tom had been there to aid or commend him. But the boys' make-believe at rescue becomes a travesty, for Miss Watson had granted Jim his freedom—he was no longer a slave. The narrative ends hurriedly, as if embarrassed to linger while loose ends were tied. Huck's father is dead—Jim had known that since the first stage of their journey but in kindness had withheld the knowledge. One threat to Huck's freedom is gone, but another remains, for good people again pity the brave pariah boy and offer to adopt him. But Huck will not have it: "I can't stand it," he said. "I been there before."

Much has been made of these last chapters, in condemnation or approval. To some readers they certify Clemens' inability to control plot, to others they reveal a compulsive attraction toward elaborate inventions such as Tom Sawyer loved, but to still others they are exactly right, supplying an inevitable rounding out of tale and theme. And much has been made of the development of Huck's character, his initiation, or his disillusionment with the world and its ways, and especially the change in his attitude toward the Negro Jim, whom he finally recognizes as a fellow being, more decent and honest than most of the white people who hold him and his kind in slavery. A few find special charm in the assumption that Huck does not develop in any fundamental sense at all, because as a child of nature he is changeless. But to all, it is Huck and his view of the world which secure for this book its high place among American writings.

For one of the things to notice about *Adventures of Huckleberry Finn* is that Mark Twain is not the narrator. Huck makes that plain in the first paragraph: Mr. Mark Twain had written of him in *The Adventures of Tom Sawyer*, he said, but this would be his own story. And the first-person narrative which follows allows Huck to misspell and mispronounce words in a manner which could delight admirers of Mark Twain, and to act sometimes in a manner which he thought would have delighted Tom Sawyer, but it is his voice which speaks, authentically and without posturing. Sometimes Mark Twain's accents are heard, as compellingly humorous as ever, tempting attention away from the boy who, with no humor at all, struggles to make himself understood. But Huck is finally the better witness, infinitely better than Tom Sawyer, whose vision is blurred by boyish trickery very different from Huck's protective deceit.

Boyish Tom, however, seems to have been Samuel Clemens' favorite. He wrote of him again in *Tom Sawyer Abroad* in 1894 and in *Tom Sawyer Detective* in 1896, contrived books, imitative of earlier successes, and crowded with imagined adventure rather than experience. Yet, with boyhood behind him, even Tom was not to be envied. Boys grew up to become men, and men were molded by temptations that a boy could never know. Innocence became a remembered thing, to be cherished—but only as a memory of times long past.

But if old times in backcountry America were idyllically best, older times in Europe certainly were not. Far too many of his countrymen, Clemens thought, were beguiled by romantic notions popularized by Sir Walter Scott, which made overgrown Tom Sawyers of them all. Scott was "so juvenile, so artificial, so shoddy," not once "recognizably sincere and in earnest." His characters were "bloodless shams," "milk-and-water humbugs," "squalid shadows." Nor were American romancers, bred under Scott's influence, appreciably better. Among the most persistently anthologized of Clemens' short pieces is the humorously perceptive dissection of "Fenimore Cooper's Literary Offenses," in which he finds that "in the restricted space of two-thirds of a page, Cooper has scored 114 offenses against literary art out of a possible 115." He speaks of Cooper's "crass stupidities," his lack of attention to detail, and his curious box of stage properties which contained such hackneyed devices as the broken twig: "It is a restful chapter in any book of his when somebody doesn't step on a twig and alarm all the reds and whites for two hundred yards around. . . . In fact, the Leather-Stocking Series ought to have been called the Broken Twig Series." Surely, Clemens reasoned, history could be presented without such twaddle.

So Clemens wrote of the adventures of a sturdy, practical nineteenth-century mechanic who is knocked unconscious by a blow on the head and awakes to find himself under a tree near Camelot, amid a landscape "as lovely as a dream and as lonesome as Sunday." But *A Connecticut Yankee in King Arthur's Court,* published in 1889, was double-edged in satirical intention. The Yankee proves himself a better man than the magician Merlin and he overcomes the best of knights in single or multiple combat. He provides what he called "a new deal" for downtrodden common people, transforming Arthur's England into a technically efficient going concern in which gunpowder and mechanical skills triumph over superstition, injustice, and oppression. But "this Yankee of mine," explained Clemens, "is a perfect ignoramus; he is boss of a machine shop, he can build a locomotive or a Colt's revolver, he can put up and run a telegraph line, but he's an ignoramus nevertheless."

A Connecticut Yankee has been called Mark Twain's finest possibility, combining satire, the tall tale, humor, democracy, religion, and the damned human race. Loosely picaresque and brightly anecdotal, it was an attempt, Clemens explained, "to imagine and after a fashion set forth, the hard condition of life for the laboring and defenseless poor in bygone times in England, and incidentally contrast those conditions with those under which civil and ecclesiastical pets of privilege and high fortune lived in those times." But what finally emerges from beneath the contrast between Yankee ingenuity and medieval superstition is the portrait of an American. He is unlearned, with "neither the refinement nor the weakness of a college education," but quick-witted and completely, even devastatingly successful. Consciously created or not, it is the image of Samuel Clemens and of many of his friends. And it explains something of the nature of the literature which he and his fellows produced.

Meanwhile Clemens had thought for years that he might write a comic story about Siamese twins, one of whom was good, the other a rake, imagining that sidesplitting situations could result when, for example, the rake drank to excess and the teetotaler twin became intoxicated. Perhaps no idea was more grotesquely unfavorable for fiction, and Clemens never developed it fully, partly because, as he said, "A man who is not born with the novel-writing gift has a troublesome time of it when he tries to write a novel. . . . He has no clear idea of his story; in fact he has no story. He has merely some people in his mind, and an incident or two, also a locality . . . and he trusts that he can plunge those people into those incidents with interesting results."

When he did put shreds of this tale together in *Those Extraordinary Twins*, he pretended jocosely to reveal something of his casual literary method, particularly in dealing with characters who became lost amid the intricacies of plot. One female character named Rowena, for example, began splendidly but failed to keep up: "I must simply give her the grand bounce," he said. "It grieved me to do it, for after associating with her so much I had come to kind of like her after a fashion, notwithstanding she was such an ass, and said such stupid, irritating things, and was so nauseatingly sentimental." So he sent her "out into the back yard after supper to see the fireworks," and "she fell down a well and got drowned." The method seemed perhaps abrupt, "but I thought maybe the reader wouldn't notice it, because I changed the subject right away to something else. Anyway it loosened Rowena up from where she was stuck and got her out of the way, and that was the main thing." Successful once, he resolved to try the stratagem again with two boys who were no longer useful ("they went out one night to stone a cat and fell down the well and got drowned") and with two supernumerary old ladies ("they went out one night to visit the sick and fell down a well and got drowned"). "I was going to drown some of the others, but I gave up the idea, partly because I believed that if I kept it up I would attract attention, and perhaps sympathy with those people, and partly because it was not a large well and would not hold any more anyway."

This was pure Mark Twain, in mood and language which many people liked best. Part of the fun was that what he said was so true or seemed so true in revelation of the shambling way he really wrote or liked to have people think he wrote stories. And the laugh was on him, or seemed to be, at the same time that it mocked conventional or sentimental writers who had no convenient wells in their back yards. Almost everybody agreed that Mark Twain made most sense when he was funniest. He could double people over with laughter as he pointed to their shortcomings or his own or those of people not quite so clever as they. The laughter was cleansing, but quieting also, for surely such amusing peccadilloes needed no correction.

Those Extraordinary Twins appeared in 1894 as an appendix to *The Tragedy of Pudd'nhead Wilson,* a better story which unaccountably had grown from it. Using the same device of the changeling which had provided the plot for *The Prince and the Pauper,* he told now of two children born on the same day in the Driscoll home at Dawson's Landing, one the son of the white master of the house, the other of a mulatto slave named Roxana, who switched the babies in their cradles so that her tainted son was brought up as Thomas à Becket Driscoll, heir to estates, while Tom, the white boy, became a slave. The bogus Tom grew to be a wastrel, a thief, and finally a murderer. When his mother threatened to expose him if he did not change his ways, he sold her to a slave trader.

The mulatto Roxana dominates the book, sentimentally perhaps, but illustrating again qualities of nobility like those which Huck discovered in the Negro Jim. But her attitudes on race are ambiguous and have puzzled people who would relate them to Huck's attitude or Jim's. When her son proved himself in every respect bad, she told him, "It's de nigger in you, dat's what it is. Thirty-one parts o' you is white, en only one part nigger, en dat po' little one part is yo' soul. 'Taint wuth savin', 'taint wuth totin' out in a shovel en throwin' in de gutter." Perhaps it is a mistake to expect consistency in a writer like Clemens. Or perhaps the greater mistake is to think that any one book of his can be used as commentary on any other.

Potentially more significant is the title character, a lawyer fond of philosophical maxims, but considered queer, a Pudd'nhead, by the rest of the community because he fails to conform to village standards. Among his strange hobbies is that of taking fingerprints, and he had years before made prints of the baby boys before they were changed about. When the trial for the murder which the bogus Tom had committed is held and Italian twins (the remnant of the Siamese twin idea) are blamed for it because they have the misfortune of being foreigners and strangers in the village, Pudd'nhead defends them, dramatically revealing by means of his prints that the true murderer is Roxana's villainous son.

The Tragedy of Pudd'nhead Wilson is filled with familiar failings, false starts, and rambling excursions. The title makes us wonder why it is Pudd'nhead's tragedy. But it contains excellencies also, of a kind which Sherwood Anderson was to use in writing about village people, and which have earned for it a reputation as "the most extraordinary book in American literature," filled with intolerable insights into evil. Even distorted by drollery, it penetrates toward recognition of social ills not unlike those which William Faulkner was later to probe. Beneath the burlesque which peoples the sleepy village of Dawson's Landing with representatives of decayed gentry bearing such exuberant names as Percy Northumberland Driscoll and Cecil Burleigh Essex runs a vein of satire which allows recognition of these people as ancestors of the Satorises and Compsons. Pudd'nhead himself might have sat as model for Faulkner's Gavin Stevens, who comments on tradition-ridden life in Yoknapatawpha County. The octoroon who masquerades as white can be thought of as a tentative fore-shadowing of Joe Christmas in *Light in August* or Sutpen's half-caste son in *Absalom, Absalom!*

Its failure is literary, the failure of words, not of ideas. Mark Twain is telling a story according to a familiar pattern, incident strung on incident as if they might go on forever. Humor, pathos, sentiment, anger, and burlesque rub shoulders with intimacy bred of long acquaintance. *Pudd'nhead Wilson* is serious in intention, for all its belly laughs and tears. It faces up to problems made by the venality of man. Seldom is it more plainly evident that Mark Twain's eyes rarely twinkle when he laughs. A social conscience here is plainly showing. Scorn looks boldly out from behind the burlesque. But the words do not come true, as Huck's words did or as Clemens' did when he remembered apprentice days on the river. He is saying what he wants to say, but in accents which ring false because they speak now as people expected him to speak.

Perhaps it is even possible to suppose that Mark Twain, who was responsible for so much of Clemens' incomparable contemporary success, became finally an encumbrance. As Stephen Crane once said, two hundred pages is a very long stretch in which to be funny. And the stretch is more enervating when the humorist understands that what he writes about is not of itself funny, but only seems so because of the way he writes about it. Man was more likely than not to be mean and do wrong—this even Huck knew, who was not humorous at all. Clemens seems to have known it also, and for a long time.

But Clemens had never kept his observations on the venality of man completely in focus, not even in *Adventures of Huckleberry Finn*. Whether his seasoning of humor and relaxed excursions into anecdote are uniformly successful or not, they do reveal a distinctly practical approach to literature. I can teach anyone to write a successful story, he once advised a literary friend. All that needs to be done is catch the reader's attention with the first sentence and hold it by whatever means are possible to the end. The story flows, he said, as a stream flows, and the storyteller's responsibility is to pilot the reader in safety and comfort through its often meandering channel.

During the twenty years between 1875 and 1894 Samuel Clemens was happiest, and wealthiest, and he wrote his best books. He lived then in luxury among a group of well-to-do littérateurs in Hartford. He lectured, assumed an occasional editorial commitment, and sought attractive books for distribution by his publishing house. His income was breathtaking, probably mounting more than once to one hundred thousand dollars a year. But money went as fast as it came, especially in speculative enterprises like the typesetting machine into which he poured much of his earnings. He dreamed like Colonel Sellers of making millions, as many of his contemporaries did, but by the mid-1890's he was bankrupt. A world tour then brought him increased fame and respect, produced *Following the Equator* in 1897, paid his debts, and provided new financial security. But at sixty, his effective literary career could be considered finished.

While resident in Europe he completed the writing of *Personal Recollections of Joan of Arc*, an account so seriously intended as the expression of a lifelong admiration that it was published in 1896 without Clemens' familiar pseudonym for fear that readers might expect another comic book from Mark Twain and laugh. The innocent faith of the Maid of Orleans represented a quality pitiably absent from modern life. She seemed "easily and by far the most extraordinary person the human race has ever produced." Untrained and without experience, she had within herself a capacity for goodness so pure and successful that it was condemned as heresy by men whom the world named good. But, hampered perhaps by the necessity of keeping close to what he had learned through years of reading of Joan's history, Clemens did not tell her story well, and few readers have agreed with him that it made his best book.

Grief and increasing bitterness had begun to close in upon him, to darken the rest of his life. His daughter Susy died suddenly while her parents were abroad, Mrs. Clemens was distressingly ill for years and then died, and his youngest daughter died suddenly one Christmas Eve. During the fifteen years which preceded his own death in 1910, Clemens lashed out often in anger at a world which had wounded him or reminisced with increasing compulsion on a world which was gone. He could not bear to return to Hartford, where he had been happily successful, but moved restlessly from place to place, from residence in New York, to Florence in Italy, to Bermuda for his health, and finally to Stormfield in rural Connecticut, writing furiously at more projects than he could ever complete.

Readers who found Tom Sawyer silly or Huck Finn finally a profitless model were moved to wry approval of *The Man That Corrupted Hadleyburg*, which in 1900 presented Clemens' most trenchant testimony to the fundamental dishonesty of man. Piercing the shell of respectability which traditionally had made each small town seem inhabited by kindly hearts and gentle people, he demonstrated how easily even prominently moral citizens could be led beyond temptation when confronted with opportunity to acquire wealth dishonestly but undetected. None were exempt, for every contest was rigged. No more astringent or cynical condemnation of contemporary mores had been issued by an American; even Stephen Crane's *Maggie* eight years before and Theodore Dreiser's *Sister Carrie* of the same year seem tempered with sentiments which Clemens could no longer feel. A year later, in *A Person Sitting in Darkness*, he struck savagely at the militant morality of missionaries, and in *King Leopold's Soliloquy*, in 1905, scornfully denounced pious exploitation of underdeveloped countries. *Extracts from Adam's Diary* in 1904 and *Eve's Diary* in 1906 were whimsical accounts of the dependence of even the first man on the superior management of women, and spoke feelingly by indirection of the loneliness of life without connubial and familial affection.

In 1906 he began to dictate his autobiography, reviewing, often without any defense of humor, incidents and personalities remembered from his rambling career. Some parts were so forthright that he thought they should not be published for a century after his death, but other parts were sent off for immediate serialization in the *North American Review*. Selected portions have been put together for *Mark Twain's Autobiography* in 1924, *Mark Twain in Eruption* in 1940, and *The Autobiography of Mark Twain* in 1959, each adding its effective extension to the image of a favorite American, who grumbled and growled, who smoked too much and cadged Scotch whiskey from his wealthy friends, but who had been places and who was known and loved all over the world.

In 1906 he also issued privately and anonymously what he called his "wicked book," *What Is Man?* which contains his most astringent diagnosis of man as a mechanism, the plaything of chance, his brain "so constructed that it can originate nothing." Man is a chameleon who "by the law of his nature . . . takes on the color of the place of his resort. The influences about him create his preferences, his aversions, his politics, his taste, his morality, his religion." All that he knows, all that he does, is determined by one inexorable law: "From his cradle to his grave a man never does a single thing which has any first and foremost object but one—to secure peace of mind, spiritual comfort, for himself." He is what he is, and nothing will change him. Self-seeking, self-admiring, he babbles of free will and love and compassion, which are fictions made to ensure his satisfaction with himself. "Whenever you read of a self-sacrificing act or hear of one, or of a duty done for duty's sake, take it to pieces and look for the real motive. It's always there."

The book is not wicked, but it is tired, like the posthumous *Letters from the Earth*. Its words speak forthrightly, despairingly, echoing the words of other men who testified to man's slavery to forces beyond himself. They are palliative as well as condemnatory, as if their writer were explaining to himself as much as to other men why it was necessary for all men to do what he and they perforce had done. Resolution is not lacking, nor is anger. On its level, the book argues well. It presents its case. What is no longer there is the power of the inevitable word which is in so intimate a relation to the thing of which it speaks that meaning spills over to intimations which ordinary words can never reach. Once Clemens' words had clung thus close to things, but now they gestured and had less to say.

Six months before his death Clemens released an *Extract from Captain Stormfield's Visit to Heaven,* a favorite tale over which he had been puttering for many years. In it almost every contrivance of humor, sentiment, or dissection of human frailty that Mark Twain had ever used was expended again on the adventures of a crusty, matter-of-fact mariner who went flashing through the air like a bird toward paradise, racing a comet on the way as steamboat pilots used to race on the Mississippi. He has difficulty in finding wings that fit or a harp that suits him. He seeks long before finding the proper resting place for people from a planet so little valued by angels that they call it the Wart. He has trouble conversing with people who speak ridiculous languages, tumbles terribly in learning to fly, is surprised to find Jews and Moslems in heaven, and pleased that Shakespeare is placed "away down there below shoe-makers and horse-dealers and knife-grinders" to make room for an unknown tailor from Tennessee who "wrote poetry that Homer and Shakespeare couldn't begin to come up to; but nobody would print it, nobody read it but his neighbors, and they laughed at it." Recognition of wisdom masked by such burlesque is usually considered a test of an admirer of Mark Twain.

As a philosophical humorist he spoke on two levels, now one, now the other, seldom blending them to unity of tone or consistency of insight. Henry Nash Smith is correct in describing Mark Twain's popularity as a result of his exploitation of the comic contrast between things as they might be and things as they are. But Louis Budd is also correct in discovering Clemens neither original nor objective as a social philosopher. Convictions he had in plenty, and courage also; but he had a place to preserve and boyhood visions to sustain. His miseries were subtly compounded and his sense of sin extended as young dreams exploded to recriminatory nightmares at last.

No subtlety of interpretation is required for recognition of the bleak despair of Clemens' posthumous *The Mysterious Stranger*. The scene is Austria in 1590, where in the village of Eseldorf, a paradise for play like that which Tom and Huck had known, three boys are joined by a visiting angel, namesake and nephew of the fallen Satan. He entertains them with miracles, making little creatures of clay, breathing life into them, and then mashing them down as if they were flies. It seems cruel to the boys, but Satan explains that it was not cruel, only capricious and, as far as man could understand, ordained. Crippled by moral sense, in bondage to circum-

stance, his vision distorted by illusion, man pampers himself
with ideals which exist only when he imagines them. What
an ass he is! How hysterically mad are his expectations: "No
sane man can be happy, for to him life is real, and he sees
what a fearful thing it is," for "there is no God, no universe,
no human race, no earthly life, no heaven, no hell. It is all a
dream—a grotesque and foolish dream. Nothing exists," said
the angel, "but you. And you are but a *thought*—a vagrant
thought, a useless thought, a homeless thought, wandering
forlorn among the empty eternities."

Nothing remains of the Widow Douglas' reliance on the
religion of love or Huck's possibility of escape from the world
through flight. Again Clemens speaks, as he had in 1885, of
ideas which unsettled many people of his time, but now others
voiced them better than he, for some magic of language has
disappeared from these late sputtering insights of anger and
despair. The angel Satan speaks, but the words are Clemens',
in reprimand as much to himself as to those who read him:
"You have a mongrel sense of humor, nothing more," he
charged; "you see the comic side of a thousand low-grade and
trivial things—broad incongruities, mainly; grotesqueries, ab-
surdities, evokers of the horse-laugh." But the "ten thousand
high-grade comicalities" made by the juvenilities of man are
sealed from your dull visions. "Will a day come when the
race will detect these juvenilities and laugh at them—and by
laughing destroy them?" In a perfect world there is no room
for laughter, but this world is not perfect, and man in his
poverty "has unquestionably one really effective weapon—
laughter. Power, money, persuasion, supplication, persecution
—these can lift at a colossal humbug—push it a little—
weaken it a little, century by century; but only laughter can
blow it to rags and atoms at a blast."

"Humor," Mark Twain once wrote when in another mood,
"is only a fragrance, a decoration." If it is really to succeed in
survival, it must surreptitiously teach and preach. Perhaps that

is why so sober an admirer as James T. Farrell sees in Huck and Tom "two accusing fingers pointing down the decades of America's history," relentlessly questioning why it is in America, or perhaps anywhere else, that a man so rarely becomes what the boy gave promise of becoming. Samuel Clemens did see the world as a boy sees it, in its infinitude of possibilities for freedom and fun and in its darkened depths of disillusionment. And, like a boy, when embarrassed he laughed; when tentatively serious he laughed first, so that the responding laugh could be with, not at, him; even in tantrum, he seemed somehow comic, an object which in brighter spirits he might have ridiculed. "From a boyhood idyll of the good life to a boy's criticism of that life," says Wright Morris in accusation, "is the natural range and habitat of the American mind." Mark Twain's charm of innocence did isolate him from maturity. What he achieved artlessly so well that he invented a theory of storytelling art to explain it was received with riotous applause by his countrymen. With so natural a talent why should he then not attempt more? Clemens' inability to respond to that question explains much of Mark Twain and the milieu which made him possible. But it fails to explain all, or even what is most important.

Samuel Clemens created or became Mark Twain, who boundlessly created laughter, but he was more than a buffoon. As comic realist he applies for place beside Laurence Sterne, Dickens, Joyce, Faulkner, and Camus, for his eyes like theirs have seen beyond locality to qualities which men universally, sometimes shamefully, share. To remember him only as a creator of boyhood adventure or as a relic of an American frontier or the voice of native idiosyncrasy is to do him disservice. His accomplishment finally contradicts his thinking, thus certifying his literary achievement. Much that is excellent in American literature *did* begin with him, and Lionel Trilling is correct when he says "that almost every contemporary American writer who deals conscientiously with the

problems and possibilities of prose must feel, directly or indirectly, the influence of . . . [his] style which escapes the
fixity of the printed page, that sounds in our ears with the
immediacy of the heard voice, the voice of unpretentious
truth."

But he was anticipated also, ten years before his first triumphant entry to public notice, by another native observer
who admitted men "victims of illusion" and life "a succession
of dreams." Samuel Clemens, Mississippi pilot, had not yet
become Mark Twain, but Emerson had someone much like
him in mind when he described "a humorist who in a good
deal of rattle had a grain or two of sense. He shocked the
company by maintaining that the attributes of God were two,
—power and risibility, and that it was the duty of every pious
man to keep up the comedy."

Perhaps it was a basic lack of piety in the sense of dedication to the demands of literature ("and all that bosh") which
deprived Samuel Clemens of an ability consistently to keep up
the comedy. Laughter is not joy, funny fellows are notoriously
prone to tears, and the comic view has never sustained man's
highest vision of himself or his possibilities because, as Baudelaire once said, the comic is imitation, not creation. But his
countrymen seldom chide Mark Twain for what he is not;
what he was is good enough, and plenty. It is probably true
that the sense of the comic, the ability to laugh, is in him who
laughs, and not in the object which excites his laughter. If the
thousand low-grade and trivial things which quickened mirth
among his countrymen were more often displayed than Samuel Clemens' occasional genuine and high-grade comicalities,
the fault was not his alone, and he is not to be blamed for his
anger, except that it came too late, when his words were
tired. He shocked his countrymen by explaining what they
were, and they laughed. Their continuing laughter measures
his genius and their own, and the limitations they have shared
together.

2

❧

Mark Twain's Wound:
Standing with Reluctant Feet

MY SUBTITLE derives from a parody of Longfellow's familiar lines made by an impious friend of mine who spoke one evening of "Standing, with reluctant feet, Where Brooks and Bernard meet." For the warfare between partisans of Van Wyck Brooks and Bernard DeVoto has seemed long-drawn and debilitating to many people—including, I suspect, Van Wyck Brooks, who never publicly returned a blow. To people like my friend, the question of the extent to which Samuel Clemens was a wounded man stands quite apart from the fact of his literary achievement. All men, they say, are wounded, but all men are not artists. Whether a writer has been warped by wine, women, or wayward circumstance seems to them less important than whether he has succeeded in arranging words in such a manner that what they say seems inevitable and authentic. The mark of a minor literature, they tell us, is that its critics find so little in it to admire that they turn instead to an examination of the men who made it, so that criticism becomes exploration of personality, and Mark Twain's misadventures are made to seem more important than *Adventures of Huckleberry Finn,* and Melville's unhappy quest becomes a key to *Moby Dick,* Thoreau's idiosyncrasies an index to *Walden,* and Whitman's eccentric sexuality the explanation of *Leaves of Grass.*

Literature in the United States has perhaps unavoidably carried a large burden of commentary of this kind. Native writing arose during a period when the revelation of national traits or national spirit was considered the proper function of literature. It was watered to first flowering by the "new" thought of early nineteenth-century Europe which considered effective writing the effervescent expression of free spirits who, in discovering themselves, discarded inherited restrictions. It blossomed in a series of books which seem personal indeed: "I become a transparent eyeball," "My name is Arthur Gordon Pym," "I went to the woods," "Call me Ishmael," "I celebrate myself." Evaluation of this literature assumed self-conscious postures of maturity under the direction of critics like Hippolyte Taine who argued that writers were formed by time, place, and circumstance—that French writers, nourished on veal and wine, were necessarily different from English writers, who preferred beef and beer. Psychoanalytic methods appropriated from Freud and, later, from Jung were applied and misapplied to explain the influence of a writer's total experience on his art. Many came to think that American writers were distinguished from others because the United States was a frontier land, rough and demanding, and destructive of art, or because it was a Puritan-tainted land, at once prudish and prurient.

Through much of the history of writing in the United States—from Philip Freneau and Brockden Brown, through Cooper, Hawthorne, Henry James, and Whistler, to Ezra Pound and T. S. Eliot—patriotic American eyes have turned from native crudities toward European standards of taste. Voices over many generations have been raised to demand that transatlantic standards of discrimination be superimposed on indigenous Yankee or Western or Southern strength. It was not surprising then that by 1908 young Van Wyck

Brooks should discover for himself that in Europe "the premise of an artistic life [was] really taken for granted," while America, he explained that year in *The Wine of the Puritans*, was either too "rough" or too "polished"—or, as he would later say, too "lowbrow" or too "highbrow," without opportunity for serious investigation of the quiet middle region which, as Lionel Trilling would explain, is inhabited by art. Brooks spoke hopefully of *America's Coming of Age* (1915) and tendentiously, like a latter-day Shelley, of *Letters and Leadership* (1918). Then he wrote three more books: one, *The Ordeal of Mark Twain* (1920), to show how native environment stultified the artist; another, *The Pilgrimage of Henry James* (1925), to illustrate the stifling isolation which can engulf a writer who quits his native shore; and a third, *The Life of Emerson* (1932), to show a man who stayed home but allowed his mind to range intelligently. Since the Civil War, Brooks argued, America had lost literary integrity. Pushed about, on one side by the decayed fervor of Puritanism, on the other by the boisterous vulgarity of democratic mass opinion, writing in the United States stumbled and swerved and almost always fell flat.

High-minded and messianic, Brooks and his friends sought cultural salvation for a spiritually impoverished land. Like H. L. Mencken and Waldo Frank and all their associates in founding or reviving brave new literary magazines, he had occasional glimpses of a fair, fresh dawn rising over the intellectual darkness of the United States. He and his kind scolded and were scolded by schoolmaster critics like Stuart Sherman, Brander Matthews, and William Lyon Phelps. They chafed under the placid pronouncements of William Dean Howells, the "dean" perhaps of American letters, but subject to all of any dean's proverbial backward-looking timidity. They were embarrassed by the mincing, unmasculine verbal precision of Henry James. New men—like ponderous Theodore Dreiser, Edgar Lee Masters, who played effectively only in one key, or the unpredictable Sherwood Anderson—were none of them what the young critics wanted them to be, but they were better and braver than the old-line, polite men of letters, and were therefore worthy of encouragement and correction, and of being warned about the danger of stumbling. Mark Twain was particularly an embarrassment. Though dead ten years, he was still in 1920 doggedly present, every common man's favorite, remembered as a writer with little nonsense about him, a real person who had been places, done things, and made money. His books still appeared—*The Mysterious Stranger* in 1916, *What Is Man?* in 1917—and tantalizing, revelatory new chapters from his *Autobiography* were promised. Mark Twain's "mind was of universal proportions," said John Macy. Brander Matthews ranked him with Cervantes, Molière, and Chaucer. Howells spoke of him as the Lincoln of our literature. But the younger critics would have none of this. "Mark Twain—the humorist—America's funny man!" scoffed somber Waldo Frank. So clever, so appealing, so popular, what a shame it was, said Van Wyck Brooks, that Mark Twain had not done better. What caused so talented a man, so mercurial—now up, now down—to trade his superb skills for the plaudits of a multitude which filled his pockets with cash to be spent on gaudy homes and harebrained inventions? In 1910 Howells had written of him as *My Mark Twain.* He was everybody's Mark Twain. And every young critic's natural target.

Later cultural historians have recognized Brooks as the first among them successfully to demonstrate the degradation of living in an acquisitive society. Yet he spoke like many others of his generation: Sinclair Lewis' *Main Street* appeared in the same year as *The Ordeal of Mark Twain,* and T. S. Eliot's *The Waste Land* two years later. "Brooks's long lament over Mark Twain's tribulations," explains Alfred Kazin, "came at a time when the revolt against Victorianism was being led by the debunkers, and in their own way the intellectuals read his book as they read Claude Bowers's *The Tragic Era, The Education of Henry Adams,* and the many fictional studies of Emily Dickinson—for solace and malicious amusement."

Very few shared his feeling for Mark Twain, his lofty indignation at the repression of a great artist, his characteristic and moving insistence on the spiritual importance of great art. They were content to applaud his solemn attack on Olivia Clemens and Elmira, New York: the "brutish" frontier and the parochialism and vulgarity of contemporary taste. That Brooks's history took no account of the vitality of thought during the Gilded Age, that his psychoanalytic flights were a subtle form of wish fulfillment, that his humorless condemnation of the whole period of American life was a little absurd, did not matter to them. Out of his profound conviction of Mark Twain's unhappiness and failure Brooks had written a brilliant study of the meanness and poverty against which artists had to rebel in America, and it was enough.[1]

Nor was Van Wyck Brooks the first to suspect some flaw in Mark Twain. Many years before, Walt Whitman had said, "I think he mainly misses fire. I think his life misses fire; he might have been something; but he never arrives." And Mark Twain himself, in letters and in bantering conversation, had often seemed to support charges of being influenced by his wife and friends. "Livy would skin me, if I said that," he was fond of remarking. It appeared to be part of an affectionate game they played together, for him to picture his gentle wife as an ogre, and for her to twit him about his irresponsible brashness. "I was a mighty rough, coarse, unpromising subject," he once admitted, "when Livy took hold of me." She called him "Youth" and took loving pride in instructing him. And Mrs. Clemens had a quietly persuasive ally in Howells. When that friend read a draft manuscript, probably of *Tom Sawyer,* in 1874, he mildly suggested that certain words be

---

[1] Alfred Kazin, *On Native Grounds: An Interpretation of Modern American Prose Literature* (New York: Reynal & Hitchcock, 1942), 283.

deleted. His letter came by accident to Mrs. Clemens' hands, who, reported her husband, "lit into the study with danger in her eye and this demand on her tongue: Where is the profanity Mr. Howells speaks of? Then I had to miserably confess that I had left it out when reading the manuscript to her. Nothing but inspired lying got me out of this scrape with my scalp." "Does your wife," he asked Howells, "give you rats like this . . . ?"[2]

Writing to another friend in 1891, Mark Twain explained that he confined himself to life with which he was familiar "when pretending to portray life":

I confine myself to *boy*-life on the Mississippi because that had a peculiar charm for me, and not because I was not familiar with other phases of life. I was a soldier for two weeks once at the beginning of the war, and was hunted like a rat the whole time. . . .

Yes, and I have shoveled silver-tailings in a quartz-mill a couple of weeks, and acquired the last possibilities of culture in *that* direction. And I've done "pocket-mining" during three months in the one little patch of ground in the whole globe where Nature conceals gold pockets—or *did* before we robbed all of those pockets and exhausted, obliterated, annihilated the most curious freak Nature ever indulged in. . . .

And I've been a prospector, and know pay rock from poor when I find it—just with a touch of the tongue. And I've been a *silver* miner and know how to dig and shovel and drill and put in a blast. . . .

And I was a newspaper reporter four years in cities, and saw the inside of many things; and was a reporter in a legislature two sessions and the same in Congress one session, and thus learned to know personally three sample bodies of the smallest minds and the selfishest souls, and the cowardliest hearts that God makes.

And I was some years a Mississippi pilot, and familiarly knew all the different kinds of steamboatmen—a race apart, and not like other folk.

[2] *Mark Twain–Howells Letters: The Correspondence of Samuel L. Clemens and William Dean Howells, 1872–1910*, ed. Henry Nash Smith and William M. Gibson (2 vols.; Cambridge: Harvard University Press, Belknap Press, 1960), I, 54.

And I was for some years a traveling "jour" printer, and wandered from city to city—and so I know that sect familiarly.

And I was a lecturer on the public platform a number of seasons and was a responder to toasts at all the different kinds of banquets—and so I know a great many secrets about audiences—secrets not to be got out of books, but only acquirable by experience.

And I watched over one dear project of mine for years, spent a fortune on it, and failed to make it go—and the history of that would make a large book in which a million men would see themselves as in a mirror; and they would testify and say, Verily, this is not imagination; this fellow has been there—and after would cast dust on their heads cursing and blaspheming.

And I am a publisher, and did pay one author's widow (General Grant's) the largest copyright checks this world has seen—aggregating more than £80,000 in the first year.

And I have been an author for 20 years and an ass for 55.[3]

When Albert Bigelow Paine brought together things like this in his three-volume biography published two years after Clemens' death, he provided fuel to feed the fires of those who disliked Mark Twain as well as those who admired him. Paine had been Clemens' secretary and had talked with him (or been talked to by him) almost every day during the last five years of the humorist's life. Paine knew the elderly Mark Twain, the whimsical, growling, quick-tongued but slow-moving, perspicacious popular favorite, whom Upton Sinclair called "the uncrowned king of America"; but Paine relied largely on what Clemens wished to reveal (or was able to remember) of his origins, his experiences in the West, the early years of his marriage in Elmira and Hartford, his adventures as a publisher, and his shrewd discovery of the way to wealth, then his fall to bankruptcy, and his almost ten-year climb to wealth again. The result was a book as many-faceted, and sometimes as factually unreliable, as Mark Twain himself,

[3] Quoted in Albert Bigelow Paine, Mark Twain, A Biography: The Personal and Literary Life of Samuel L. Clemens (3 vols.; New York: Harper & Brothers, 1912), II, 915–16.

without a critical center, but filled with anecdotes and evidences of mood which provided inadvertent revelations of a
kind that lay readers of an author's personality or motives
have always clutched at eagerly, with humorless delight.

Paine spoke of the affection and influence of Mrs. Clemens.
He talked, as every biographer of Mark Twain must, of the
assistance and long friendship of Howells; of Mark Twain's
dissatisfaction with a steady job in California, New York,
Washington, or Elmira; of the community in Hartford where
Mark Twain moved familiarly among faddish late-Victorian
people who were interested in a variety of reforms, some of
which to a later generation have seemed tentative or silly; of
his grief and despair and self-accusation on the death of a
brother, a son, two daughters, and a wife; of his perky dis-
claimers of interest in "literature and all that bosh." Paine
relied on the memory of Clemens' daughter that many a
"delightful terrible part" of *Huckleberry Finn* had been deleted at the command of Mrs. Clemens. He showed the experienced Howells giving shrewdly practical editorial advice.

Van Wyck Brooks pounced on all of these, but especially
on Paine's dramatic account of the death of young Sam
Clemens' father, when the boy, barely in his teens and
wracked with grief and remorse, tearfully promised his
mother, as they stood together by the dead man's bedside, to
be a good boy and to become as successful (and wealthy) as
his father would have wished; and how then Sam was so disturbed that for nights afterwards he walked in his sleep,
until released from somnambulism by the touch of his mother's hand and the sound of her voice. Such an influence, such
a traumatic experience, left scars, Brooks thought, which
time never healed, but which were aggravated by Mark
Twain's contacts with the money-grabbing, celebrity-seeking,
laughter-intoxicated, irresponsible late nineteenth century.

For most people, Mark Twain remained what he had been

for Howells, "a comic force unique in the power of charming us out of our cares." [4] Certainly, his spirit still lived—and in a very real sense: a former Columbia University professor had spoken to it in a seance, and had received table-rocking assurances from the ghost of Mark Twain that never during his earthly existence had he ever had to suppress a single word he wanted to say. [5] Professor Stuart Sherman, from the University of Illinois, was fond of speaking and writing about "The Democracy of Mark Twain," [6] and with knowledge of what was unmistakably "polite" in American letters, borrowed Emerson's term to call Mark Twain "one of our great representative men":

He is the fulfilled promise of American life. He proves the virtues of the land and the society in which he was born and fostered. He incarnates the spirit of an epoch in American history when the nation, territorially and spiritually enlarged, entered lustily upon new adventures. In the retrospect he looms for us with Whitman and Lincoln, recognizably his countrymen, out of the shadows of the Civil War, an unmistakable native son of an eager, westward-moving people— unconventional, self-reliant, mirthful, profane, realistic, cynical, boisterous, popular, tender-hearted, touched with chivalry, and permeated to the marrow of his bones with the sentiment of democratic society and with loyalty to American institutions. [7]

Such polished professorial rhetoric seemed empty, if not pretentious, to men of Van Wyck Brooks's persuasion. "I am glad you are going to get at Twain," Sherwood Anderson had written him in the spring of 1918. "It is absurd that he should

---

[4] William Dean Howells, "Mark Twain: An Inquiry," *North American Review*, CLXXI (1901), 321; reprinted in Howells, *My Mark Twain* (New York: Harper & Brothers, 1910), 166–85.
[5] James Hervey Hyslop, *Contact with the Other World* (New York: Century Co., 1919), 249–81.
[6] Stuart Sherman, *On Contemporary Literature* (New York: Henry Holt & Co., 1917), 15–19.
[7] Stuart P. Sherman, "Mark Twain," in Sherman and others (eds.), *Cambridge History of American Literature* (4 vols.; New York: Macmillan Co., 1917–21), III, 2.

have been translated as an artist by a man like Howells or that fellow Paine. There was something about him no one has got hold of. He belonged out here in the Middle West and was only incidentally a writer." A few days later, he wrote again:

As far as Mark Twain is concerned, we have to remember the influences about him. Remember how he came to literature—the crude buffoon of the early days of the mining camps—the terrible cheap and second-rate humor of *Innocents Abroad*. It seems to me that when he began he addressed an audience that gets a big laugh out of the braying of a jackass and without a doubt Mark often brayed at them. He knew that later. There was tenderness and subtility in Mark when he grew older.

You get the picture of him, Brooks—the river man who could write going East and getting in with the New England crowd—the fellows from barren hills and barren towns. The best he got out of that bunch was Howells and Howells did Twain no good.[8]

Meanwhile, another of the group got to Mark Twain before Brooks did. Waldo Frank was the first to suggest in print that Clemens had been victimized by his frontier environment, to become "a defeated soul":

Out of the bitter wreckage of his lone life, one great work emerges by whose contrasting fire we can observe the darkness. This work is *Huckleberry Finn.* . . . The balance of his literary life, before and after, went mostly to the wastage of half-baked, half-believed, half-clownish labor. And underneath the gibes and antics of the professional jester, brooded the hatred and resentment of a tortured child. Mark Twain, in his conscious mind, shared his people's attitude of contempt for "art and spiritual matters"—shared their standards of success. Mark Twain strove to make money and to please! This great soul came to New York and felt ashamed before the little dancing-masters of the magazines; felt humble before Richard Watson Gilder and William Dean Howells! Shared their conviction that he was only a crude, funny writer, from Missouri; changed the texts of his books to suit their fancy. Mark Twain did not believe in his soul, and his soul

[8] *Letters of Sherwood Anderson*, ed. Howard Mumford Jones and Walter Rideout (Boston: Little, Brown & Co., 1953), 30–31, 32–33.

suffered. Mark Twain believed, with his fellows, that the great sin was to be unpopular and poor, and his soul died. His one great work was the result of a burst of spirit over the dikes of social inhibition and intellectual fear.

Waldo Frank's subject was not Mark Twain, but America: the dismal failure of his country, its subservience to the machine that was a "sucking monster which, as it sucked swelled larger and so sucked more. Feed the machine of life. Do not stop. Open your veins." For "the clown tragedy of Mark Twain is prelude to the American drama. The generic Clemens was a tender and dreaming and avid spirit, in love with beauty, in love with love. But," said Frank, "he was born in the ranks of a hurling and sweating army. He forced himself to move with it at its own pace. He forced himself to take on its measures of success; to take on that distrust of life and love which so well defended the principal business of its march. For this betrayal of his soul, the soul brought him bitterness, and the mass of his works are failures." [9]

When Brooks's longer, broader, more eloquent, but equally severe indictment appeared a year later as *The Ordeal of Mark Twain*—with its thesis that Mark Twain's bitterness "was the effect of a certain miscarriage in his creative life, a balked personality, an arrested development of which he himself was almost wholly unaware, but which for him destroyed the meaning of life" and his possibilities for success as an artist —then other critics jumped immediately to the fray. Sherwood Anderson wrote admiringly to Brooks, "Twain is dead; he paid the price of caving in." But at the same time, he wrote to Waldo Frank, telling him that the longer he read in Brooks's book, the more Anderson pictured himself in Mark Twain's place, so that he began to realize "just how impossible it was for Brooks to really see the man." He wrote another, an angry letter then to Brooks (which seems not to

[9] Waldo Frank, "The Land of the Frontier," *Our America* (New York: Boni & Liveright, 1919), 37–44.

survive) accusing him—he told Frank—of using psychological trickery: "How easy to slaughter the artist Twain now he is safely dead." [10]

Other voices rose in protest. "It is a treacherous business," said Alvin Johnson, "for a critic devoid of a sense of humor to hold an incorrigible humorist too strictly to account": "There are two questions here: one whether American institutions are in fact so hopelessly corrupt as Van Wyck Brooks assumes; the other whether Mark Twain was by temperament fitted to perceive institutional corruption, and perceiving it, to understand the work of exposure. . . . [Mark Twain] accepted American institutions as a tremendous improvement on the rest of the world. . . . Therefore he could not have made himself a satirist according to Mr. Brooks's taste." [11] Critics like Brooks, temporized Henry Seidel Canby, do not understand Mark Twain's boisterousness "because it is not a literary boisterousness, nor his pessimism because it is not a literary pessimism, the first being a lecture habit by which he roused his own mind to humorous pitch and set his audience laughing, the second a direct expression of brooding thought which uses words in default of action." [12]

Carl Van Doren, who had presented a discriminating review of the *Ordeal* soon after its appearance,[13] later continued his estimate of the book: "That it is an arraignment . . . and exhibits instances of special pleading and definite animus must be admitted, even by those who, like myself, agree that the picture here drawn of our great humorist is substantially accurate as well as brilliant." Yet "one thing that makes me suspect at times the general drift of Mr. Brooks's argument is that a good many of the details of his psychoanalyzing

[10] *Letters of Sherwood Anderson*, 60–61.

[11] Alvin Johnson, "The Tragedy of Mark Twain," *New Republic*, XXIII (July 14, 1920), 201–204.

[12] Henry Seidel Canby, "Mark Twain," *Literary Review*, IV (1923), 202.

[13] Carl Van Doren, "The Fruits of the Frontier," *Nation*, CXI (August 14, 1920), 189.

look suspicious. . . . I think he has reduced Mark Twain too neatly to a dualistic pattern." [14] At another time, Van Doren suggested that Mark Twain's failure was the result of lack of discipline rather than because of some hidden neurosis,[15] a supposition in which he was later joined by Bernard DeVoto and, recently, by Albert E. Stone, Jr., who says:

One does not need to endorse fully *The Ordeal of Mark Twain* to see that the social and financial pressures of genteel living had a profound effect on Twain's method of writing and on what he wrote. The well-known habit, for example, of composing under the inspiration of the moment and then putting the manuscript aside when the original impulse slackened was in part accommodation to this social pattern. With only the summers entirely free for concentrated labor, it is not surprising that he wrote by fits and starts. As an amanuensis, he had to defer to the caprice not only of *his* daemon but to those of his house guests.[16]

John Macy had little patience with Brooks's theorizing: Mark Twain "said all he had to say, he knew how to say it, and circumstances fostered his genius." [17] C. Hartley Grattan, admitting that Mark Twain failed in literary discipline and that he was undoubtedly influenced by the acquisitive ideals of those about him, yet found him "an idealist of a most uncompromising sort," who "was strong enough to reject" whatever "violated his ideals of decency and honor." [18] Stephen Leacock was sure that the West made Mark Twain, and made it possible for him to conquer the East with his breezy gusto. As for Mrs. Clemens, Howells, and the rest—

[14] Carl Van Doren, "The Lion and the Unicorn," *The Roving Critic* (New York: Alfred A. Knopf, 1923), 45–55.

[15] Carl Van Doren, "Posthumous Thunder," *Saturday Review of Literature*, I (October 25, 1924), 225.

[16] Albert E. Stone, Jr., *The Innocent Eye: Childhood in Mark Twain's Imagination* (New Haven: Yale University Press, 1961), 127; see also Bernard DeVoto, *Mark Twain at Work* (Cambridge: Harvard University Press, 1942), *passim.*

[17] John Macy, *The Story of the World's Literature* (New York: Horace Liveright, 1925), 532.

[18] C. Hartley Grattan, "Mark Twain," *American Writers on American Literature*, ed. John Macy (New York: Horace Liveright, 1931), 275–77.

"They did their loving best to ruin his work—and failed; that's all." [19]

But almost everyone agreed that Brooks wrote with infectious verve. Even fifteen years afterwards, Edward Wagenknecht could say, "One may agree with Mr. Brooks or one may disagree with him. One may even disagree with him acrimoniously. The only thing one cannot do with Mr. Brooks is to ignore him." [20] When conservative William Lyon Phelps reviewed the *Ordeal* in the New York *Times* of June 27, 1920, he said:

> Many books have been written about Mark Twain; but with the exception of Paine's biography, this work by Mr. Brooks is the most important and most essential. Whether one agrees with Mr. Brooks's thesis or not—and I do not—one must admire and ought to profit by the noble and splendid purpose animating it. It is a call to every writer and every man and woman not to sin against their own talents. . . . The main idea of the book is that Mark Twain's career was a tragedy—a tragedy for himself and a tragedy for mankind. Every man who does not live up to his highest possibilities is living in a state of sin. Mark Twain was, therefore, one of the chief sinners, because his possibilities were so great and he fell so short. There were two villains in Mark Twain's tragedy—his mother and his wife. His mother was more eager to have him good than to have him great; his wife wanted him to be a gentleman. Between them, they tamed the lion and made him perform parlor tricks.

Most of the younger men believed that Brooks had hit square to the mark. Alfred Kreymborg admired his intellectual honesty in exposing Mark Twain as "America's last buf-

---

[19] Stephen Leacock, *Mark Twain* (New York: D. Appleton & Co., 1933), 21, 64.

[20] Edward Wagenknecht, *Mark Twain: The Man and His Work* (New Haven: Yale University Press, 1935), 173. When Mr. Wagenknecht revised his book a quarter of a century later (Norman: University of Oklahoma Press, 1961), he also revised this opinion, saying then that "though Mr. Brooks's thesis has never been accepted by anybody who knows anything about Mark Twain, it still maintains a hold over persons who are more interested in theories about literature than they are interested in literature" (164–65 n). Something of an "official" scholarly position is represented by

toon." [21] Harvey O'Higgins thought Mark Twain was proved to be "as profound a biological failure as America has produced." [22] Frank Harris savagely attacked his "shallowness of soul." [23] Upton Sinclair, himself expert as muckraker and prolific as a novelist, testified:

There were only two possible ways for [the artist in America] to survive; one was to flee to New York and be lost in the crowd; the other was to turn into a clown and join in the laughing at himself and at everything he knew to be serious and beautiful in life. This latter course was adopted by a man of truly great talent, who might have become one of the world's satiric masters if he had not been overpowered by the spirit of America. . . . Mark Twain lived a double life; he, the uncrowned king of America, was the most repressed personally, the most completely cowed, shamed, tormented, great man in the history of letters.[24]

However severe the arguments against it or the loyalty of its defenders, *The Ordeal of Mark Twain* has remained now for more than fifty years one of the most challengingly acute and fructifying literary studies of the first half of the twentieth century—"an American classic," says Malcolm Cowley, "that gains in force and more clearly seems permanent when read in its historical context." [25] Not only did it invigorate and intensify studies of Mark Twain and of the effect on him of

E. Hudson Long, *Mark Twain Handbook* (New York: Hendricks House, 1957), 60: "Much of the book is pseudo-science, an attempt to substitute psychological theorizing for common sense, and a tendency to make something mysterious out of the obvious."

[21] Alfred Kreymborg, review of *The Ordeal of Mark Twain*, *Spectator*, CXXX (1923), 701.

[22] Harvey O'Higgins, *The American Mind in Action* (New York: Harper & Brothers, 1924), 26–29.

[23] Frank Harris, "Memories of Mark Twain," *Contemporary Portraits*, Fourth Series (New York: Brentano's, 1923), 173.

[24] Upton Sinclair, *Mammonart: An Essay in Economic Interpretation* (Pasadena: privately printed, 1925), 326–33. Matthew Josephson and Theodore Dreiser, among other author-critics, have agreed on the dual quality in Mark Twain's personality; see Josephson, *Portrait of the Artist as American* (New York: Harcourt, Brace & Co., 1930), 158–61, and Dreiser, "Mark the Double Twain," *English Journal*, XXIV (1935), 615–26.

[25] Malcolm Cowley, Introduction to Van Wyck Brooks, *The Ordeal of Mark Twain* (New York: Meridian Books, 1955), 8.

environment, especially the far-ranging, tradition-free atmosphere of the frontier West (and also in the ignorance of greenhorn Easterners about what the West really was like); it sent critics scurrying deeper into the backgrounds and peccadilloes of other writers, to reveal them wounded also and transmitting to art the awesome memories of their wounds.²⁶ The simplest way of expressing Brooks's effect on literary scholarship and speculation is to say that neither has been or has wanted to be what it was before he blasted them both from complacence. If at first they skipped about petulantly under his prodding, each finally learned to mind its manners, and—agreeing often, in spite of the bruises Brooks had administered to native pride, that much he said was correct— then to look beyond for better reasons than his for explaining the indubitable charm, the egregious great lapses, and the continuing presence of Mark Twain.

"Is Van Wyck Brooks too harsh?" asks Alexander Cowie, for one example, and then replies temperately that perhaps he was. In his own mind, Mark Twain "never 'sold out' to special interest. In fact comparatively early in his career he looked forward to the time when he could 'stop writing for print.' This he planned to do 'as soon as he could afford' it." Yet, Cowie adds, "he deferred this expensive pleasure of saying plainly what he thought. Most of his early books reflected his radical views chiefly in the mirror of history, often rather remote history. The fact is that most of his radical publications appeared during the last ten or twelve years of his life and some of the most cogent things appeared posthumously." That is, Cowie seems to say, and many have agreed with him, Brooks was certainly correct, but somewhat unworldly:

²⁶ See, for example, two entirely dissimilar books, Henry Nash Smith's *Virgin Land: The American West as Symbol and Myth* (Cambridge: Harvard University Press, 1950), and Philip Young's *Ernest Hemingway* (New York: Rinehart & Co., 1952), both of which derive, the one at tangent, the other directly, from Brooks.

In approaching the problem of suppression, one must bear in mind Mark Twain's rather delicate position. It is comparatively easy for a social outcast or an economic derelict to attack the system he thinks responsible for his failure. But Clemens was a successful writer almost from the first. As a successful author he was caught up in and to some extent dependent on the web of the very system which he castigated as so iniquitous. He was living among the pillars of the very structure he sometimes wished to demolish—an irresolute Samson. How could the man who invested in market tips from Henry Rogers [the Standard Oil Company executive who came to Clemens' financial assistance when the writer was bankrupt] arraign the capitalistic regime? Was it graceful for the bosom friend of Joseph Twichell, a Hartford minister, to say in print that the latter's profession was hollow mockery? Moreover it was hard for Clemens to go counter to the wishes of one he revered so much as he did his wife, and there is no doubt that on scores of occasions Mrs. Clemens either persuaded Clemens not to publish an item which she regarded as potentially harmful to his reputation or forced him to drain off its bitterness before he gave it to his public. Then there was Howells, dear Howells. Storms never came up in Howells's mind —only temperate breezes—and his mild editorial influence more than once helped to calm Mark Twain—especially when the latter was raging against the Almighty.

"All these," concludes Cowie, "were restraining influences and there was no doubt that Mark Twain the writer was modified by them." It was the sensible and decent and loyal thing to do—to be modified. "It is likely, too," says Cowie, "that in doing so he created in himself a state of exasperation that was only partially relieved by private expression, often extremely profane, in conversation and in letters." [27]

Much academic criticism has been of this kind, temperately accepting the thesis of the *Ordeal,* then turning to an explanation of how Mark Twain, being what he was (wounded?) and living when he did, could not, indeed should not, have turned out to be anything other than what he became. How Ameri-

[27] Alexander Cowie, *The Rise of the American Novel* (New York: American Book Co., 1948), 631–33.

can! Brooks might often have replied (but did not); how profoundly and precisely and ineluctably characteristic of exactly the kind of chameleon compliance the *Ordeal* spoke of; how ineradicable the malaise of American society!

Like many others, Stanley Edgar Hyman—a man of indestructible wit—discovered the greatest weakness of the *Ordeal* to be Brooks's lack of a sense of proportion, his "absolute and lifelong humorlessness." But Hyman also finds "much of the book . . . very perceptive; among other things, Brooks's recognition that the symbol of the Mississippi pilot was the archetype of freedom and creative satisfaction, even of art, for Twain . . . ; his awareness that Twain's later receiving in bed was a retrogressive pattern, like Proust's cork-lined room; his identification of Twain's concern with dual personality in such stories as 'Those Extraordinary Twins' as essentially cycloid; his observation that *The Gilded Age* is essentially a discussion of business in religious imagery." But "the book also contains," says Hyman, "a good measure of foolishness, distortion, and oversimplified use of Marx, Veblen, Freud, and whatever theoretical club comes to hand, even a rather corny moral to the effect that since the system did this to Twain, writers, revolt!" The *Ordeal's* greatest flaw was that "to fit Twain perfectly into the Procrustean bed of his thesis, Brooks is forced to stretch and lop off, that is, to underestimate Twain's accomplishments vastly, calling him the author of works 'of inferior quality' appealing to 'rudimentary minds,' while at the same time insisting that he could have been a Voltaire, Swift, or Cervantes." [28]

Brooks's use of Freudian analysis has seemed to Alfred Kazin sporadic, declamatory, and without logical coherence, and his literary criticism distorted by the assumption which Lionel Trilling has remarked as common among most literary

[28] Stanley Edgar Hyman, *The Armed Vision: A Study in the Methods of Modern Literary Criticism* (New York: Alfred A. Knopf, 1948), 113–14. Hyman presents (114–16) an informative but incomplete reading of the revisions Brooks made for a new edition of the *Ordeal* in 1933.

Freudians, that the "meaning" of a work is to be discovered in
its author's intention, not in its effect. Yet, says Kazin,

Brooks's conception of the Gilded Age was not false; it was a
great literary myth, like Henry Adams's glowing interpretation of
twelfth-century culture, or Nietzsche's Dionysian portrait of Greek
drama—one of those primary hypotheses by literary men that give
a design to history and awaken its imagination. But as he applied
it to Mark Twain it rested on a curious amalgamation of social
history and literary psychoanalysis that was so dazzling and new
in 1920, still so fundamentally a challenge to old conventions,
that it was at once unconvincing and incontestable. . . . Like the
Freudians, Brooks was writing to a thesis; but it was not a Freudian thesis. His aim was to dramatize a great artist (Mark Twain)
degraded by a narrow, prudish, greedy, hostile environment (the
Gilded Age, Olivia Clemens, the frontier, and so on). In that
aim, certainly, he succeeded brilliantly, and by his own sensibility and seriousness invested the whole context of late
nineteenth-century letters in America with a tragic and unforgettable force.[29]

As time has gone on, Brooks has been corrected, point by
point, by people who have more carefully investigated the
historical background of Samuel Clemens. "Mark Twain
knew more of his America than his more scornful successors,"
said one anonymous early commentator. "Perhaps that is
why he liked his country in spite of the defects of his countrymen."[30] Looking back over the years, many have agreed
with Frederick W. Dupee:

It is one thing to muckrake a period, as Brooks here so effectively
muckrakes the genteel era, pointing out its stultifying effects on a
writer of genius, but it is quite another thing again to assume that
in happier conditions your writer would be a Tolstoy. That is
more or less what Brooks does assume, with the result that the
historical Mark Twain is everywhere dogged by the shadow of an
ideal or potential or Unconscious Mark Twain, a kind of spectral

[29] Kazin, On Native Grounds, 284–85.
[30] "Mark Twain, Radical," Saturday Review of Literature, I (November
1, 1924), 241.

elder brother whose brooding presence is an eternal reproof to the mere author of *Huckleberry Finn.*[31]

To counter Brooks, Minnie Brashear in *Mark Twain, Son of Missouri* (1934) made perhaps extravagant claims for the cultural climate of Clemens' native state and hometown. "The real Hannibal," mediated Dixon Wecter, "was neither the cultural desert imagined by Van Wyck Brooks nor the seat of the muses patriotically conceived by Minnie Brashear" on the strength of casual advertisements of books for sale which appeared in local newspapers: "The basic culture of Sam Clemens's Hannibal was literate not literary." [32] Ivan Benson, who followed Mark Twain's trail assiduously through the West, said:

Brooks has made much of the supposed mother-complex which exerted a powerful influence on Sam Clemens and his literary career. Yet certainly there is no evidence of this psychological factor during Clemens's Western years. Samuel Clemens's letters during the first year in the West, and, in fact, during the whole five and one-half years of his Western period, are anything but intimate love letters. They are rough, businesslike, only moderately informal letters addressed rather generally to the folks, or to his mother and sister—occasionally to "My Dear Mother"—full of boisterousness, slapstick, good and bad humor, with the ordinary amount of information a normal boy would write. It requires a lively imagination to find any mother-complex in the Western Mark Twain.[33]

Max Eastman, who had lived there as a boy, defended Mark Twain's Elmira from Brooks's charge that it had been

[31] Frederick W. Dupee, "The Americanism of Van Wyck Brooks," *Partisan Review,* VI (Summer, 1939), 69–85. This essay, the most maturely professional estimate of Brooks's achievement, is reprinted in *The Partisan Reader, 1934–44: An Anthology,* ed. William Phillips and Philip Rahv (New York: Dial Press, 1946), and in *Critiques and Essays in Criticism, 1920–1948,* ed. Robert W. Stallman (New York: Ronald Press Co., 1948).

[32] Dixon Wecter, *Sam Clemens of Hannibal* (Boston: Houghton Mifflin Co., 1952), 209.

[33] Ivan Benson, *Mark Twain's Western Years* (Stanford, Calif.: Stanford University Press, 1938), 43.

a bourgeois, backward community.[34] Mark Twain's niece and nephew defended his mother, Jane Clemens.[35] DeLancey Ferguson, who was to become Mark Twain's most perceptive biographer, and Cyril Clemens, distantly related to the humorist, both defended Mark Twain's wife.[36] "How often," said his daughter, "did my father express his gratitude at the marvelous fate that had given him such a companion, one who was as deeply absorbed in his work as he was himself, one who had a pure instinct for the correct values in literature as well as in life, and one whose adverse criticism proved invariably to be a just criticism because her intuition—born of a large heart and mind—hit the target plumb on the center." [37] Dixon Wecter later ridiculed the whole "silly Freudian controversy," which supposed that some ordeal made Mark Twain "into a kind of hen-pecked Rabelais." [38]

Richard Burton, a friend and neighbor of Mark Twain's at Hartford, jumped quickly to the defense of that city,[39] and Kenneth R. Andrews, in a detailed study of the congenial, well-intentioned people who lived there in Clemens' neighborhood, seconded him firmly:

It has often been said that the gentility of Hartford, supposedly hostile to the burgeoning of Mark Twain's satiric power, helped warp him as a satirist of his own time and imposed upon him a mediocre conventionality that emasculated his work and frustrated his spirit. The obvious untruth of such a judgment does not

[34] Max Eastman, "Mark Twain's Elmira," *Harper's Magazine*, CLXXVI (1935), 620–32.
[35] Doris and Charles Webster, "Whitewashing Jane Clemens," *Bookman*, LXI (1925), 531–35.
[36] Cyril Clemens, "The True Character of Mark Twain's Wife," *Missouri Historical Review*, XXIV (1929), 40–49, and DeLancey Ferguson, "The Case for Mark Twain's Wife," *University of Toronto Quarterly*, IX (1939), 9–21.
[37] Clara Clemens, *My Father, Mark Twain* (New York: Harper & Brothers, 1931), 67–68.
[38] Dixon Wecter (ed.), *The Love Letters of Mark Twain* (New York: Harper & Brothers, 1949), 1–15.
[39] Richard Burton, "Mark Twain in the Hartford Days," *Mark Twain Quarterly*, I (Summer, 1937), 5.

mean that Mark Twain was unaffected by the standards of taste operative in Hartford and in Elmira. . . . The gentility of Hartford . . . was more flexible, amiable and genial than sinister. The narrowness, complacence, sterility, and Grundyism sometimes thought to have vitiated the literature of the post-war decades and to have prevented Mark Twain from attaining his full greatness do not appear to have been decisive at Nook Farm.[40]

What first brought criticism tumbling in torrents about Brooks's heady suppositions was the growing interest of historians, even literary historians, in testing Frederick Jackson Turner's theories of the influence of the frontier on the development of American society and its culture. In a pioneer study, Lucy Lockwood Hazard spoke of Mark Twain as a free-spirited man of the West, greatly more untamed and uninhibited than Brooks had thought him.[41] Vernon Louis Parrington celebrated the humorist as rising triumphant from "The Backwash of the Frontier," the spirit of Mike Fink within him stubbornly refusing to be tamed by Olivia Clemens or anyone else: "Here at last was an authentic American—a native writer thinking his own thoughts, using his own eyes, speaking his own dialect." [42] Constance Rourke insisted that Mark Twain's was "consistently a pioneer talent," firmly bedded in frontier comic tradition.[43] Granville Hicks, however, supposed that the "frontier humorist and realist might have become a great novelist" only by "transcending the limits of his tradition"—which he never quite did.[44] "American humor," countered Walter Blair, "gave Mark Twain his materials, his methods and his inspiration." His genius was in

---

[40] Kenneth R. Andrews, *Nook Farm: Mark Twain's Hartford Circle* (Cambridge: Harvard University Press, 1950), 188, 198.

[41] Lucy Lockwood Hazard, *The Frontier in American Literature* (New York: Thomas Y. Crowell Co., 1928).

[42] Vernon Louis Parrington, *The Beginnings of Critical Realism in America* (New York: Harcourt, Brace & Co., 1930), 88.

[43] Constance Rourke, *American Humor: A Study of the National Character* (New York: Harcourt, Brace & Co., 1931), 209.

[44] Granville Hicks, *The Great Tradition* (New York: Macmillan Co., 1933), 38–49.

recreating the "poetry of folk speech" with the precision and imagination of an artist who deftly "reproduced the rhythms of conversation and evoked the most effective imagery for the purposes of laughter." [45]

V. F. Calverton, though convinced that Mark Twain never really did "sell out" to the upper bourgeoisie, nonetheless did think that the humorist lost something of power when he left the West:

Beginning as a pure frontier product, reeling off his prose all the spontaneity of that region, its hilarious gaieties and irresponsible enthusiasms, he ended in the East as a convinced pessimist and dyspeptic philosopher not less desperate in his despairs than Leopardi. In a way, he was the Charlie Chaplin of American literature. Ever eager, especially in his latter days, to be a Hamlet, he was forced to remain a Falstaff. There were, thus, two Mark Twains and not one, and those who have tried to interpret the contradictions in his character have tripped up very often by their failure to see that this dichotomy in his personality had as much to do with the environment as with the immediate conflict of his soul. The youthful Mark Twain of the West, the avatar of the frontier, who loved pilots, and miners, and the common run of people, who felt himself part of the region he described, and who in a humorous form gave life to those people and to that region— that Mark Twain was an optimist, a lover of life, a devotee of the soil and of the country which he cherished with such childish pride. The other Mark Twain who was successful, had lost the optimism and zest, and lost the faith of his youth. The America that he saw growing up about him was not the America of his dream. The promise of the frontier had begun to grow stale. . . . Indeed, there was little left of the America which he once loved. . . . Carping psychological conflicts and heart-shaking tragedies too had come on Twain, and embittered his personal outlook. To have remained the same man then, to have retained the same philosophy, through all these vicissitudes of change, would have been impossible to any but the most insensitive personality.[46]

---

[45] Walter Blair, *Native American Humor*, 1800–1900 (New York: American Book Co., 1937), 147–62.

[46] V. F. Calverton, *The Liberation of American Literature* (New York: Charles Scribner's Sons, 1932), 319–21.

But the strongest wind that blew on Brooks came gustily down from Harvard in searing words from Bernard DeVoto, a historian who knew and cherished the West, who resented Brooks's implication that it had been a cultural Sahara, and who boiled over with facts to refute him. DeVoto wrote *Mark Twain's America* in eloquent anger, and referred to his book as an "essay in the correction of ideas." "I wish that this able study were not so controversial," complained Henry Seidel Canby in the *Saturday Review of Literature* on October 29, 1932. "I wish that Mr. DeVoto had thrown his stones in a pamphlet and written the book afterward. It is too good a book to be tripped off its balance by the violence of his attack on critics who have misrepresented Mark Twain but are only obstacles in the author's way, not his objective, which is a truer estimate of Twain."

Many agreed with Mary Ellen Chase, who remarked in *Commonweal* on January 11, 1933, that "the element of controversy . . . lends unfortunately a childish aspect to the book"; but others, like Constance Rourke, who reviewed it in the New York *Tribune* on September 11, 1942, enjoyed its "warm eloquence of partisanship, lavishly evoking a whole mind and an era." Mark Van Doren in the *Nation* on October 19, 1932, thought that

Mr. DeVoto would have written a better book if he had known the kind he was writing—if he had known that in his book, too, thought was required. Charging blindly into territory which Mr. Brooks has long dominated by virtue of a beautiful and sinuous intelligence, he leaves himself open on every side. And he never really answers Mr. Brooks, since the only thing that can answer a theory consciously held is another theory consciously held. Mr. DeVoto thinks he is meeting a theory with facts, but as is usual in such situations he only gets tangled in a profusion of data.

DeVoto's thesis in *Mark Twain's America*, most simply stated, is that "Mark Twain was a frontier humorist. His literary intelligence was shaped by the life of the frontier and found expression in the themes and forms developed by the humor of the frontier." Here, in America's expanding West, men knew "intense pleasure in the variety of the world—an exuberant delight which sprang from the frontier's energy."

There was also the frontier's sharp perception—its ability to understand behavior and the motives which produce it. These form the basis of frontier humor which worked out in obscure newspapers the first formidable realism . . . in our literature. What this humor required was some one native to its pleasures and perceptions who could express them on the level of genius. . . . [And Mark Twain] was . . . the expression of this humor at its highest level. . . . It was the basis of his mind, as it was the framework of his books. He was always a frontier humorist, who devoted himself to the promotion of laughter. If he had not been that, he could not have become the satirist and realist who is remembered.

How impertinent, said DeVoto, was the tendency of critics who followed Van Wyck Brooks "to think of Mark Twain not as a writer of books but as a man who either betrayed something sacred or was betrayed by something vile." [47]

John Chamberlain in the New York *Times* on September 11, 1932, wondered "how Mr. Brooks's thesis that Mark Twain was a 'frustrated' writer" could possibly survive "the shock of Mr. DeVoto's scansion." To M. A. DeWolfe Howe in the *Atlantic Monthly* for January, 1933, the book had an authentic ring; but to Newton Arvin in the *New Republic* on October 5, 1932, it seemed shallow and romantic: "It is impossible to accept its views of Mark Twain as merely a humorist." Almost everyone agreed that DeVoto was a better historian than critic. "Unquestionably," said a reviewer of *Mark Twain's America* in the *Forum* for December, 1932, "Mr. DeVoto knows the frontier and unquestionably many of his criticisms of Brooks are justified. Presumably this book is no more completely authoritative than the *Ordeal*—certainly his

[47] Bernard DeVoto, *Mark Twain's America* (Boston: Little, Brown & Co., 1932), 259–60, 298.

estimates of Twain as an artist are sometimes a little lame." But it was a fascinating book DeVoto had written, just the kind, thought a critic in the Boston *Transcript*, that Van Wyck Brooks would most enjoy.

East rose against West in pursuit of the quarrel, as when Arthur Hobson Quinn of the University of Pennsylvania supposed it indeed a good thing that Mrs. Clemens and Howells had trimmed some of the rough edges from Mark Twain: his Western writings were vulgar.[48] "Clemens was the kind of spirit that needed a certain amount of suppression," said Henry Seidel Canby from Yale, "without which he would have fizzed through life like an uncapped soda spring." [49] Clarence Gohdes, a Texan teaching in North Carolina, dourly dismissed the whole "hullabaloo" as inconsequential because as "a thinker, Mark Twain is too inconsistent and too shallow to be of much importance." [50] And Fred Lewis Pattee of Pennsylvania State College thought that "to say that Mark Twain was hamstrung by the East and that as a result he lived his later years a thwarted genius is to argue that ignorance . . . should be quarantined from all contact with art and culture lest its originality be vitiated." [51] Pattee peremptorily dismissed Brooks's contention that Mark Twain's Samson locks had been shorn by his Delilah wife as "Nonsense! Twaddle!" It was "a brilliant half-truth undoubtedly, but one not dangerous. The most damning thing about it is the mosquito swarm of echoing voices it has aroused. . . . It was the East that made Mark Twain. What would he have written had he remained in San Francisco? . . . The Mark Twain that has endured was born in New England. He needed restraint, literary ideals, suggestion, and publication in ade-

[48] Arthur Hobson Quinn, review of Ivan Benson's *Mark Twain's Western Years*, *Pacific Historical Review*, VII (1938), 282–83.

[49] Henry Seidel Canby, "Mark Twain," 201–202.

[50] Clarence Gohdes, "Mirth for the Million," in *Literature of the American People*, ed. A. H. Quinn (New York: Appleton-Century-Crofts, 1952), 710ff.

[51] Fred Lewis Pattee, "On the Rating of Mark Twain," *American Mercury*, XIV (June, 1929), 183–91.

quate magazines. That New England prudishness and puritanism took from his work the element of truth is nonsense." [52]

Nonsense indeed, politely said Walter Blair of Chicago, who knew the West and its humor better than most men: "Consider the claim that Sam's first sketch, 'The Dandy . . . ,' shows that 'even in his teens his ambition was to write humor, and not polite, bookish, Irvingesque humor, but rough, fullbodied humor of his native region'—a claim which hardly seems to square with the fact that a major fault of the sketch is the use of painfully stiff and elegant 'literary language.' " [53] To Edgar M. Branch of Ohio, however, the habits which Mark Twain picked up as a journalist in Nevada and California were responsible for some of his most reprehensible literary defects: "Farce, caricature, and banter replaced his earlier attempts to portray authentic, humorous character. Verbal trickery was preferred to the free flowing, colloquial language he knew so well. It is truer to say that much of what he learned in Washoe went into his mature work—often to its detriment—and that its very presence was often a mark of literary immaturity. When he left Nevada, Mark Twain was a far more practiced writer than he had been before, but too much of his practice had been along harmful lines." [54]

And so the argument continued, niggling at times, but hotly pursued, and gathering small new force from each voice which spoke variations on pronouncements from one side or the other.[55] Through it all, the fervent ingenuity and appeal of

[52] Fred Lewis Pattee, *Mark Twain: Representative Selections* (New York: American Book Co., 1935), xxvii, xxix.

[53] Walter Blair, review of DeLancey Ferguson's *Mark Twain: Man and Legend*, *American Literature*, XVI (1944), 144.

[54] Edgar M. Branch, *The Literary Apprenticeship of Mark Twain* (Urbana: University of Illinois Press, 1950), 174.

[55] The controversy had what Stanley Edgar Hyman in *The Armed Vision* (p. 117) has described as its "comic sequel in 1944 when DeVoto, a decade crustier, wrote a book called *The Literary Fallacy*, a study of the sins of our contemporary writers, which devoted almost half of its one hundred and seventy-five pages to attacking Van Wyck Brooks," who was a Johnny-come-

Brooks's central thesis—that Mark Twain was wounded and that life as lived in the United States aggravated that wound—he remained alive, not because Brooks was right, but because as an artist he created, as Alfred Kazin has said, "a great literary myth," and because as an artist he created it with words more skillfully arranged than those of any of his detractors. Perhaps, one might say, literature does finally prove to be superior to history, depriving fact, in Emerson's terms, of its shining angularity.

"All his critics and biographers seem agreed on Mark Twain's doubleness," observes Richard Chase, "whether they go on to say, with Van Wyck Brooks, that his inner contradictions thwarted and ruined a literary genius or to say, with Mr. DeVoto, that they did not. Probably all his critics agree too that Mark Twain's habit of mind was originally derived from the small-town life on the river that he knew as a boy and from his feeling about it. When Mark Twain invoked Hannibal, Mr. DeVoto says, 'he found there not the idyl of boyhood, but anxiety, violence, supernatural horror, and an uncrystallized but enveloping dread.'" [56] DeVoto did say this, and more besides, sometimes with the authority of a historian who knew the West intimately and from long study, but sometimes with the unreasoning anger of a native son who resented strangers telling him what his home country was like, and who therefore threw mudballs after them, even after they had retreated and gone. "Mr. DeVoto has been chided frequently for not being polite," said Walter Blair, "but it may

lately in disapproving of modern writing only since 1940 (see his "On Literature Today," New York, 1941, an address given at Hunter College the year before) compared to DeVoto, who had hated the stuff for twenty years. Sinclair Lewis, who had also been attacked, replied with an ill-tempered article, "Fools, Liars, and Mr. DeVoto," *Saturday Review of Literature*, XXVII (April 14, 1944), 9–12. Sparks flew, igniting some tempers, but no one was burned, especially not Brooks, who brought to question the often repeated charge that he had no sense of humor by quietly watching the small tempest blow itself out.

[56] Richard Chase, *The American Novel and Its Tradition* (New York: Doubleday Anchor Books, 1957), 149.

be that his bellicosity has some justification in that it does more to knock down error than does the sweetly reasonable American scholarship." [57] As Lewis Mumford once said, "About the *facts* of pioneer life, Mr. DeVoto and Mr. Brooks are . . . in substantial agreement: the slight discrepancy in their points of view comes from the fact that what Mr. Brooks calls Hell, Mr. DeVoto calls Heaven." [58]

In broad outline, the question asked was whether Mark Twain was a sensitive literary artist whose genius had been deformed or whether he was a genuine product of Western America, a folk artist, the kind of unrestricted man whom Emerson had called for, the democratic literatus described by Whitman, a writer who reflected his society with such patient discernment that Ernest Hemingway could say in *The Green Hills of Africa* (1935) that all American literature really began with Mark Twain's masterwork. In the heat of argument, each side overstated its case. Edgar Lee Masters produced in *Mark Twain: A Portrait* (1938) a caricature of the frustration theory: "He tried," says Roger Asselineau, "to do with a bludgeon what Brooks had done with a scalpel. . . . He evaluated Mark Twain's literary activity from a strictly proletarian point of view, blamed him for embracing bourgeois ethics and politics, and deplored that he refused to become a satirist at a time when American society needed one so badly." [59] The result, even in the eyes of conciliatory men like Edward Wagenknecht, was "the worst book ever written on Mark Twain." [60] Those who saw Clemens as only a humorist or a folk artist spoke strongly also. "Criticism which emphasizes

[57] Walter Blair, review of Bernard DeVoto's *Mark Twain at Work*, *American Literature*, XIV (1943), 447.

[58] Lewis Mumford, "Prophet, Pedant, and Pioneer," *Saturday Review of Literature*, IX (1933), 573–75.

[59] Roger Asselineau, "The 'Debunking' of a Hero—or Mark Twain as a Psychic and Social Problem," *The Literary Reputation of Mark Twain from 1910 to 1950: A Critical Essay and a Bibliography* (Paris: Marcel Didier, 1954), 43.

[60] Wagenknecht, *Mark Twain: The Man and His Work* (Norman: University of Oklahoma Press, 1961), 164n.

the esthetic value of literature," said Grant C. Knight, "will spend little time on Samuel L. Clemens." [61] Mark Twain, repeated DeVoto almost fifteen years after the publication of *Mark Twain's America,* "had no conscious esthetic"; he was "not fully a literary artist." [62] If he was, said Dixon Wecter, "Mark Twain the artist had always been a kind of pocket miner, stumbling like fortune's darling upon native ore of incredible richness and exploiting it with effortless skill—but often gleefully mistaking fool's gold for the genuine article, or lavishing his strength upon historical diggings long since played out." [63]

Amid all the skirmishing, Mark Twain as a man of letters, even of excellence in folk-letters, often became lost. Inevitably his love life came under scrutiny, until even Wecter, who rejected Brooks's theories almost entirely, proposed a Freudian supposition of his own which suggested that Mark Twain's low sexual vitality was somehow connected with his inability to face adult dilemmas maturely.[64] Clemens' reticence about sex in his books, to which DeVoto had several times pointed, was extended by Alexander E. Jones to a sense of guilt which extended even to relations with his wife.[65] Connubial privacy was indeed invaded when Edward Wagenknecht supposed that "Mrs. Clemens's health being what it was, . . . there must have been many periods when a physical relationship between them was impossible." [66]

Poor Mark Twain, poor Huck, poor bumbling Colonel Sellers, but especially poor Tom Sawyer, who became inno-

[61] Grant C. Knight, *American Literature and Culture* (New York: Ray Long and Richard R. Smith, 1932), 358.

[62] Bernard DeVoto (ed.), *The Portable Mark Twain* (New York: Viking Press, 1946), 20.

[63] [Dixon Wecter], "Mark Twain," in Robert E. Spiller and others (eds.), *Literary History of the United States* (3 vols.; New York: Macmillan Co., 1948), II, 939.

[64] *Ibid.*

[65] Alexander E. Jones, "Mark Twain and Sexuality," *PMLA,* LXXI (1956), 595–616.

[66] Wagenknecht, *Mark Twain: The Man and His Work,* 156n.

cently a foil representative of everything thwarted or distorted or diverted in Samuel Clemens' character! Was Mark Twain an adolescent, an innocent, a poseur, an aging *enfant terrible*, a vaudevillian eager for top billing, a huckster grasping for the fast buck, an artist who sold out for a mess of royalties, or a man who hid behind his comic mask a vast profound disillusionment with the whole "damned human race"? Which of these was Mark Twain—"Mark the Double Twain," as Theodore Dreiser called him? Or was he all of these things? Or none—only a man who wanted to write well, when circumstances or mood or spirit allowed him?

DeLancey Ferguson first called halt to the wild horses which strained almost out of control on either side, by declaring simply that "Mark Twain was not a folk humorist but a highly skilled man of letters . . . a humorist who knows what he is doing and making the most of his materials," [67] and by demonstrating that most of the manuscript changes in *Huckleberry Finn* were made, not in the interest of morals or taste, but of art.[68] Since then Ferguson and Gladys Bellamy, Edgar M. Branch, Richard P. Adams, James M. Cox, and many others have turned to what seems today the legitimate province of literary criticism—concern with what a man wrote rather than with why he wrote it. The pendulum of opinion has settled slowly toward a middle position, still swinging, but less widely. Leo Marx today discovers a "lapse of moral vision" in Mark Twain, and Kenneth S. Lynn finds him deriving from Western humor; but each writes as a critic with his eye focused on the literary object.[69] Outdoing DeVoto in

[67] DeLancey Ferguson, review of Walter Blair's *Native American Humor*, *American Literature*, IX (1938), 482–84.

[68] DeLancey Ferguson, "Huck Finn Aborning," *Colophon*, III, n.s. (1938), 171–80; see also Walter Blair's informed study of the composition of *Huckleberry Finn* in *Mark Twain and Huck Finn* (Berkeley: University of California Press, 1960).

[69] See Leo Marx, "Mr. Eliot, Mr. Trilling, and *Huckleberry Finn*," *American Scholar*, XXII (1953), 423–40, and Kenneth S. Lynn, *Mark Twain and Southwestern Humor* (Boston: Little, Brown & Co., 1960).

gusto, vying with Brooks in sensibility and control over what can sometimes seem (though it is not) a wildly obstreperous language, Leslie Fiedler has found them both right, and both wrong; pushing further in each direction than either had been willing or able to go, Fiedler finds Mark Twain wounded, but not fatally, a literary figure of dignity, limitations, and power.[70] Daniel G. Hoffman has extended and documented some of Constance Rourke's suggestions of the influence of folk background on Mark Twain, to show how he, like Cooper, Hawthorne, and Melville, has been molded by indigenous tradition.[71] Sidney Kraus's study of Mark Twain's literary judgments demonstrates his place in and his attitude toward intellectual tradition.

Many minds have changed. DeVoto moved finally closer to Brooks's position, and Brooks closer to DeVoto.[72] "I wish you would indicate," writes Granville Hicks about what he said of Mark Twain in *The Great Tradition* [73] thirty years earlier, "that it does not fully represent my present opinion. The chief difference is that I should say more today of what Mark Twain did accomplish, though I have much the same opinion of what he didn't and why." "Too much of the critical writing on Mark Twain," once said James T. Farrell, "has stressed his failure and limitations." [74] But this seems no longer completely true. Bolstered by the commendation of Ernest Hemingway and the sensitive, informed criticism of James M. Cox,

70 Leslie Fiedler, *Love and Death in the American Novel* (New York: Criterion Books, 1960), 553–74.

71 Daniel G. Hoffman, *Form and Fable in American Fiction* (New York: Oxford University Press, 1961), 317–42.

72 See DeVoto's *Mark Twain at Work* and *The Portable Mark Twain*, and Van Wyck Brooks's *Howells: His Life and His World* (New York: E. P. Dutton & Co., 1959), and *The Times of Melville and Whitman* (New York: E. P. Dutton & Co., 1947), in which he describes Mark Twain as a great folk artist, a "serio-comic Homer" (448–65).

73 Granville Hicks, *The Great Tradition* (New York: Macmillan Co., 1933), 39–49.

74 James T. Farrell, *The League of Frightened Philistines* (New York: Vanguard Press, 1945), 25.

Richard Chase, T. S. Eliot, and Lionel Trilling, the man who wrote and spoke as Mark Twain is being more surely evaluated, no longer as an eccentric whose frustrations must be explained, but as a writer who wrote conspicuously well.

After all the argument about what he might have been or should have been dies down, his books remain, as well as the character called Mark Twain who was the inspired creation of a talented man named Samuel L. Clemens. The argument has not been unuseful; its distorted emphases on one side or the other plot the fluctuations of the self-fascinated or society-fascinated critical mind as it has moved, often through honest misjudgments, sometimes almost imperceptibly, toward better understanding of itself, its environment, and its proper study. An examination of the controversy over Mark Twain's wound provides in miniature a history of the developing thought of our century, through its enchantment with suggestions offered by men like Marx and Freud and Van Wyck Brooks and Bernard DeVoto, who have fed it and wished it well. In reviewing the controversy, the person of informed humility will remind himself that what he is reading is the story of how men's minds have reacted to Mark Twain, his achievements, and his limitations, and that it is not really about Mark Twain at all. That is another subject, which will be longer with us, and more absorbing.

3

❧

The Bankruptcy of Mark Twain

SAMUEL CLEMENS HAD a cold when he landed in New York on September 7, 1893, hurrying home from Europe to see what could be done in this panic year about his investments in the Paige typesetting machine and in his publishing company which floundered now in—he thought—the incompetent hands of an incompetent nephew. To cure the cold, he drank "almost a whole bottle" of whiskey, went warmly to bed, and got up the next morning, he boasted to his daughter, "perfectly well." His throat was a constant trouble to him—even giving up smoking every night did not cure it; but he was acquainted perforce, and gladly, with Dr. Clarence C. Rice, a jovial fellow-member of the Players Club, and a specialist in such matters who did or would cure the throats of other celebrities, like Edwin Booth, Enrico Caruso, and Lillian Russell. He was "a physician of great reputation," thought Clemens, "and one of the choicest human beings in the world."

He stayed with Dr. Rice at his home at 123 East 19th Street during his first weeks in New York, while he scurried about on Wall Street and among the banks, trying desperately to raise money for his ailing enterprises. None was to be had, not "at any rate of interest whatever, or upon any security, or by *anybody*." Seeing his friend's distress, Dr. Rice came to his rescue. He had another patient who was wealthy ("a rich friend of his who was an admirer of mine," Clemens later explained), and he told him of the straits Mark Twain was in, and then he introduced him to the rich friend, and neither Samuel Clemens nor Mark Twain was ever quite the same again.

They were indistinguishable, these two—Samuel Clemens, who thirty years before had invented Mark Twain, and Mark Twain, who could play the fool, could laugh at and laugh away the failures which Samuel Clemens had made, to become the innocent at home or abroad who could tell the most outrageous whoppers and get away with them: "I didn't say that," Samuel Clemens could say, "Mark Twain said that. Don't blame me." For Mark Twain became a mask behind which Samuel Clemens could hide; and Samuel Clemens, always something of an entrepreneur, a kind of literary confidence man, supplied Mark Twain with all the proper virtues: he was a man's man, gruff and laconic; he had been places and done things, and he spoke of them in the language of men, but he respected women and he flattered them, and he was a little henpecked by his wife. Mark Twain was a riverman's term for water which was safe, but just safe, for navigation; and Clemens' Mark Twain was only just safe as a literary commodity. He had great successes and horrible failures; he was marvelous at his best when guided by recollection and sentiment, but jejune and embarrassing at his worst when Clemens interrupted him by thinking.

For Samuel Clemens was insistently beguiled into thinking that he should be a rich man. He had just missed riches in the silver fields of Nevada, the gold fields and timberlands of California; he had not made it as a newspaperman in Buffalo; but he had nurtured Mark Twain so well as a wandering reporter and lecturer and as a writer of books which were peddled from door to door by subscription agents that by the time he reached his forties Clemens had a big house in Hartford, a circle of friends which included Beechers and Stowes and even the local clergyman, and there he lived a quiet life, productive and extremely profitable. His best books had been written then, but he did not yet know that. His happiest years were behind him.

For soon this comfortably respectable world had fallen to pieces around him. Restless and unsatisfied with what he had, he wanted more. Mark Twain's books should sell more widely —his publisher, he thought, was robbing him: "A publisher," he explained, "is by nature so low and vile that . . . from the bottom of my heart I wish all publishers were in hell." So he had become his own publisher, and was on his way now toward the hell of bankruptcy. For years he had also been supplying money, sometimes as much as $3,000 a month, toward the support of an inventor who was going to perfect a typesetting machine which would make them both rich. But Samuel Clemens was not an astute businessman. Nothing worked, except when Mark Twain could be funny, or write good books.

By the early 1890's he was frantic, and facing financial disaster. He had left Hartford and taken his family abroad where they might live less expensively, and he worried and fretted and swore and beat his brow as he felt financial ruin nipping at his heels. But then he met Dr. Rice's rich friend, who steered him through bankruptcy and upward toward riches again. But at a price—for the story of the friendship between these two takes on Faustian overtones, as Clemens in a very real, very human, and very fallible sense exchanged moral for financial bankruptcy.

The rich friend was Henry Huttleston Rogers, and he and Clemens hit it off splendidly, and at once. They were two of a kind, and they even looked alike. Each had been a poor boy; each had risen in the true American tradition; each was

now, in his own right, famous. Rogers was of New England
background, and he had known the oil fields of Pennsylvania
much as Clemens had known the silver fields of Nevada and
the gold fields of California, and now, in 1893, he was executive head of the gigantic Standard Oil Company, known with
John D. and William Rockefeller, John D. Archbold, and
Henry M. Flagler as one of the more wealthy and most ruthless men of his time. "Hell-hound Rogers," he was called, a
pirate and a butcher, a malefactor of great wealth. "No pun-
ishable offense," said the New York *Times,* had ever been
formally proved against him, but his "share in the unfair and
abhorrent methods of Standard Oil was so considerable that
he ought therefore to have suffered increasing torments of
remorse; and undoubtedly he did not so suffer."

Rogers' Midas touch in speculation was one which Colonel
Sellers, or Samuel Clemens, might well envy. The capitalist
who manipulated monopolies in oil and copper and railroads
seemed not unlike the Boss from the Hartford firearms shop
who in *The Connecticut Yankee* with equal bravado and
native skill, and with some explosive help from gunpowder,
bested Merlin and routed the enemies of King Arthur. How
close and warm and rakish became the friendship between
these two; they were cronies in every best sense. Rogers was
the kind of man Clemens most admired—bold, swashbuck-
ling, with a sense of humor, and with millions on millions of
dollars: "He is not only the best friend I have ever had, but
is the best man I have known."

Whatever his public image, Rogers was in private, among
his friends and in his family, the kindliest of men, a good
companion, quietly witty, and warmly responsive. He loved
good stories, and told them well, and he loved the theater; he
had even a few years earlier published a volume of homely
verse—but he never said much about that. Among friends,
he was a man's man, who played poker and billiards, liked
boxing matches and fast racing yachts (and bought himself

one that could outrun even Pierpont Morgan's famed *Corsair*). He was a gruff and affectionate companion, and he and Clemens greeted each other with affectionate, unprintable insults when they met, swapping yarns and schemes for getting Mark Twain out of financial trouble. Clemens envied his new friend, the way he got things done—"no grass grew under his feet"—and the way he manipulated people (like Tom Sawyer, only ever so much more profitably). He liked to lounge in Rogers' office at 26 Broadway, listening entranced to the manipulations of high finance. He dreamed sometimes that he might manipulate that way.

But even Rogers' magic touch and helpful money could not immediately save Clemens. When the publishing company went bankrupt and the typesetting machine proved impractical, debts mounted to over two hundred thousand dollars. Could they be paid, and Clemens approaching sixty? Rogers thought that they could and should be. Clemens was not sure on either count; he seems to have been tempted more than once to cut and run—some of his creditors were scoundrels, he thought, deserving nothing. He cursed them in private. But Mark Twain was a man of public gestures, and he let it be known that he would travel around the whole world, old as he was and ill as he was, and that he would lecture and lecture until every creditor was paid in full. Privately, he did not think it could be done, but the newspapers cornered him, and he made a bold front of it: "The law," he told them, "recognizes no mortgage on a man's brain, but I am not a business man, and honor is a harder master than the law." So, and at Rogers' insistence and with Rogers' encouragement, he made the trip, and preserved the image of Mark Twain among his admirers.

While he was away, Rogers handled Clemens' business affairs, alternately fighting off and paying off creditors, investing for him in copper and railroads and oil, so that by 1900, when the Clemens family returned to the United States, their debts were done away with, and they were back where Clemens always wanted to be, on the road toward wealth. But by that time he was really ill and old and bitter. While they had been away in Europe his oldest daughter had died; and he learned that his youngest daughter was an incurable epileptic; and he saw that Mrs. Clemens was worn and weak and ill, and that embittered him more. "I cannot think," he wrote, "why God, in a moment of idle and unintelligent folly, invented this bastard human race. And why after inventing it, he chose to make each individual in it a nest of disgusting and unnecessary diseases, a tub of rotten offal."

The tenor of Clemens' life now changed. He who had been a family man, fond of home and the discrete circle of friends at Hartford, became now (as he had been earlier during his Western years) a man of masculine affairs, in which Mrs. Clemens and his daughters had little share. Of his devotion to Mrs. Clemens there can be no doubt; but she was ill and his presence tired her, so that he was allowed to see her during one awful period only for a few minutes each day. But he spoke often of her in public—in after-dinner speeches and lectures which he was increasingly called on to give; his friends and his audiences admired him for the depth of his admiration for his wife. He was Mark Twain, a public man, and his husbandly devotion became a public thing. His whole life was public now—he enjoyed being seen with Rogers and William Rockefeller at prizefights; he was proud when Stanford White took him to Jim Corbett's dressing room at the New York Athletic Club; he liked being seen riding down Fifth Avenue in her new automobile with Henry Rogers' attractive daughter-in-law. He liked especially the trips on Rogers' steam yacht, the *Kanawha*, and the poker and horseplay and good masculine fun that was there enjoyed.

Samuel Clemens had always wanted to be a millionaire, and now he was, vicariously: he lived like one, and he was seen often in the company of bona fide, class A, genuine products. One part of him hated it; the other part lapped it up greedily: he became more and more and more spoiled—a kind of private jester to the Rogerses and the Rockefellers and the Flaglers and their friends. He called Andrew Carnegie St. Andrew, and Carnegie called him St. Mark, and each knew that the joke of it was that neither was saintly at all. Their jokes together were fun. Because Carnegie was a Scotchman, Mark Twain held him responsible for supplying him with Scotch whisky; but in private Mark Twain wrote Carnegie down as less than benevolent, at the same time that in public he let himself be publicly used.

It was good for these wealthy men to be seen with a person so popularly loved as Mark Twain. They liked him, and they were all boyish brigands together, each of his kind; but it was also good for their public image. He rode with them to public hearings at which their honesty was impugned; he was seen with them at testimonial banquets and at sporting events. Surely, no man could be all bad, if Mark Twain liked him. And Clemens did genuinely like these people, and like being seen with them. Newspapers might know Rogers as a "Standard Oil fiend," but Clemens knew him as a friend, and was proud to be privileged to drop in on him or on other members of his family whenever he wished, to be petted and waited on and spoiled. Rogers was the "only man I care for in the world; the only man I give a damn for." He was "lavishing his sweat and blood to save me and mine from starvation and shame."

But knowing the Rogerses and their friends was not something which Clemens shared with his family. The Clemens girls seem not to have known the Rogers girls at all, and Mrs. Clemens seems only to have met Mrs. Rogers when the Rogers yacht was put at Clemens' disposal so that he could take his ailing wife away from the New York heat for the summer. It may be that Clemens unconsciously believed that by keeping his family secluded, away from the kind of public and fawning life which he led, he was keeping them from contamination. For he became pulled quite asunder, more bitter than he had ever been, in scorn of all mankind—that damned human race—and in conscience-ridden condemnation of himself: "What a man sees in the human race," he said, "is merely himself in the deep and private honesty of his own heart. Byron despised the human race because he despised himself. I feel as Byron did and for the same reason."

His increasing bitterness distressed Mrs. Clemens, who not many weeks before she died in 1904 wrote him a note which is filled with wifely devotion and genuine concern, wishing that he would show the world the sweet, dear, tender side that she knew. But then she died, and he exploded, and later was to write: "There is *nothing*. There is no God and no universe; . . . there is only empty space, and in it a lost and homeless and wandering and companionless and indestructible thought. And God, and the Universe, and Time, and Life, and Death, and Joy and Sorrow and Pain only a grotesque and brutal *dream*, evolved from the frantic imagination of that insane thought." And what a thing was man: "Hypocrisy, envy, malice, cruelty, vengefulness, seduction, rape, robbery, swindling, arson, bigamy, adultery, and the oppression and humiliation of the poor and helpless in all ways have been and still are more or less common among both the civilized and uncivilized peoples of the earth."

This world, he wrote, "is a strange place, an extraordinary place, and interesting. . . . The people are all insane, the other animals are all insane. Man is a marvelous curiosity. When he is at his very best he is a sort of low grade nickel-plated angel; at his worst is unspeakable, unimaginable; and first and last and all the time he is a sarcasm. Yet man, blandly and in all sincerity, calls himself 'the noblest work of God.' . . . He believes that the Creator is proud of him; he even believes that the Creator loves him; has a passion for him; sits up nights to admire him; yes, and watch over him and keep him out of trouble."

Like Walt Whitman, he compared man to the animals: "Indecency, vulgarity, obscenity—these are strictly confined to man; he invented them. Among the higher animals there is no trace of them. They hide nothing; they are not ashamed. Man, with his soiled mind, covers himself. . . . Man is the Animal that Blushes. He is the only one that does it—or has occasion to. . . . Of all the animals man is the only one that is doing it. Man is the only animal that deals in that atrocity of atrocities, War. He is the only one that gathers his brethren around him and goes forth in cold blood and with calm pulse to exterminate his kind. . . . Man is the only slave. And he is the only animal that enslaves. . . . Man is the only Patriot. . . . Man is the Religious Animal. . . . He is the only animal that has the true religion—several of them. He is the only animal that loves his neighbor as himself and cuts his throat if his theology isn't straight."

> Onward, Christian soldiers
> Marching unto war,
> With the flag of progress
> Going on before. . . .
>
> On, ye true believers
> Put them into flight
> Charity dispensing
> Mixed with dynamite.

Clemens was bitter and discouraged, and he began detailing his bitterness for posterity, in writings which would not be read for a hundred years, for he dared not speak these thoughts in his own day, to his friends who, he thought, were as crass and sinful as he. The world was greatly with him, and it pulled him apart. The face he showed was a clown's face, a serious and sharp-tongued clown, but one not to be held responsible for what he said. The aging, compromising Mark Twain does not present a pretty picture, but perhaps no man does. His writing deteriorated during these late years. It became pointed and plain, saying what it had to say with vigor, but with no overtones, only anger and despair as he whipped himself and whipped his friends and contemporaries in frenzies of disgust.

In public, he posed and preened, spoiled and pampered. He played the wounded lion, and displayed his wounds for all to see. He was a funny man, good to have around to laugh or grouse with. He must have known that in an important sense he had sold out, and that respectworthy people (like Stephen Crane, for one) were beginning to scorn him as a public clown. Soon younger men like Sherwood Anderson, Waldo Frank, and Van Wyck Brooks would be speaking of the wastage of his powers—his half-baked, half-believed half-buffoonery. Ten years after his death, Van Wyck Brooks gave reasoned explanation of what Clemens had allowed to be done to the genius of Mark Twain. His indictment has needed only small revision even in the fifty years since it was first made. Like many of his countrymen, before or since, Clemens did sell out—it was, and perhaps still is, the customary, if not the expected thing for a man to do.

But there were, of course, other things—including growing older—which contributed also to what seems to me the spiritual bankruptcy of Mark Twain—it had better be said, of Samuel Clemens—after he gave himself over to Rogers and his friends and his influence and his wealth and tempting ministrations, in exchange for or in gratitude for release from financial bankruptcy. Hardly anything that Clemens wrote after 1890 is moving or aesthetically right, not even "Eve's Diary," which is marred as he submits even his grief over the death of his wife to conventional poses and what he must have recognized as sentimental silliness. He continued to write occasionally well, for he was a professional who knew his business; and he became perhaps even a little more popular than he had been before, and that may be because he wrote what other people thought, or what other people thought he should write. He hardly ever attacked anyone except patsies, like Boss Tweed and Jay Gould and missionaries, whom it was fashionable to attack; his snub of Gorki was two-faced and just as public as it could be; his recriminations against King Leopold were as safe from public opposition as was his public friendship with Booker T. Washington and Helen Keller and little girls—and, oh, that poor cabman who dared overcharge a Clemens retainer!

Clemens of course was old and he had reasons in plenty for his sorrow and his bitterness; in a literary sense, his anger was the best thing left to him, when it was real and lyrically explosive, as the anger of a later, also aging, Ezra Pound was explosive and often lyric. What charm was left was a learned charm, carefully maintained, with an entrepreneur's canny skill. The wastage of his powers of which Brooks was to speak came, I would think, now—not in those early years, or as a result of traumata from those early years, of growing up in midland America or searching wealth in the Pacific West, and certainly not during those years in the seventies and the eighties when he did his best work, but in the almost twenty years which followed when he found himself controlled by, and loyally liking, a new set of counselors—not Howells so much any more, not Twichell in Hartford, who presided at marriages and funerals, and on whom Rogers and Clemens played boyish tricks, but men of wealth (malefactors was not a word which Clemens would use in describing them) who made it profitable for him to be their private jester and public companion.

And of course his writing suffered, for one does not write well under duress, even when one accepts and is partly pleased by the conditions of duress. Surely, it was the humanitarian rather than the critic in Leslie Fiedler which allowed him to name *Pudd'nhead Wilson* as Mark Twain's second-best book. *The Mysterious Stranger* was put together from what Clemens never quite finished; *What Is Man?* turned out to be as jejune in its way as *Captain Stormfield's Visit* was in its; and the writings that were so bitter that they could not be made public for a hundred years, as now issued, turn out to be Mark Twain's last joke—just more of the same complaints of man's inadequacy, with only a snigger of sex added, and just a little excrement.

The shimmer was gone, and the magic which transformed Huck and the great river into things which are not forgotten because never completely spoken, and which are set before us with more love than anger. It may be charitable to think that Mark Twain had been dead for over a decade—make it sixteen years!—when the twentieth century opened, and that it was a pasteboard mask through which Clemens spoke during the ten years more that Clemens lived in masquerade. But that will not do, because it was Clemens who spoke all the time—a forgotten man in our literature, this Samuel Clemens, who must have the praise for creating Mark Twain and the blame also for allowing him to be tempted toward corruption. Mr. Mark Twain, he told the truth, mainly; but not Mr. Clemens.

Pulled this way and that, saying sometimes what he must say and sometimes what he thinks he must, torn asunder by conflicting loyalties, knowing that the comfortable bland thing was the wrong thing but that it was easier and better applauded, he showed himself a man fitted to our season, discontented, unsure, emasculate, shouting curses to drown out the murmurings of conscience, weak, vacillating, well-meaning, and self-seeking—our brother and our mask: Mark Twain, who speaks for us precisely because he is human and fallible, available to corruption.

4

୧

On Writing about Writers: Especially Mark Twain

To EXPLAIN ANY writer is perhaps a task too large for criticism to undertake. Yet the temptation to biography is constantly, perhaps inevitably, with us. The author, the man, the mind, behind the writing looms larger than the sum of his parts. What he has intended to do and why he intended it becomes somehow the measure of his success in requiring our attention. This, we have been told, is peculiarly an American attitude: not having great writings to confront, we discover instead great individuals who write, maimed men who in another situation would have done better. We may even find a kind of theological justification for such an attitude as we recall that traditionally the creator is superior to the creature. And when writings speak so poignantly, yet so falteringly, of the condition of man, we are emboldened to think that there must be, beyond the writings, circumstances in the experience of the writer which bespeak their failure. The critic gathers together what he knows of Freud or Jung, of social aspirations or the state of society, or simply his own experience or instinctive apprehension of human nature, and from this puts together a reasonable explanation of the man who has written. The question of whether this is a defensible literary enterprise may not concern us; it certainly can be appreciated as an intellectual exercise, often of great vigor; it is what we ask for, and gladly receive.

What I have said above is simplified beyond what consideration of so complex a subject requires. It may stand however as indicative of an attitude, and as preface to what I have to say of two books, one of which seems at first glance to adhere to the attitude which I have outlined and which in my judgment, and for reasons which I hope to be able to set forth, succeeds as useful literary commentary, and the other of which, pleading aversion to such an attitude, fails. One reason for this may be that the first is about Mark Twain, a devious and enigmatic character, whom even Samuel Clemens probably never completely understood, but who, though perhaps only occasionally, is universally a delight, while the other is about William Dean Howells, who may have been more consistently pleasing, but was seldom so delightful a man.

James M. Cox in *Mark Twain: The Fate of Humor* [1] has the better chance, for in one sense the man about whom he writes never existed, except as Samuel Clemens without remarkable consistency made him. He was a voice and a costumed presence, which dared be outrageous or scoffing or sentimental because there was not beneath the costume a person who could seriously be held accountable for what he said. He could therefore afford irresponsibilities. As jester to his generation, and latterly as pampered private jester to wealthy friends, he had a kind of privileged immunity. He gave something more than lip service to their gods; he strove and sometimes despairingly to placate givers of good fortune; unabashedly he lay his gifts before them, and became atheist only when gifts were denied.

Or did he? Mr. Cox recognizes, or seems to recognize, more

[1] James M. Cox, *Mark Twain: The Fate of Humor* (Princeton: Princeton University Press, 1966).

than most of us, that if we are to talk about the writer, Samuel Clemens is our man: he, the creator; Mark Twain, the creature. The entrepreneur from Hannibal was not much perhaps, and it was undoubtedly comforting to him to be able finally to become virtually obscured by his creation; he grasped in almost every direction at more than he could hold —as a family man, in business, as writer, and as an aging admirer of young girls. He had successes perhaps finally in each, but more often than not he patched and postured. What he did do was to invent Mark Twain, a grand achievement, partly because being a character who lived largely plotless, he is not greatly susceptible to consistent critical interference. Improvising his way through a variety of often comic, but sometimes distressingly serious, guises, Clemens put together and lived with and in a sense finally became such a personage that, even during his lifetime, there were probably more people who knew Mark Twain than there were people who had read what he was said to have written. If Clemens was not consistently a good writer, nor a good father, nor a good investor, he was a showman, self-conscious from first to last, and desperately conscious of impressions which he could profitably make. He was a professional, and a canny one, too, who, if he was satisfied to allow his creature to receive applause which might have been his, also avoided much of the blame.

To distinguish between Samuel Clemens and Mark Twain requires more discrimination than even he was finally able to apply, for creature quite consumed creator. Mr. Cox's accomplishment is with remarkable consistency to have kept the two apart—and without needing to speculate more than casually on the prevalence of twins or twinlike characters in writings signed by Mark Twain. In his view, Mark Twain sprang, if not full-blown, at least with full potential, from the forehead of Samuel Clemens on February 3, 1863, when the pseudonym was first used. He was necessary as an agent of fulfillment, for Clemens at twenty-eight had not done well. His adventuring on the way toward wealth had been erratic: "He had to fail as a prospector and later as a speculator so that he could succeed as a writer." Clemens had been "the fool of his illusion," and he could not easily admit it, but Mark Twain could, and did, so that he became "an extension, an addition by means of which Samuel Clemens was able to enlarge and fulfill himself." He became a surrogate whose humor was "pervasively concerned with repression, censorship, dreams, the conscience, and self-approval," reflecting at first "the extravagant and grandiose dreams of territorial glory," and then of other dreams which became illusion. "For Mark Twain," explains Mr. Cox, "was neither a character who seized reality from Samuel Clemens, nor a persona which masked his identity; . . . far from losing his identity in his new name, Samuel Clemens had found it. Thus the life of Mark Twain which was to be written was the imaginative life of Samuel Clemens." But Samuel Clemens was still there, no matter how bewilderingly he came to identify himself with his creation—this, I think, Mr. Cox does not always make consistently clear; it was Clemens, released and defended by the personality which he created, who was able then to reorganize his own sometimes shabby past into the legend which has become the life of Mark Twain. One result has been that, as Mr. Cox says, "the reader is constantly in the process of reconstructing Samuel Clemens out of Mark Twain."

To some extent this is what Mr. Cox, perhaps inevitably, does. As he traces the emergence of the white-garbed, shaggy, irreverent, spoiled, but beloved personage, called King in his own household, who could be rude or condescending or unbelievably kind, and who has become an abiding public image of a man who was never there but who became a presence more real than of the man who made him, Mr. Cox undertakes a difficult but necessary task, and, perhaps as well as anyone can, keeps the creator and the creature apart. His intention is clearly literary, to explain how Clemens in creating the myth of Mark Twain engaged progressively "in the activity of inventing himself." As the fool of his illusions, he recognized that the language of illusion was the language of cliché, spoken sometimes melodiously by other, more pious fools, and he exposed their reverence by impersonating it; and he exposed himself through his guise of innocence, his expectations, real or assumed, unfulfilled. Perhaps it is not necessary to ask, whose illusion? Mr. Cox makes careful distinction about who it was who drew his wife, and his children also, into the masquerade by referring to Olivia Clemens as the muse, not of Mark Twain, but of Samuel Clemens. When she censored his writings, if indeed in any real sense she did, her husband never suggested that it was Mrs. Mark Twain who pulled him up short; whatever her involvement in his disguise, she was allowed to keep distance as Mrs. Clemens—cast as "the figure representing all the social and artistic values antithetical to Mark Twain's native genius." Poor Susy became more involved, and distracted; and Clara, when she wrote of her father, spoke of him as Mark Twain.

Mr. Cox mainly avoids such confusion. But when he says that Mark Twain is "not a writer who uses myths; he invents them," I think it may not be too carping to wish that the words had been more carefully chosen, for it is possible to suppose that Mr. Cox's excellent explanations might have been sharpened if throughout he had allowed the reader constantly to remember that Mark Twain was not in that sense a writer but a protective projection. The distinction is not minor, and it becomes more important as, increasingly, Clemens himself was unable to make it. Mark Twain was indeed allowed to expose illusion as defined by "the false pieties and platitudes of the adult world," and to disclose as truth his outrageous whoppers "told not to deceive the listener but to make him see that the only truth which can be told is the lie which reveals rather than conceals the fact that it is a lie," disclosed in "a world where play, make-believe, and adventure are living realities." Samuel Clemens in his own voice could not have enforced these attitudes so well; he could not afford levity. Insofar as he remained himself, he was abidingly serious; but as Mark Twain, through burlesque, impersonation, and the outrageous lie, he could take the reader in, "making him vaguely but pleasantly suspicious that he has been 'sold,'" moving him to laughter, rousing him to skepticism. That was the function of his humor.

In this view and this structure, humor is engaging; seriousness is not—when Mark Twain fails, it is because the serious one, Samuel Clemens, intrudes; just as when Huck, bedeviled by the platitudes of society, decides that he will help Jim escape from slavery even if he must go to hell for it, and then, in fact, does go to a living hell as through the interminable final chapters of his *Adventures* he endures Tom Sawyer's play, which has become platitude and which intrudes as the cruelest cruelty in the book. For the fate of humor is that it becomes platitude; when an aging Samuel Clemens, increasingly less the fool than the suffering, embittered victim of illusion, began seriously to assume responsibilities or opportunities of the role he had invented, then he allowed Mark Twain to speak as an agent rather than as catalyst. The fate of humor is that it becomes serious at last. This, explains Mr. Cox, "forces humor to serve a noble purpose instead of forcing all noble purposes to serve humor." Samuel Clemens, who made him, was finally responsible for the downfall of Mark Twain: "the more Samuel Clemens attempts to be 'serious,' the more he betrays his genius, Mark Twain," for "insofar as Mark Twain *is* present, the impulse necessarily is toward humor—which is to say the impulse to discover the world as entertainment. . . . For in commercializing himself, Samuel Clemens was wasting his genius, in trying to be serious he was failing to believe in it . . . he put truth, virtue, and morality before pleasure."

Pleasure may or may not be a legitimate end; the freedom from conscience which Huck sought may in truth be evasion; but these represent attitudes, practical or not, which have attracted admirers and distracted critics of Mark Twain. Mr. Cox with few false steps has followed a difficult path to its inevitable conclusion, and has produced the most thoughtful —though serious—and most thought-provoking study of Mark Twain of his generation. Perhaps I may be allowed to rise to a point of personal privilege as a member of a generation older, to suggest that simpler reasons than those which he has adduced may be brought forward to explain the ultimate deterioration of Samuel Clemens or Mark Twain or almost anyone else who ages. Most men moving into their sixties promise more than they can achieve, worry about extending themselves beyond mortality, find the world a less pleasant place than once, and are likely to become common scolds, niggardly and jejune. Perhaps the fate of humor is the fate of man.

Because he holds his ground, keeping his eye on the creation which is Mark Twain, explaining it as an imaginative extension of his creator, Mr. Cox performs a useful literary task; but George C. Carrington, Jr., in *The Immense Complex Drama: The World and Art of the Howells Novel*,[2] though he claims more, does less well. He is "primarily interested in novels as works of art," and he applies a modified Fryeistic formula to discover "what happens if we look at them with the irreducible minimum of external reference, and examine them for meaning." Well enough, and good; that is the critic's choice. But to read Howells against such standards becomes indeed a challenging task, which Mr. Carrington valiantly pursues, demonstrating that Howells can be revealed as a "craftsman of perception," and as more of a thinker, a technician, and a modernist than many readers

[2] George C. Carrington, Jr., *The Immense Complex Drama: The World and Art of the Howells Novel* (Columbus: Ohio State University Press, 1966).

have allowed themselves to realize. The exercise involves him in some strain, and tempts him to rhetorical flashes which set Howells forth as heir of Melville and harbinger of Faulkner, but what finally comes through is not a fresh or clarified reading of the novels, which do not stand well under the weight of examination, but another familiar apology for another "neurotic artist . . . harmed but not controlled by defects in his psychic economy."

Howells, I think, was as good a critic, and comes to much the same conclusion. Writing to Clemens—he almost always wrote to Clemens, not Mark Twain; and Clemens almost invariably signed his letters to Howells "Mark"—writing to Clemens in 1904 when both were in their sixties, he observed, "You are dramatic and unconscious; you count the thing more than yourself; I am cursed with consciousness to the core, and can't say my way out." If I read him correctly, Howells is saying that he could never get beyond himself to say what he wanted to say without remembering that what he said and the way he said it would inevitably determine what readers would think of William Dean Howells. Samuel Clemens was not bothered by this to the same degree: Mark Twain could take the buffeting and the applause. This is not to say that Howells needed a persona—he had one, of dignity and faultless respectability. It merely underlines what needs no underlining, our understanding that Howells was not so successful an artist as Clemens; his genius was, as he said, restricting. Whatever his personal alienation, his hypochondria, his sense of evil or of self-hatred ("Lately I have felt," he wrote Clemens, "as if I were rotting with egotism. . . . I am sick of myself")—however revealed or cautiously concealed, these attitudes do not come through in his fiction. He avoided "the black heart's-truth," and wondered whether in writing his (or Mark Twain's) *Autobiography* Clemens would not also avoid the "black truth which we all know of ourselves in our hearts."

Of course he would, and did, though he pretended otherwise; and James Cox explains how, entrepreneur to the last, Samuel Clemens played a final and profitable joke on us in the expectation which he aroused that Mark Twain had such wondrous truths to tell that they must wait a hundred years before they could be made public. It was the kind of slick trick that Huck might have enjoyed. But its having to be explained to us suggests one reason why it may not have been such a good joke after all.

5

Tom and Huck:
Innocence on Trial

ONE CANNOT SERIOUSLY quarrel with DeLancey Ferguson when he says that *The Adventures of Tom Sawyer* violates every rule, past, present, and future of the "art novel," for in its context Mr. Ferguson's statement points out something which is important and true about that book. Taken out of its context, however, as I am afraid it has often been taken, this judgment and others like it have been seriously misleading. There is, of course, a great deal of apparent looseness about *Tom Sawyer*. Characters like Alfred Temple and Cousin Mary are needlessly or belatedly introduced. Toward the latter part of the book, time does seem mangled until some critics find more summer days following the Fourth of July than either the weather or the school calendar of Missouri would have allowed. The story is desperately episodic. The parts—the whitewashing incident, the graveyard horror, the adventure in the cave—remain more prominently in our memory than the whole to which they should be contributory. These are commonplaces, plain to almost every reader.

Yet, episodic, loose, and shambling—as Mark Twain was loose and shambling—the book is not without artistry beyond the surface artistry of the raconteur who, as Bernard DeVoto has said, engraves minor realisms about provincial society for all time. There is another artistry, of theme and structure, which makes *Tom Sawyer* more than a charming narrative which transcends its own weaknesses. It is not, I think, a planned structure or a consciously articulated theme. But planned or not, the structure and the theme are there, expressive of a deeply underlying principle which haunted Mark Twain and which helps to explain why Tom Sawyer remained all his life Mark Twain's favorite character.

Mark Twain admits that the story moves on two levels. His first purpose, we are told in the preface, is to tell a tale which will hold boys and girls; his second, "to pleasantly remind adults of what they once were themselves." The boy adventures—the whitewashing, the love in the schoolroom, the Jackson Island runaways, the school examination days— these, we may suppose, were for adults mainly. The murder, the murder trial, the cave adventures, almost everything about Injun Joe—these were for the boys and girls. The story line, the plot, the excitement were for them, the secret, the pursuit, the capture. The episodes were for the reminiscent adults. But a close reading of *Tom Sawyer* reveals more than this. One of the things I want to suggest as we reexamine its structure is a third, a more tantalizing and penetrative level. Let us, then, review the story briefly, with Mark Twain's often maligned time-sense as one of our principal guides.

The book is divided into three almost exactly equal parts. There are ten chapters in the first part, ten in the second, thirteen in the third. The first part is separated from the second and the second from the third, each by an interchapter. Within the three parts events are detailed carefully, time moves slowly, incident by incident, day by day. In the interchapters time is accelerated, so that weeks go by within a few pages. Each of the three parts is different from the others in tone, in the kind of adventure in which Tom involves himself, and in the ultimate relationship of these adventures to what I hope can be demonstrated as the theme which unifies the whole.

The first part begins on a Friday afternoon when Tom is discovered by Aunt Polly to have been in the jam pot. It continues through Saturday morning when he promotes his whitewashing coup, through Saturday afternoon when he meets the new girl in town, through the two Sunday chapters, one of the Sunday School, the other of the church service, the beetle and the poodle. It then proceeds to a full-packed Monday when, off to school minus the tooth he had pled as reason for staying home, Tom meets Huck Finn, exchanges the tooth for a wood tick which gets him and Joe Harper into trouble, pauses for a romantic moment over the noontime tryst with Becky Thatcher, details an afternoon of hooky and imaginative schoolboy play, and finally ends on Monday night when Tom and Huck in the graveyard witness the murder of young Dr. Robinson by Injun Joe.

Seldom in any fiction have three and a half days been more expertly packed with what we must know in order to follow the rest of the tale with understanding. Tom is established, the murder known, the picnic which provides the climax planned. Seldom has time been better articulated. We know throughout where we are and just when every incident happens. There is unity of time, of place. It is the Aristotelian beginning, self-contained. Nor are the incidents told for their own sake alone, but weave one into the next to a pattern which creates a unity of tone for this whole first part. Its purpose? The recreation of boyhood adventure. Its theme—that innocent boyhood adventure, the brave curiosity of the imaginative boy, leads from innocence to knowledge of evil. Tom and Huck have eaten of no forbidden fruit. They do go out at night in defiance, at worst, of grownup disapproval, and they go where, in the strictest sense, they have really no right to be. But they go to the graveyard essentially in innocence, bravely, and adventuresomely, and the evil which is revealed to them and which will cloud and lengthen the whole summer for them is outside of them and in no manner of their making.

Then comes chapter eleven, an interchapter. Time is no longer exactly chronicled, but accelerated. Muff Potter is arrested. Two weeks pass.

The second part of the novel, chapters twelve to twenty-one, is divided into two episodes—the Jackson Island adventure and the last day at school. Again time slows down, so that the first episode begins on a Wednesday and ends on Sunday morning when the boys confuse the adults by attending their own funeral, and the second episode begins on Monday morning and moves to its climax with the artful prank of lifting the schoolmaster's wig. Each episode details imaginative boyhood adventure, each is an extension of the adventures of the first part of the novel, not precisely the same, but nonetheless much the kind we have been led to expect from a boy like Tom.

Are we too long diverted from the plot, which is concerned with the discovery of the murder, the capture of the murderer? If so, what is established? The two episodes which make up this second part of the novel have this in common: in each the boy in his prank wins out over the practical, matter-of-fact adult. And the tone of the adventure is now different. It is less innocent. It is no longer the simple, imaginative play of boys among themselves for their own ends. Tom's escapade on Jackson Island is in part the result of his reaction to a certain fall from innocence typified in his initiation to the bewildering attitude of girls. The schoolroom prank is a result of boyhood's revolt against conventional authority, against punishment for something of which Tom is not really guilty, against the kind of adult standards which the schoolmaster represents. In each, it is revolt against what the world inevitably holds in store for boys as they grow beyond innocence to knowledge of the world, of society, of its bewildering complications, its restraints, its insistence on regulations which would, without imagination, put everything in its place.

Then comes chapter twenty-two, another interchapter. It is vacation time, into which so many things are packed that a particularizing reader can count, at very least, thirty-seven days following the 4th of July and estimate, therefore, that the murder trial which opens the third part of the novel could not have taken place before the middle of August. And yet this second acceleration of time, of time into which too much is crowded, is perhaps justified. With guilty knowledge on his conscience, with fear in his heart, Tom may well have found that summer long, blighted with length. Restlessly he sought one consoling activity after another. He joined the Sons of Temperance. He gave up smoking and swearing. He kept a diary, for he was troubled with knowledge of himself. He played at soldier, at minstrel show, and at circus, as any boy might, but then he went to bed with measles for two weeks and got up to discover himself isolated, as indeed with his guilty knowledge of Muff Potter's innocence he was, from the rest of the community which had undergone a religious revival, so that Joe Harper was "studying a Testament," Ben Rogers was "visiting the poor with a basket of tracts," and even Huck Finn was quoting scripture. For three weeks more he was in bed with a relapse. Bernard DeVoto suggests that Tom was sick too much. He had reason to be.

The last part of the novel, the final thirteen chapters, is again unified in time, but not so concisely as the first two parts. The story moves now of its own power toward climax. The "sleepy atmosphere of the town was stirred—and vigorously: the murder trial came on in court," and continued through three exciting days until Tom gave his surprise evidence and Injun Joe escaped through a window. The boy was a hero, and up to a point he loved it: "Tom's days were days of splendor and exultation to him, but his nights were seasons of horror." He was entering, as everyone who grows to maturity must, the world of an adult where nights are often filled with horror. And so the "slow days drifted on," and Tom's fear changed and increased. He had squared his conscience with confession: that was right and proper and decent, but it led to menace even more real, the vengeance of Injun Joe.

These final chapters round out the plot and articulate the theme. From chapter twenty-five to the end, the time sequence is again precise. It begins on Thursday afternoon, when Tom and Huck first go treasure hunting on Cardiff Hill. If their adventure is not so innocent as it had been before, in the first part of the novel or even the second, it is as bravely pursued, in spite of the threat which the presence of Injun Joe and his companion provides. Evil is no longer something unknown, nor is it something which simply gnaws at the conscience to make nights filled with horror. It is real, it is present, it is consciously recognized and guarded against.

The boys are beginning to act as adults would act, and not only in seeking now a treasure which is real and not an imagined product of boyish play. On Saturday, when they discover that Injun Joe is disguised as the "old deaf and dumb Spaniard," they stalk him and watch for him at the head of the alley from Monday through Thursday in something approximating a serious, commonsense, adult manner. But with no results. (It may be worth noticing that, for some reason, Sunday is omitted from this sequence: we move from Saturday night directly into Monday. Is Mark Twain nodding, or did he cannily slip something by us? Either way, we may read into the omission remembrance that Sundays sometimes seem very important to boys, if only because they are restricted and uncomfortably miserable on that day, but that as one grows toward maturity and is occupied with more sophisticated adult activities, then Sundays can be less important or even hardly Sundays at all. But we must not labor this point.)

With chapter twenty-nine, when the Thatchers return on Friday to town and announce their picnic for the next day, the story for the first time forks into parallel lines of action—with Tom and Becky in the cave, and with loyal, practical Huck at the same time conscientiously shadowing the murderer. Mark Twain's handling of the picnic-cave episode has not perhaps been adequately admired. It is prepared for early in the book, when Becky, eleven chapters and many weeks before, promises it during that crowded last day of school which ends the first part of the novel. As for the episode itself, it takes a second, even a third reading to discover how intricately the author has woven bumbling adult planning into a pattern of suspense ingeniously effective. It takes perhaps another reading to realize that it is this adult planning which goes astray and allows Tom and Becky to be lost for many hours before the search begins, that the adult search does not find the lost children, any more than it captures the murderer, but that it is Tom's brave, thoroughly impracticable, romance-bred explorations at the end of a string which ultimately lead them to safety.

Here, I think, the theme is most effectively pointed up: it is not the practical and methodical Huck, who acts as an adult would act and who is doggedly faithful in watching for the murderer, who accomplishes any more in relation to the evil personified by Injun Joe than scaring it off, driving it into hiding from which it may escape to strike again. It is the irresponsible and irrepressible Tom, who leaves the chase for a picnic, who explores beyond common sense into the cave, who bravely but quite inadvertently leads to the capture of Injun Joe. The adults do seal the mouth of the cave, but not to trap a murderer, only to prevent a recurrence of Tom's kind of adventuring. And the boy who had been in the cave which became a tomb for three days, from Saturday afternoon to Tuesday afternoon, ascended from it not essentially a different, but a more decently mature person. Two weeks later, when the body of Injun Joe was found, Tom's "pity was moved." He knew from his own experience "how this wretch had suffered."

Tom was not in the strictest sense reborn, but he was growing up, to knowledge and understanding of evil. Most important, however, he retained, as many who approach maturity do not, the secret of avoiding evil. It is boyhood adventure again, in the final two chapters, which leads Tom and Huck to the discovery of Injun Joe's treasure, as they play themselves at being robbers. It is Tom's imaginative play, not Huck's common sense, which brings to each of them the stupendous wealth of a dollar a day for life. That is security, indeed. Tom revels in it and is happy. But Huck is further rewarded. For his adultlike activities in tracking Injun Joe to the widow's house and then, scared but sensible, running for help as a responsible person should, Huck is adopted and ultimately made unhappy as the widow attempts to "sivilize" him.

We thus discover within the three parts of *The Adventures of Tom Sawyer* meanings which underlie the plot and which our examination of the structure of that book have made clear. In the first part we find that boyhood adventure leads innocently to knowledge of evil. In the second part we are shown that, even when it is self-consciously in revolt, adventure wins out over prosaic, adult methods of doing things. In the final part we discover that adventure, which is compounded in part of the spirit of make-believe, imagination, illusion—that adventure, and not common sense, leads finally to the wiping out of evil. Is this why *Tom Sawyer* was Mark Twain's favorite among his books? Is this also the theme, expanded and in some degree amended, of *Adventures of Huckleberry Finn,* and a reason why the hero of that book is identified in the subtitle as "Tom Sawyer's Comrade"?

The Huck Finn of *The Adventures of Tom Sawyer* is not essentially different from the Huck Finn of its sequel, *Ad-*

ventures of Huckleberry Finn. He is brave and loyal and with just enough imagination to be badly scared in the first book, just as he is brave and loyal and often scared in the second. In practical matters of managing for himself he is perhaps more learned than Tom. Yet when a situation becomes tense or when Huck surprises himself by doing better than he thought he could, then he wishes Tom were with him, for advice or praise. For all his self-reliance, Huck is anxious for the approval of his contemporaries. When he admits to Tom in the first book that he is friendly with Mr. Rogers' Negro Uncle Jake, who likes him, as Jim was to like him in the second book, "becuz I don't ever act as if I was above him," and when he further admits that he has eaten with the Negro, Huck cautions Tom, "But you needn't tell that. A body's got to do things when hungry he wouldn't want to do as a steady thing."

Lionel Trilling, T. S. Eliot, Ernest Hemingway, and many others have made sufficiently clear the virtues of *Adventures of Huckleberry Finn,* in style, in mythic quality, and in penetrative illumination of human conduct. American literature, as Hemingway has said, at least much that is admirable in contemporary American literature, did begin here. These excellencies have been permanently established, and it is not the intention of this essay further to underline them. What has not so often been examined is the relationship between Tom and Huck in the second book.

Almost everyone will recognize that *Huckleberry Finn* is not so well-made a novel as *Tom Sawyer,* or even *The Prince and the Pauper.* Yet we are not misled by Mark Twain's admonition that "Persons attempting to find a motive in this narrative will be prosecuted; persons attempting to find a moral in it will be banished; persons attempting to find a plot in it will be shot." In *Huckleberry Finn* Mark Twain achieved the looseness of design to which his talents were best adapted.

Structure and content are integrated, for one of the things which the book is about is the breaking of just such conventional patterns as those which we associate with the "well-made novel."

Yet it does not, except in its central portion, the river odyssey, quite create a pattern of its own. Form of a sort is imposed on it by its author. The first eleven chapters detail the adventures of Huckleberry Finn on land, in and around what Dixon Wecter has so well convinced us really was Mark Twain's Hannibal, before Huck begins his voyage down the river on the raft. Tom Sawyer plays a prominent part only in the earliest of these adventures. He remains with Huck just long enough to establish himself and his kind of romantic, traditional, book-fed play as a necessary part of the story —for the point is, I think, that Mark Twain did find Tom and his attitude necessary to the complete telling of this second tale. The next twenty chapters take us to the river— Huck and Jim alone for seven chapters, until some of the evils of society catch up with them and they are joined by the King and the Duke for thirteen chapters. Tom Sawyer is not there, but he is not forgotten: Huck remembers him in moments of crisis or triumph; perhaps we may even read the King and the Duke, and the Grangerfords, and Colonel Sherburn as changes played on what a talent like Tom's might become if carelessly pursued. There, but for the grace of circumstance, goes Tom! Then the last twelve chapters, on land again, involve us in the interminable connivings through which Tom leads Huck, and the reader also, as he contrives the "emancipation" of Jim. The structure of this novel, then, has been likened to that of a gigantic dumbbell, with adventures on shore, in many of which Tom Sawyer takes part, bunched at each end, and with the adventures on the river the long shaft between. There is detail of conventional plot at the beginning and, even tiresomely, at the end. Joining the beginning to the end is a river, a raft, a boy, and his companions. And a contrast between the land adventures and the river adventures is one of the things the book is about.

There is also, as Edgar M. Branch has recently made clear, important thematic structure in *Huckleberry Finn*. Hardly anyone fails to recognize that one of the more prominent threads running through the narrative is a consideration of the problem of individual freedom. Huck seeks freedom for himself—he will not be "sivilized." He is bothered also about the problem of freedom as it applies to Jim. How free may the Grangerfords and the Shepherdsons be, how free is Colonel Sherburn, and how much freedom may be allowed to people like the King and the Duke when that freedom approaches anarchy?

If this is one of the themes of *Huckleberry Finn*, it is also Emerson's theme, and Whitman's, and Thoreau's, and many another's. Someone has said that it is the theme of any thinking man living in a democracy. It is the problem of the self-respecting individual amid the pressures of society. In Emerson and Whitman and Thoreau and Mark Twain it is perplexed by the question of how far the individual can or should maintain his precious gift of individuality and to what extent, through personal concession or through force, this individuality must be curtailed in the interest of society. The question for Huck is whether the Widow Douglas, Aunt Sally, or anyone else will "sivilize" him.

Emerson and Whitman, I think, suggest a solution; Thoreau perhaps does not. And Huck Finn does not solve it. At the end of the tale, not unlike Natty Bumppo at the end of many of the *Leatherstocking Tales*, he is off into the unknown, the uncontaminated, where society cannot shackle him. He learns that his father, who has led him most brutally but most persuasively also toward individual freedom, is dead. The tempter is gone. One menace is gone, but society remains. Huck is still the rebel, beloved as a symbol of the rebellion which lies perilously close to the surface in our own struggles with conformity; "Aunt Sally's going to adopt me and sivilize me, and I can't stand it. I been there before."

Tom does solve it, not very well perhaps, and certainly not in any really satisfying philosophical manner. But he does as well as he could do, as well as Mark Twain could. That, I think, is the point of those dreary final twelve chapters which may be something more than "an artificial manoeuvre to conclude the action" or "Mark Twain's payment for some earlier sins against the logic of plot." Tom Sawyer's solution really does not solve anything, so far as Jim's freedom is concerned. Jim had been freed in a natural course of events contrived through the balance between greed and contrition in an adult world. Tom's solution may even be read as one of the reasons why Huck, who finally had his fill of such make-believe contrivings, threw up his hands and retreated to complete nonconformity. Huck had been exposed to nearly every solution which society seemed to offer. Religion had no answer, certainly not the religion which tried to frighten him to approved behavior with threat of hellfire. Pride, tradition, cleverness which becomes chicanery—none of these things which he had known on the river satisfied him. Huck was a decent person, honest and forthright. He responded, within limits, to the Widow Douglas' doctrine of love and to Jim's loyalty. He reacted in the right way to the right things, when they were called to his attention. He was frightened by the right things. He had the kind of imagination which bred fears. But not Tom Sawyer's kind.

Tom Sawyer's solution is in the direction of Henry James's solution, of James Branch Cabell's, even of Ernest Hemingway's. It is escape through avoidance of what one wishes to avoid by creation of values of one's own which transcend reality because they seem finally more real than reality. Find in human behavior in its purest form, least contaminated by the noisy chaos of actuality, some secrets of renunciation, perhaps, which make life in essence ultimately a fine thing. Recognize the illusion, but cherish it. Simplify—drink, make love, be brave. Any of these effectively lead away from the disruptive chaos which men have wrought. "Man," said Mark Twain, "is a museum of diseases, a home of impurities; he comes today and is gone tomorrow; he begins as dirt and departs as stench." Tom Sawyer's solution is the solution of escape to a world of his own. It is not, as I have said, a good solution or a satisfying one. I think it did not satisfy Mark Twain, who escaped himself to restless traveling and restless adult activities in which he never became skilled, and who escaped also to humor: "There is no humor," he said, "in Heaven." We do not like Tom's solution. Huck is what we would like to be, and his hold on us is powerful. Tom, we suspect, is what we must be.

For if Huck is changeless, not very different at the end of the second book from what he was when we first met him on page seventy-five of the first, Tom Sawyer, in his book, grows from innocence of a kind that Huck never really enjoyed to a response to evil not unlike Mark Twain's. Huck is frightened by evil, he is repelled by it, he wants no part of it, but in other respects he hardly learns from evil at all. Tom, with more sensitive imagination, becomes master also of a means of defeating it, through illusion, through compromise which is escape to a world made as he wants it to be, because he made it. But in the second book Tom's solution, like Huck's running away, is finally no solution at all, for now evil remains. No wicked men are adventitiously destroyed, even indirectly as a result of Tom's imaginings. Nothing happens, except that Tom gets shot. He has no knowledge at all of the varieties of evil which Huck has confronted. In the face of Huck's experience, Tom's solution becomes innocent indeed. We suspect that it is unsatisfying as an ending to *Huckleberry Finn* because it now began to seem unsatisfying to Mark Twain also. It would do for boys, not for men. Mark

Twain had admitted several years before that he would like to be a boy again, but only if he could be assured of dying at fifteen. The boy is the hero, the adult the bumbling villain still. Man who has suffered to maturity finds no better solution than Tom's—yet Tom's would not do.

Perhaps that is why Mark Twain some years later, in 1891, contemplating briefly an extension of the story of Tom and Huck, wrote in his notebook that "Huck comes back sixty years old, from nobody knows where—and crazy." He imagines himself a boy again and he watches everyone who passes to find one of his boyhood friends. Then Tom returns also, from years of "wandering in the world and attends Huck and together they talk of old times." Neither has succeeded: "both are desolate, life has been a failure, all that was lovable, all that was beautiful is under the mold. They die together." Whichever road one took, of running away or of compromise through illusion, there was no solution. But because Tom's attempt at solution was Mark Twain's attempt, he placed it painstakingly and honestly, without irony, at the end of *Adventures of Huckleberry Finn*.

We need not suppose that Mark Twain was hammering out a moral, in either book. He was not that kind of writer. But the problem was there, unsolved and a personal problem, and it bothered him. What is romance, he once wrote, but adorned autobiography? Among things lovable and beautiful to Mark Twain was innocence—a favorite word, whether he used it to describe his own experiences during his journeyman days, or Tom's irrepressible innocence, in which Mark Twain seems never to have ceased to believe, or the innocence of Joan of Arc, which was so convincingly wise and simple that men whose lives become complicated must rid themselves of it. In a world bereft of innocence Mark Twain might yet encourage innocence to triumph in the better world which he as a writer could create. But the world he lived in impinged on Mark Twain until even fiction was a lie, and the illusion of innocence in make-believe and boyhood play became in *Huckleberry Finn* an empty thing.

Yet, paradoxically, it is the inadequacy of the answer which Mark Twain has Tom Sawyer suggest to us and, I think, Mark Twain's own never completely expressed sense of its inadequacy which combine with other elements to make the second book, as Huck drifts down the river untouched by the necessities of plot, inestimably the finer of the two. The contrived innocence of Tom Sawyer fails. The questing spirit of Huckleberry Finn, who would be impatient at our even raising the question of innocence, lives on.

6

❦

The Lovingoods:
Notes Toward a Genealogy

SUT LOVINGOOD and his escapades, as described by George
Washington Harris, have never been quite forgotten. But
during the past several years they have been splendidly and
generously memorialized, and most often in a manner which
would have pleased Sut completely. Four books about him,
who reminds us of "the depravity ove man, when he am a
boy," [1] have appeared since 1954, only one before that date;
more than thirty articles have seen print since 1950, as opposed to five recorded in the previous half-century; a Sut Society has been formed, and four issues of *The Lovingood
Papers* presented in annual volumes; and at least nine candi-
dates have received advanced graduate degrees by writing
learnedly about him. His admirers have become legion, for
Sut is them and Huck Finn and an advocate of measures
which neither they nor Huck would have dared.

But Sut has not been without enemies who have called
attention to his violence, his sadism, his lack of polite taste.
"A dreadful bestial lout," he has been called, in whom "all

[1] George Washington Harris, *Sut Lovingood's Yarns,* ed. M. Thomas
Inge (New Haven, Conn.: College and University Press, 1966), 60. Here-
inafter citations from this source are given parenthetically within the text
immediately following the quoted material or reference.

111

that was lowest of the South found expression." [2] Even his ability to speak as he should has been questioned; his vagaries in spelling have been thought "disastrous to his fame," [3] though they certainly can be thought to exemplify that fine American assumption, variously attributed to Benjamin Franklin and Mark Twain, that no man can be considered educated who cannot spell a word in at least two different ways. But, even worse, he has been accused of speaking as a Yankee speaks, his use of "du," "intu," "fer," and other such words said to have been learned from the New Englander Hosea Biglow. [4]

Not even all of his friends have been consistently respectful. More than one in quoting him have taken polite pains to correct Sut's orthography so that he might seem to speak more plainly and be less confusing to modern readers. But true lovers of Lovingoodeana recognize that of course Sut is confusing and sometimes confused, just the same as anyone else, and as who in situations such as he finds himself would not be. Confusion is part of his character, even of his intention, and should not be tampered with. No more than his

[2] Edmund Wilson, "Poisoned," *New Yorker*, XXXI (May 7, 1955), 138–42, 145–47, reprinted in *Patriotic Gore: Studies in the Literature of the American Civil War* (New York: Oxford University Press, 1962), from which I quote, pp. 509, 517. Brom Weber, in "A Note on Edmund Wilson and George Washington Harris," *Lovingood Papers*, I (1962), 47–53, has proved, I think, that Mr. Wilson did not read Sut carefully. Henry Watterson, however, in *Oddities in Southern Life and Character* (Boston: Houghton, Mifflin and Co., 1883), 415, though a qualified admirer of Sut, partially disowns him as belonging "to a class which is but little known . . . in the South."

[3] E. Hudson Long, *Mark Twain Handbook* (New York: Hendricks House, 1957), 2. J. Thompson Brown, in *The Library of Southern Literature* (Atlanta: Martin & Holt Co., 1909), V, 2101, may imply something of the same, but is certainly more correct, when he says, "Sut Lovingood has his own dialect." For myself, I would plead with all tamperers to allow him to keep it. As Walter Blair has said, in *Native American Humor, 1800–1900* (New York: American Book Co., 1937), 96n, "Sut's dialect is mastered after a little effort"; my experience tells me that the effort is worthwhile.

[4] Jay B. Hubbell, *The South in American Literature* (Durham, N.C.: Duke University Press, 1954), 679.

relative Huck did Sut want to be drawn to book learning or civilized: "ove all the fools the world hes tu contend wif, the edicated wuns am the worst; they breeds ni ontu all the devilment a-gwin on," and he further wisely cautions, "Ef yu ain't fond ove the smell ove cracklins, stay outen the kitchin" (25)—a statement which Sut, being human, may have purloined from a verse of the mountain fiddle tune, "If you don't like my peaches, stay outa my tree."

Nor has he been without other admirers who threaten to turn his head completely. To be told that his stories possess "on the comic level something of what Melville does on the tragic" would have caused Sut to choke on his chitterlings, though he might have preened on hearing that his language was closer than that of "any other writer to the indigenous and undiluted resources of the American language, to the common man himself." [5] To place him beside Falstaff and the Wife of Bath [6] would have appalled his not unplacid sense of his unsullied monosexual personality. To hear himself described as a neglected, lost, and lonely child [7] would have sent him gagging behind the woodshed. He might not have understood all the implications when he was called "a peasant squatting in his own filth," [8] surely the most genteelly scatological image contrived in our time by a major critic, but he surely would have agreed that he was indeed a "genuine roughneck mountaineer riotously bent on raising hell." [9] And

[5] F. O. Matthiessen, *American Renaissance* (New York: Oxford University Press, 1941), 644, 637.

[6] M. Thomas Inge (ed.), *High Times and Hard Times*, by George Washington Harris (Nashville: Vanderbilt University Press, 1967), 3.

[7] Milton Rickels, *George Washington Harris* (New York: Twayne Publishers, 1965), 129–31, has taken Kenneth S. Lynn properly to task for this kind of sentimental designation of Sut in *Mark Twain and Southwestern Humor* (Boston: Little, Brown and Co., 1960), 129–35; Mr. Lynn seems to me more temperate and closer to fact in his briefer treatment of Sut in *The Comic Tradition in America* (New York: Doubleday Anchor Books, 1958), 192–93.

[8] Wilson, *Patriotic Gore*, 510.

[9] Franklin J. Meine, *Tall Tales of the Southwest* (New York: Alfred A. Knopf, 1930), xxiv.

he just might be proud to be reminded that in his often outrageous tales "the antebellum humor of the South reaches its highest level of achievement before Mark Twain." [10]

But most admirers of Sut seem to me to take him too seriously. He does descend to intolerable depths, particularly in his treatment of the Negro—see, for an example, "Sut at a Negro Night Meeting" (128–37), but especially in "Sut Lovingood Come to Life" (280). But he rises sometimes also to minor heights: certainly "Mrs. Yardley's Quilting" (114–22) and probably "Sicily Burns's Wedding" (76–83) and "Sut Lovingood's Chest Story" (90–96) belong in any anthology of American short fiction, humorous or not. But so each of us have our heights and depths, though often not so candidly revealed, or so successfully set forth. Read rightly, this "natral born durn'd fool" (83) reveals cousinship with us all. It may be somewhat fancy to name him the victim-hero of "scape-goat ritual and the nightmare dream . . . that concentrates our fears and hates" in, and of, a society where "injustices are an inseparable part of existence," [11] though there is certainly something about him to which the tatterdemalion in almost everyone responds. It seems proper then briefly to review his lineage and his family ties, and to review them simply, without stopping to designate literary antecedents.

When Sut first appeared in 1854, and side by side that year on few library tables with Thoreau and his better-controlled adventures in wildness beside Walden Pond, the family name was Lovengood, which was probably the way Sut pronounced it; it was changed from an aural, or oral, to a visual signification by the time the yarns were collected in 1867, and has remained so ever since. Of all the family, how-

10 Blair, *Native American Humor*, 101.

11 As Milton Rickels does in *George Washington Harris*, 65, drawing for definition of the *pharmakas* from Northrop Frye's *The Anatomy of Criticism* (New York: Oxford University Press, 1957), 41–45; the quotations from Frye are, however, mine.

ever spelled, Dad was most often in Sut's mind, in admiration or filial terror. As the young man exercised his "tremenjus gif . . . fur breedin skeers amung durned fools" (26), he had trouble enough with Barbelly Bullen, the "Passun," who was an "infunel, hiperkritikal, pot-bellied, scaley-hided, whisky-wastin, stinkin ole groun'-hog" (52–53); with Dr. Gut-Fatty Gus Fagin, who called on Sut's old sweetheart when her husband was away (93); with Sheriff Dalton, who seemed not always as honest as he might be; with old Clapshaw, the "suckit-rider," whom Squire Bullen cuckolded; and with other burly, usually overweight, scoundrels, and all the thin ones, who were peddlers, Irishmen, or Yankees whose moral values were subject to correction. But his dad was more trouble than most: "he allers wer a mos' complikated durned ole fool" (35). When Ticktail, his horse, died, "starv'd fust, and froze arterwards" (so stiff, said Sut, that "we hed tu wait ni ontu seventeen days fur 'im tu thaw afore we cud skin 'im"), Sut's dad decided, "I'll be hoss *mysef*, an' pull the plow, whilst yu drives me." And he did, after "a-studyin pow'rful . . . how tu play the kar-acter ove a hoss puffectly" (34–35); another time he disguised himself as a cow in order to train Sut's puppy to hold fast—and almost lost his nose in doing it. Only a true-blue but transported Southerner could have recognized that "man reduced to the level of beast" is "crucial to the meaning" of the Sut stories.[12] Sut might have expanded that observation simply by saying, Man am beast.

For that reason, I think that readers must resist the more recent suggestion that in some symbolic sense Hoss Lovin-good—that's Dad—is meant to represent a heavenly father: such an attribution is unfair both to father and son, and would have shocked Sut immeasurably. Lest anyone be tempted to the further step, it certainly cannot be docu-

[12] See Hennig Cohen, "Mark Twain's Sut Lovingood," *Lovingood Papers*, I (1962), 22.

mented that Sut was his father's only begotten son, on either side of the blanket. To attribute to him "supernatural characteristics" or to find in his escapades a "mythic quality" [13] places upon him responsibilities greater than he would be comfortable in accepting. Even without being sure of the meaning of all of the words, he would have responded to the better, though Yankee-born, assurance that "no cosmic relations about mythology disturbed Sut Lovingood." [14] He seems to me all boy, primitive, vengeful, ingenious.

But back to Dad. His playing horse or playing cow, "hit cudn't a-been did by eny uther peopil on this yearth, but us," for Lovingoods were all, from the beginning of their line, "plum clarified darn fool, frum aind to aind" (206). "Hit am an orful thing," said Sut, "tu be a natral born durn'd fool . . . an' all owin tu dad" (83), for he was the "king ove all durn'd fools" (77) and his influence was large; his perpetual proximity to trouble was inherited.

Even Dad's wife thought him an old fool who played "hoss better nur . . . husband," though she only "sed so when he warn't about" or when as horse he kicked at her. For Hoss Lovingood was "dod-dratted mean, an' lazy, an' ugly, an' savidge, an' durn fool tu kill" (35). Sut had reason to keep all the space he could between himself and his dad. When Sut was a boy and Dad "fotch home a durnd wuthless, mangy, flea bitten, grey old fox houn, good fur nothin but tu swaller up what orter lined the bowels ove us brats," Sut "natrally tuck a distaste" to the dog, "an hed a sorter hankerin arter hurtin his feelins an discumfortin ove him every time dad's back wer turnd."

What Sut did to that poor dog does not bear retelling— it was awful, even by Sut standards: he gave him no "more peace ove mind nur a suckit rider dus in a baptis neiborhood at sacramint time when the ruver am up in good dippin order" (235). As a result, Dad turned his meanest, and "durn

13 Rickels, George Washington Harris, 85.
14 Matthiessen, American Renaissance, 641.

his onsanctified soul! flung five or six hundred onder my shut with the dried skin ofen a bull's tail, an gin me the remainder nex day with a waggin whip what he borrered frum a feller while he wer a waterin his hosses" (236). Later, when Sut taunted his father for acting like a horse stung by hornets (which Dad had done, and certainly had been), "knowin dad's onmollified nater," Sut set out for the copper-mine country of Tennessee (38), astride a "nick tailed, bow necked, long, poor, pale sorrel horse" of his own (33).

There we first meet him, "a queer looking, long legged, short bodied, small headed, white haired, hog eyed, funny sort of genius . . . who reined up in front of Pat Nash's grocery, among a crowd of mountaineers full of fun, foolery, and mean whiskey" (33). From this time on, Sut ("half dandy, half devil") was on his own, prey to all, and all his prey. He was often duped, but usually outduped the dupester, and his long legs—"the Lovingoods, durn em! knows nuffin but tu run when they gits skeerd" (57)—allowed him to live to dupe another day. Bees were his allies, and rampaging bulls, not people generally, certainly not those who got in the way of his own simplified notions of right and wrong. Almost always he is the only witness to what happened to him or to what he made happen to other people, and it can be suspected that he sometimes allowed imagination to improve on fact.

Like most of us, he had trouble with words: "Now why the devil can't I 'splain myself like yu?" he asked his friend George. "I ladles out my words at randum, like a calf kickin at yaller-jackids" (114). He recognized himself to be only "a rack heap ove bones an' rags. . . . I'se nuffin," he admitted, "but sum newfangil'd sort ove beas', a sorter cross atween a crazy ole monkey an' a durn'd wore-out hominy-mill" (89). With few illusions, he knew of himself,

Fustly, that I haint got nara a soul, nuffin but a whisky proof gizzard, sorter like the wust half ove a ole par ove saddil bags. *Secondly*, that I'se too durn'd a fool tu cum even onder millertary lor. *Thudly*, that I hes the longes' par ove laigs ever hung tu eny cackus, 'sceptin only ove a grandaddy spider, an' kin beat *him* a usen ove em jis' es bad es a skeer'd dorg kin beat a crippled mud turkil. *Foufly*, that I kin chamber more cork-screw, kill-devil whisky, an' stay on aind, than enything, 'sceptin only a broad bottum'd chun. *Fivety*, an' lastly, kin git intu more durn'd misfortnit skeery scrapes than enybody, an' then run outen them faster, by golly, nor enybody (138).

Through all of his adventures and all of his skeers, even when he went traveling with Abraham Lincoln and saw New York—"that cussed n'isey, skary, strange-lookin' country" [15] —Sut seldom forgot his family in the clearing above the creek. If Hoss Lovingood was remembered more than most, it was, as has been suggested, with good reason. He was the root of Sut's troubles, having handed down the "famerly dispersishun tu make a durn'd fool ove myse'f jis' es ofen es the sun sets, an' fifteen times ofener ef thar's a half a chance. Durn dad evermore, amen!" (72–73). When old Burns's fox-hunting sons came after Sut "with hosses, houns, ho'ns, muskits, shotguns, cur dogs an' all," Sut got away by running fast, but he thought now his time "mos' cum"—fifty dollars reward was on his head, and it was Dad's fault: "I is one ove dad's explites at makin cussed fool invenshuns. . . . I blames him fur all ove hit. . . . He hes a heap tu count fur" (89).

"I'se allers hearn that hit tuck a mons'us wise brat tu know hits daddy," said Sut, "an' I thinks hit takes a wiser daddy tu know his own brats" (64). And Hoss had a cabin bulging full—seventeen children, including "the baby that haint named yet," and not including the "Prospect" which Betts Lovingood then carried. Sut tallied them carefully on his fingers, naming himself five times: "me . . . an' Sall, an' Jake (fool Jake we calls 'im fur short), an' Jim, an' Phineass, an' Callimy Jane, an' Sharlottyan, an' me, an' Zodiack, an' Cashus Clay, an' Noah Dan Webster, an' the twin gals (Castur and Pollox), an' me, an' Catherin Second, an' Cleo-

15 Inge (ed.), *High Times and Hard Times*, 126.

patry Antony, an' Jane Barnum Lind, an' me, an' Benton
Bullion, an' the baby . . . an' me" (34). He did not commit himself on the paternity of his younger brothers and
sisters, but of his own he was sure, though not always unequivocally. Most readers recognize him as the eldest son of
Hoss and Betts Lovingood, as indeed he does seem to be.

However, in "Rare Ripe Garden Seed" he remembers his
mother as holding him in her arms in such a way that he
would be sure to get his infant's share of mush, because, Sut
explains, "Whar thar ain't enuf feed, big childer roots littil
childer outen de troff, an' gobbils up thar part" (174), which
seems to imply that there were children older than he. It
could be supposed that there were older siblings who did not
survive, except that Sut's tally of the family corresponds exactly with Dad's later statement that, in addition to Sut,
"Seventeen other brats we cotch in my net, an' strung on
my string" (300). One may reasonably assume that, like
Mark Twain, Sut told the truth mainly, but was capable of
an honest "stretcher" when a good story required it. Whatever the provenance of his brothers and sisters, Sut had no
doubt of his own legitimate Lovingoodness: "Dad never wud
speak sartin about eny ove our famerly but *me*, an' he
counted fur that by sayin I wer by a long shot tu cussed a
fool tu belong tu enybody else, so I *am* a Lovingood" (64).

Betts suspected Hoss of having been too friendly with "old
Missus Simmons, what lived a mile below" (287) on the
same creek which the Lovingoods used, and once the two
had a hair-pulling, dress-ripping altercation, though ostensibly
not for that reason. It was not, as has been said, "a fight . . .
over dad," [16] for though Betts Lovingood did have suspicions
about the origin of Sall Simmons' "cum by chance childer,"
the immediate cause of animosity was that Betts had mud-
died the creek which the two housewives used in common by
washing Sut in it: Sut it was who warned his dad, "I think

[16] Rickels, *George Washington Harris*, 91.

they'se fightin' 'bout *you*" (289); Dad preferred to think not.

Sut always remembered his capable mam with affectionate awe. She was good with fist and fingernail, and had a quicker "lick with a hickory, or a clapboard, ove eny 'oman" (299), but she was in other respects a comfort. He recalled as a youngster "a standin' atwixt her knees" while she fed him "mush an' milk, wifout the milk": "I kin feel the knobs ove her jints a-rattlin a-pas' my ribs yet" (174). When the sheriff came "levyin ontu the bed an' cheers," Sut darted for safety "on all fours onder mam's petticoatails," so frightened that he failed to gobble down the bowl of mush she had hidden there: "I'se mad at mysef yet, fur rite thar I showd'd the fust flash ove the nat'ral born durn fool what I now is. I orter et hit all up, in jestis tu my stumick an' my growin" (175).

Mam was a slender woman who had not many teeth and too many children and not enough to feed them with, but she was a good mother, ambitious for her brood and not unwilling, when circumstances were right, to encourage them in devilment. Once she set Sut up as a merchant, "(I were about thuteen year ole I recon) wif a willer basket ove red ginger cakes an' sour apples." When the enterprise proved to be "a splendid failur" because Sut "et up the las' durn'd one, apples an' all, an los' the baskit a playin' mumble-the-peg," then Mam "got hostile" and applied appropriate and vigorous correction (287). At another time, however, when Sut was sixteen, old enough for simple pranking, she encouraged him in placing a Jimson burr under the tail of the horse on which intruded Squire Haney, who was fond "ove squelchin sin in the neighborhood" (212) and who now would squelch a Lovingood "*privit soshul famerly 'musement*" which had poor Hoss in trouble. Betts had a strong arm and a quick, sharp tongue, and she could use either of them or both, in correcting a family or a husband, in pummeling a neighbor into admitting that, yes, Betts was "a nat'ral born'd lady, every inch" (289), or in telling off this meddlesome

Squire who dared announce all Lovingoods as depraved and tormentors of varmints (213).

But Sut mostly remembered his mam as a quiet woman "standin wif her arms cross'd a-restin em on her stumick" (35). Her concern was with "kitchen insex, bakin hoecake, bilin greens, and runnin' bar laiged" (77)—sometimes Sut was ashamed "ove mam's bar laigs" (211). As a mother, she was efficient and painstaking. Sut remembered once sitting on the fence "a-shavin seed-ticks ofen my laigs wif a barlow knife," watching her "in the yard . . . wif three ur four ove the childers' heads in her lap, bizzy rite in the middil ove a big still hunt arter insex" which she cracked "vigrusly atwixt her thumbs, an' then wiped her nails ontu her gown along her thighs"(207). She was even graceful as she "peaner'd her fingers down thru the har . . . clost arter a knowin old insex, what hed been raced before" and was scooting toward "the wrinkil onder the year-flap, but he never got thar," for Mam thumped him with her finger and "he got hissef busted like ontu a 'cussion-cap" (208).

As wife also, she assumed proper responsibilities. After Dad and Sut had done the plowing, "she and the brats," her husband conceded, "kin plant, an' tend, ur jis let hit alone, es they darn pleze" (35). He called her "Old Quilt," presumably because she was a warm comfort in bed. Surely it was from observation of his parents that Sut learned that "Men wer made a-purpus jis' tu eat, drink, an' fur stayin awake in the yearly part ove the nites; an' wimen wer made tu cook the vittils, mix the sperits, an' help the men du the stayin awake." There were other male and female responsibilities however: "fur the wimen tu raise the devil atwix meals, an' knit socks atwix drams, an' the men tu play short kerds, swap hosses wif fools, an' fite fur exersise" (77), but these seem to have seemed to Sut less elemental.

He admired his mam: she was "the very bes' 'oman that I ever know'd, in my whole life" (327), he once said. He was grateful to her especially for the long legs she had bequeathed him, so useful for "a-runnin from under" (26) the consequences of his retributive escapades. They allowed him to remain faithful to the "rale pure Lovingood idear ove what orter be dun onder strong hurten an' a big skeer. Jis run over ur thru everthing yure durndest, till yu gits comfort, that's hit" (135). His legs and his skill in using them came naturally, a prenatal gift from Mam, who when carrying him "tuck a pow'ful skeer at a san-hill crane a-sittin on a peel'd well-pole, an' she out-run her shadder thuty yards in cumin half a mile. I speck I owes my laigs an' speed," he confessed, "tu that sarcumstance an' not tu eny fraud on mam's part" (64).

He had less to say about his brothers and sisters. It is possible to assume that "fool Jake" was mentally retarded (though not necessary so to assume), and Callimy Jane was "allers sayin sum durn'd fool thing, hevin no barin on the case"; her brother Benton hushed her by calling her—the context in which his remark is placed does not make it clear whether he spoke in affection or exasperation—a "littil narrer-tail'd tucky hen" (217). Benton was lively, but not quick enough to escape a whack from Mam which sent him "flyin outen his tracks over the fence, wif his hands flat ontu his starn" (218). None of the others are spoken of, except to be named, but Sall, perhaps the oldest after Sut, and she seemed a favorite. She was a practical girl, who picked up an ax to free Dad from a puppy which held fast to his nose (219) and made false bosoms out of gourds into each of which an acorn was stuck butt first (280). She had an "onlawful baby" (273), but she was the most helpful of all the family, except Sut, when it became necessary to bury Hoss Lovingood.

As far as Sut was concerned, the legitimate line of Lovingoods would die out, though I think it did not: "you never cotch me," he said, "foolin with ile stock, patunt rights, lottery tickets, cheap jewelry, ur marriage licunses" (276). Not that he was not, and naturally, everlastingly attracted to girls, women, and widows. Compared to most of the rest, Sicily Burns seemed to him "like a sunflower amung dorg fennil, or a hollyhawk in a patch ove smartweed," and "sich a buzzim! Jis' think ove two snow balls wif a strawberry stuck butainded intu bof on em" (69). That "ar gal cud make me . . . kill mam, not tu speak ove dad, ef she jis' hinted she wanted sich a thing dun." She "cud du more devilmint nur a loose stud hoss et a muster ground" (70). But Sicily was neither faithful nor kind, and she chose another, and was not faithful to him either.

Thereafter Sut turned to other girls, to a Sall who was larruped with a stirrup leather after Parson Bullen discovered her with Sut in a huckleberry patch (50–55), to Sal Yardley who was "fat enuf to kill," but who loved "kissin" and "wrastlin" and "didn't b'leve in corsets" (115). Like Ben Franklin, he knew the advantage of old maids—"ef yu gits one . . . out tu hersef, then she subsides an' is the smoofes, sleekes, saft thing yu ever seed." And widows!—"what they don't know, haint worth larnin" (118). He knew the difference between young girls and old girls, which was partly that the former twisted and turned and spoiled Sut's aim in kissing: "I is as awkward as a left-handed foot adze, with an injun rubber helve, when I is amung wimmen folks." As for kissing: "Hits sorter like hot soup, not very fattenin—jist a forerunnin shadder ove vittils, that's all" (329).

Indeed, Sut's preferences and adventures among women would provide matter for another definitive study. There were those whom he admired, like Wirt Staples' honest and hearty wife. There were those whom he feared, and with reason, like Betts Carr. He was attracted to those who had an occasional good word for him, like Mrs. Burns, but he avoided, when he could, those like Mary McKidrin who trapped men or who were meanly suspicious like the proprietress of Catfish Tavern. Best, however, were those who, though rough, were approachable, like Peg Davis, or even better than best, those who were fun at revivals. A calendar and a counting would reveal, I think, that like most of us Sut preferred good women for almost every occasion.

One girl he truly adored, but she "hed tu die," and slept now "onder the pea-vine an' the long grass of Big Frog Mount'in . . . in Tennessee, whar the south birds chirp and the bar growls, whar the wild harycane dus es hit pleases, an' whar thar's plenty of a'r tu breathe an' plenty ove room tu run." Kate Willis had been gentle—"she never told me a lie, never helped to sker me, an' alers stud up that I wur a human, spite of my looks an' behavior." Sut softened when he thought of her. "I haint got no soul," he admitted; "hits onpossible; an' I wouldn't hev one ef I could, only in hopes ove seein' her ag'in, an' hevin' her p'int out tu me the sunshine an' the green ove that purty place she used to talk so much about, whar nobody's arter you—whar thar's no skeer, nur no runnin', fur I railey wants tu rest." [17]

But the Lovingood line was an old one, and inevitably would survive, one way or another. Dad traced the family "back tu Joseph in Yegipt, an' sed hit wer pufeckly useless tu hunt furder fur better fool blood" (108). Sut cared less about genealogy; he had little patience with people who were always "on a fiddil string strain, a-lookin' up for a higher limb to roost on, an' wringin' in every chance far or onfar, what a h—l ove a feller that granmamey was, never seed a louse—smelt a bed bug, or hearn tell ove the eatch, in thar lives." His experience told him that "thar is some folks powerful feard ove low things, low ways, an' low pepil, an' everlastinly a-tryin' their durndest, to show that they aint low." As he saw it, "They ginerily has a pedigree wif one aind tied to thar sturn, an' tother one a-soakin' in *Noah's* flood, an' they'l trace hit back for you, round the jails, onder the galluses, apast the soap works, an' over the kitchens, ove four

17 Inge (ed.), *High Times and Hard Times*, 131.

thousin years, an' if you'l notice clost, hit makes some ove the shortest kind ove dodges, to miss 'em all; but by golly, hit does miss 'em, an' hits every durn castil, an' throne, on the whole road" (260).

His father was more interested. "Sut," he assures us, "comes of as good and as pure durn'd fool stock, as most public caracters now figurin' on top ove the pot." His "great gran'dad, arter a long life spent doin' the durndes fool things done in them durn'd fool days, killed hissef a jumpin down a bluff, two hundred feet into a rocky dry branch, jist to save a half mile gwine to the stillhouse" (298). Earliest named in the family was Sugartail Lovingood, Sut's grandfather, who "never got whipp'd," said Dad, "as I knows ove, becaze he never did eny fightin'. He jist sloshed along lazily, an' this sort ove life spiled him for finanshul business, all except multiplyin' childer, ove which I am one." Dad's mother "was an 'oman hard to beat, or forget," with a sure hand in discipline and "a sharp eye for insex. A sunshiney, Sunday mornin', was a day ove doom, to all creepin' things, an'," he remembered, "we all had sore heads on Monday, an' scratchin' scasely ever begun afore Wensday" (299).

Dad himself was born, probably in or near Bertie County, "in Old Noth Caliney, clost to Firginney line, an' tuck my fust drink ove warter," he said, "outen Tar River, whar herrins, gourd martin boxes, an' tupemtime did mos' abound." While he was still a lad, the family moved to Bunkum County, close to the mountains: "I led two houn dogs, mam toted twins, an' the chances, with a dinner pot on her back, while dad, Sugartail Lovingood, rid the bull, a toatin' a rifle gun; the rest ove the childer follered durn'd permiskusly, pickin' huckilberys, an' fightin' the hole way." Not long afterwards, they returned to Bertie, "whar," Dad explained, "I boun' myself out, to the trade ove varmint huntin', corn shuckin', an' sich" (299). Then he set out for himself, and straightway suffered "a sevear, an' perlonged attack ove

onintermitunt durn'd fool, jurin' which I got married" to
Betts Leatherlaigs, "an' we imejuntly sot in to house keepin'
in a bark camp, wher, sooner nor you would expeck, I foun'
mysef the daddy (so called) ove 'my son' Sut . . . a mos'
remarkabil son in his way" (300).

I am becoming increasingly convinced that Sut was not,
as I had supposed, a Tennessean at all, but a native Tar Heel
from the Old North State, who skipped over the line to
Ducktown in the Tennessee copper country in flight from his
dad. It was not Sut who said it, but he listened to and reported verbatim what an itinerant stranger said: "I wish I
wer back in old Noth Calina, whar onest people ken sleep
ove nites. . . . I'll tell you, mister, this yere Tennessee don't
suit me" (94). I shall appreciate correction on this point.

Then, more than thirty years later, Hoss Lovingood died.
The time pattern is obscure. Sut speaks of Dad's having
"acted hoss . . . fifteen years before" his death (323), and
it can be assumed, I think, that Sut had then been in his late
teens, though it can be argued that he was a little older. At
any rate, "Well, Dad's dead," said Sut. He "put off doing
his good thing for an awful long time, but at last he did hit,
like a white man. He died, by golly! Perfeckly squar—strait
out, an' for keep." Betts Lovingood grumbled "that he dident
ketch the idear twenty years sooner, for then, she mout 'a
done sumthin' "—like marrying again, perhaps. "But no, he
hilt on, jist to spite her, ontil she broke off her last tooth,
crackin' a corn bread crust, an' then he immegintly went"
(321). Only his daughter Sall wept for Dad; as they sewed
him into a bedspread shroud, she recalled that day when she
had stitched him into a cowskin so that he could train Sut's
pup to hold fast.

They all did what they could to bury Dad decently, but
they had kept him too long, so that his smell frightened the
steers that were to pull the funeral sled to the grave. Hoss
proved cantankerous to the end: the bouncing sled bounced
him so hard against wife and children who rode with him

that they were bounced to the ground; only Sut sat firm, guiding the runaway steers toward the grave hole into which he shot Dad, though wrong end to, as they dashed past. Sall was sorry it had ended that way—"An' us tryin' our best to be sorry, an' solemn." Mam wanted "to plant a 'simmon sprout at his head . . . on account ove the puckery taste he has left in my mouth" (325).

And then Sut died, or is said to have, though evidence of that event comes to us at second hand, and no authenticated report survives. Especially suspicious seems the tradition that Parson Bullen, whom Sut disliked almost more than almost anyone, is said to have had the last word as he spoke at Sut's funeral: "We air met, my brethering, to bury this ornery cuss. He had hosses, an' he run 'em; he had chickens, an' he fit 'em; he had kiards, an' he played 'em. Let us try an' ricollect his virtues—ef he had any—an' forgit his vices—ef we can. *For of sich air the kingdom of heaven!*" [18]

But the last word may not have been said. It is not necessary here to concern ourselves with Sut's descendants. Others have done that,[19] discovering them among characters and escapades in the writings of William Faulkner, Erskine Caldwell, Truman Capote, Carson McCullers, and Flannery O'Connor. Further evidences of kinship have been suggested, including that between Sut's "Well! Dad's Dead" and Faulkner's *As I Lay Dying*,[20] and between the bull on rampage in "Sicily Burns's Wedding" and the horses let loose in "Spot-

[18] The sketch in which Sut's death and funeral are recorded has not to my knowledge been found. Parson Bullen's brief eulogy is quoted in Henry Watterson, *The Compromises of Life and Other Lectures and Addresses* (New York: Duffield and Co., 1906), 60–61. Ben Harris McClary has discovered an obituary notice for William S. ("Sut") Miller, in the Athens, Tennessee, *Post*, August 20, 1858, whom he identifies as "The Real Sut," *American Literature*, XXVII (March, 1955), 105–106. I should prefer to think that the real Sut did not die, if indeed he did then, until fourteen years later.

[19] Notably Willard Thorp, "Suggs and Sut in Modern Dress," *Mississippi Quarterly*, XIII (Fall, 1960), 168–72.

[20] M. Thomas Inge, "William Faulkner and George Washington Harris," *Tennessee Studies in Literature*, VI (1962), 47–59.

ted Horses," and attention is called to Sut's opening sentence in "Rare Ripe Garden Seed," where he speaks of a "spotted hoss sirkus" (174).[21] Sut has been claimed "unmistakably an ancestor of Faulkner's Snopses," [22] and "Sut Lovingood's Daddy 'Acting Hoss' " to have a kind of kissing-kin relationship to a similar situation concerning the Armstids in *The Hamlet*,[23] but some have been more skeptical: these people simply grew up in the same region and heard the same tales.[24]

Robert Penn Warren seems to have read Sut, and Flannery O'Connor certainly—she told Milton Rickels so.[25] Faulkner knew him long and well. Joseph Blotner, his biographer, tells me that according to an inventory of Faulkner's books, an original (1867) edition of the *Yarns* was shelved in the living room of his house in Charlottesville, and that Brom Weber's simplified edition was in his bedroom. Yet, however he may have admired Sut, Faulkner seems not to have read him carefully, for he was only partially correct when he said that Sut "never blamed his misfortunes on anyone." [26] Surely, as has been noted above, Sut placed blame aplenty on his dad!

Walt Whitman did not like Sut's kind, though Hamlin Garland did. They were too uncommon for Whitman, too grotesque, without the good manners, quiet heroism, and generosity, or even the "good real grammar" which Whitman found among simple men, North or South.[27] Of course Mark Twain liked Sut, but William Dean Howells seemed to have some reservations about him. And Mark Twain also wrote a story of a boy, a bull, and some bees, and of their "larruping into the midst of . . . [a] prayerful congregation," so that

[21] William Van O'Connor, *The Tangled Fire of William Faulkner* (Minneapolis: University of Minnesota Press, 1954), 123.

[22] Wilson, *Patriotic Gore*, 517.

[23] Rickels, *George Washington Harris*, 45.

[24] See, for example, Carvel Collins, "Faulkner and Certain Earlier Southern Fiction," *College English*, XVI (November, 1954), 92–97.

[25] Rickels, *George Washington Harris*, 128.

[26] See Malcolm Cowley (ed.), *Writers at Work* (New York: Viking Press, 1958), 137.

[27] See Matthiessen, *American Renaissance*, 603.

"the meeting adjourns in stings and confusion" (pure Sut, with embellishments, though it may have been derived from others beside Sut), and Mark Twain intended the tale as one which the young prince's whipping boy would tell in *The Prince and the Pauper*. Advised by Howells, whose surer taste must have informed him that the tale of bulls and bees would be a distraction, boisterously out of place in a historical romance, Mark Twain withdrew it; but, always unwilling to let a good thing go, he published it in the Hartford *Bazar Budget*, and, years later, "he sneaked it into *Personal Recollections of Joan of Arc*." [28]

But closest kin of all is Huck. Almost everyone says so, but someone has yet to undertake the detailed, close study which will set forth the relationship complete. When that is done, I suspect that there may be found a genuine generation gap, so that the two will seem more different than alike, though I shall not anticipate the findings by saying why or in what respects they can be found to differ. Enough now to suggest that Sut, driven from the mountains, probably with a bounty on his head, found it advisable to feign death, flee the country, and change his name to Finn, to become, as deceit-filled as ever, Huck's deplorable Pap, whose first name is never revealed. He had some of Pap Finn's superficial attributes, including a great thirst for mountain dew and an apparent distaste for bathing.

The chronology, at any rate, is correct, if it is recalled that Mark Twain probably first put Pap on paper in the 1870's, soon after Sut's flight westward, and then, likely as not, pushed the action of what he wrote about him back some twenty years in order to disguise the relationship—telling the truth mainly—he was capable of that. (I

[28] Walter Blair, *Mark Twain and Huck Finn* (Berkeley: University of California Press, 1960), 242–43. See also E. Hudson Long, "Sut Lovingood and Mark Twain's *Joan of Arc*," *Modern Language Notes*, LXV (1949), 37–39, and, especially, D. M. McKeithan, "Mark Twain's Story of the Bull and the Bees," *Tennessee Historical Quarterly*, XI (1952), 246–53.

resist however the suggestion that as Sut Finn, down from the mountains and ready to make a new start, the North Carolinian turned Tennessean, and then Mississippian, found place, his name misspelled, in Faulkner's *Absalom, Absalom!*) It is true that Sut never mentions having a son, but no one of his admirers would be likely to expect him to. Huck never mentioned his mother either, no more than Sut ever admitted having, or wanting, a wife. That Sut is reported to have died is irrelevant, for Sut, like Huck, was perfectly capable of being a lively presence at his own funeral. In short, anyone who discounts the suppositions set forth above, simply does not know Sut and his incalculable capabilities for mixing things up: "thar's a heap of whisky spilt," he has told us, "twixt the counter an' the mouf" (36).

7

The Forlorn Hope of Sidney Lanier

SOME YEARS AGO three prominent Southern poets set upon Sidney Lanier with vehemence which might be supposed to have silenced him and his disciples forever. "His poetry," said Allen Tate, "has little to say to this century either in substance or technique." Lanier's was a "commonplace and confused mind," intellectually and morally insincere, irresponsible, and incapable of precise expression. Robert Penn Warren called him "The Blind Poet," so full of self and egocentric theory that his aesthetic perception was atrophied. Sentimental, sensual, and effeminate, his poetry, said Mr. Warren, was at best absurd. Finally, John Crowe Ransom, spokesman for a new Southern agrarianism, disowned Lanier as an apostate who had sold his rebel birthright for a mess of Yankee praise.

This was honest reaction, inevitable and healthy. It was reaction against a man who in the nineteenth century did not think and write as articulate intellectuals from their perspective in the twentieth century saw that he might have thought and written. It was reaction, also, against a reputation which had been swollen by what Lanier called "the cheap triumph of wrong praise" far beyond its proper proportions. Lanier's friends—those of them who, he explained, "do not know what I am about"—had in zeal done him great harm by presenting him as the Galahad of Southern letters, champion of the truest and best of a chivalry which had been despoiled by greed. Even his own protest, seventy years ago, that "any success seems cheap which depends so thoroughly on local pride as does my present position in the South" did little to stem the tide. His reputation grew to become an embarrassment to Southern men like Mr. Ransom, Mr. Tate, and Mr. Warren, who recognized, as he recognized, the invalidity and essential shoddiness of its origin.

Critically, Lanier has always been hard to handle. Except for the juvenile novel called *Tiger-Lilies*, the guidebook on Florida, and the compilations of stories for boys, only two volumes were published during his lifetime: a thin book of ten poems in 1877 and, three years later, the treatise on *The Science of English Verse*, which few in his time or ours have had patience to understand. His posthumous volumes were badly edited. Biographical sketches were almost without exception distorted with apology or special pleading. Here and there a careful man like Edwin Mims or Stanley Williams attempted judicious appraisal, with Lanier's faults on one side, his achievements on the other, but the scale, weighted by the critic's intention or his remembrance of past estimates, has swayed so perilously, now up, now down—sometimes in the course of a single examination—that a definitive reading has been difficult, perhaps impossible.

It is well, then, that Sidney Lanier was again to be allowed to speak for himself, as clearly and as completely as he could, of his intention and his achievement. The opportunity was given him by the university which he served two years as a lecturer, through publication in 1945 by the Johns Hopkins Press of *The Centennial Edition of the Works of Sidney*

Lanier, edited by Charles R. Anderson and prominent South-ern associates. Handsome in format and binding, these ten volumes "bring together in definitive form the body of Lanier's writings so they can be judged as a whole." The editors have been unobtrusive and skillful, particularly in the essential first two volumes, so that the principal voice through-out is that of Lanier. Only when he is hard to understand or when, as is too often the case, he does not quite seem to know what he is about, do the editors step in with comment or explanation. It is perhaps more than a coincidence that each of them is Southern-born or connected with an out-standing Southern institution: it is as if the South in this edition, which only another war prevented from appearing on the hundredth anniversary of Lanier's birth, were offering its poet in all his excellence and deficiency to the nation for new and unbiased examination. No gesture could be more ap-propriate or more significant of maturity.

Lanier was allowed to display himself for all critical pur-poses complete. The first volume contains his verse, all of it, 164 poems, 44 of them collected for the first time, together with fragments, outlines for unfinished poems, and variant readings. Here is the end product, what is essential to knowl-edge of Lanier as a practicing poet, that on which, in last analysis, he is to be judged. It is fitting that it should be placed first and that its introduction should detail so ob-jectively and with such discrimination the history of Lanier's literary career. It is equally fitting that the second volume should present not only *The Science of English Verse*, which Karl Shapiro in his *Essay on Rime* finds to contain sugges-tions of the "mines of new rhythm" explored in this century by James Joyce, but also the occasional papers on music, which are almost of equal importance for an understanding of Lanier's fumbling for prosodical method. Whatever there is of truth or significance in his theory, which explains poetic technique in terms of musical sound, is there as Lanier formally, though too hurriedly, set it down, enhanced by sixty pages of comment and authoritative explanation.

Less crucial, but also necessary for interpretation of what Lanier intended, were the next two volumes, which included the lectures delivered in Baltimore from 1878 to 1881 at the Peabody Institute and at the Johns Hopkins University. Here is a generous display of literary wares, lore on "Shakespeare and His Forerunners" and in exposition of Lanier's theory of "personality" as it developed from Greek drama to what seemed to him the apex of modern fiction, the novels of George Eliot. They were popular lectures, interspersed with great chunks of "readings" (many of which have now been wisely omitted), and, as gathered here, with errors of previous editions quietly corrected, probably reproduce as effectively as scholarly legerdemain ever can the combination of excitement and lofty sentiment that attracted so many people to Lanier as he spoke. Hastily written, sometimes pretentious, and full of ex-cathedra asides which must have been the delight of the unlearned, these two volumes are perhaps the bravest of the ten, because they present many of Lanier's ideas, half-formed and pompously inconsistent, just as they came from his pen when the deadline of next week's lecture hurried him on. They were meant for oral delivery, cadenced, we suppose, to the mellow tones of Lanier's voice. Certainly no eye was to read them until they had been cleared of debris.

Yet, cluttered as these lectures are with the repetitious and unessential, Lanier does speak to us through them of his critical theory and literary aim. Perhaps he did pontificate, posturing behind learning which he had not made his own, because he was on trial and wanted a job at the splendid new university at Baltimore; but, for all this, his own sincere prejudices and enthusiasms break persistently through. He was certainly doing more than appealing to conservative convictions of audience or trustees when, after a conventional diatribe directed against Whitman's man of brawn and muscle, he confided:

My democrat, the democrat whom I contemplate with pleasure, the democrat who is to write or to read the poetry of the future, may have a mere thread for his biceps, yet he shall be strong enough to handle hell; he shall play ball with the earth; and albeit his stature may be no more than a boy's, he shall still be taller than the great redwoods of California; his height shall be the height of great resolution and love and faith and beauty and knowledge and subtle meditation; his head shall be forever among the stars.

Perhaps it seems ridiculous that so many words are wrapped so lovingly about so small a thought, or that so well-conceived a figure is allowed to dribble off to so tenuously meaningful an end. Lanier's own head was forever among the stars, and he seems never to have learned enough of language or himself to translate what he found of vision there into other than conventional generalities. His *Tiger-Lilies* is unreadable, not so much because of bad models in Novalis and Longfellow, but because it never succeeds in saying what Lanier must have meant it to say. It is a young man's headful of ideas, allowed to churn meaninglessly because the words he had learned got in the way of his expression. So the pieces gathered as "Southern Prose," which share the same volume with his early novel, also represent Lanier at his loquacious and inarticulate worst. His models seem often the grandfathers of Senator Claghorn, and the tight-clenched sincerity of what he meant cannot, even in tolerance, gainsay such things as his approval of photography as an "etherealization" of painting because it portrays "little ones saying prayers at mothers' knees" rather than "bloody heeled conquerors soiling the plains"; or his sentimental apostrophe to "old comrades who lie sleeping about the yard beneath tomb and hillock and sculptured pillar"; or the funeral oration in which, after picturing partners, colleagues, brethren of the bar, admirers, and friends glorifying the tomb of the deceased with floral offerings, Lanier portrays himself as one who "steals in modestly and quietly, and as it were in secret lets fall his humble violet from the woods upon the glorious pile of homage, dropping thereon his unobtrusive tear." Surely, the English language and sincerity of grief have seldom been more unfeelingly profaned.

It may be unfair to Lanier to catch him up on these words, which only echo tones and phrases of his mellifluous generation. But we cannot pass them by, as we can the hack work of the volume which follows, the guide to Florida, the magazine articles on India, and other prose, which he wrote to sell so that he might have money to support him as he meditated poetry; for the honeyed tone and heightened phrase become as much a part of Lanier's personality as his straight, black beard and his deep-set, consumptive's eyes. His own words seem to have acted on Lanier much as did the playing of sweet music, suggestive of meaning never expressed. Like the tones he drew from his flute, they served as an opiate which allowed him to escape the traps of poverty, obscurity, and disease which mortality had laid for him, to soar for a moment to a pure atmosphere of his own making, where love ruled as kindly despot and where coughs and the ugly noise of trade had no place. Such luxuriance of expression was not, then, a pose struck as Lanier faced an audience: it became his natural idiom (though as a younger and more robust man he fought against it), the best he could find to communicate the warm glow of understanding with which the words themselves transfused him.

But our rational generation would make a thinker out of each of its prophets. And Lanier presents himself as a man of very few thoughts. He did draw both the evolutionary doctrines of the late nineteenth century and an earlier romantic perfectionism into his tolerant embrace to explain what he called the "etherealization" of all things from gross to spiritual manifestations, but his exposition could have convinced few, even of his generation, except as it reinforced their desire to believe that all things work together toward good. His reaction against trade and his championship of love as a panacea for earthly ills was certainly less intellectual than emotional. Even his theories of art, specifically his analogies between music and poetry, grew from his attempt to transfer to words the exquisitely sweet feelings which music induced and were the results of feeling rather than thought. Like most of us, Lanier seems to have been an enthusiastic rationalizer of what he believed to be true. Let us, he said, "feel more and think less! . . . Let us, who surely have seen and known some genuine Beauty and genuine Sorrow—let us trust these more."

As a thinker Lanier may in formal exposition deceive for a moment, but in the more than eleven hundred letters reproduced in the last four volumes of this edition he offers himself more candidly for examination. Struck off in varied tempos of exhilaration, despair, affection, or indignation, some dulled with fatigue, others hysterical with fever, these bring us as close as we have probably ever been brought to the day-by-day workings of an artist's mind. Lanier writes with no audience in view except the person to whom he is writing. Now he is the poet misunderstood, complaining of the "entire loneliness" of his literary life or ridiculing the "tobacco-sodden bosh such as Southern editors are prone to eject." Now he brags: whatever the world's estimate, he had "never yet failed to win favor with an artist." We, more properly schooled in reticence, may be embarrassed by the unrestrained outpourings of his love for Mary Day Lanier or by his proudly innocent flirtations with other women. We may be repelled by his intensity throughout. But the man finally revealed is—we must borrow his favorite words to describe him—infinitely sweet and courageous, to the point that we are again tempted to agree that Lanier's life was incomparably his greatest poem. Here, certainly, is material of which the biographer, the psychologist, and the critic can make amply effective use.

Now, as we read Lanier in moods he never meant us to discover, we are impressed with the single-minded purpose of his ambition, how hard he worked, how much he planned, how fervently he aspired toward greatness. He would tour the country with an orchestra to lecture the public into appreciation of fine music. He would organize "Schools for Grown People" in leading Eastern cities to instruct American adults in literature, art, science, and the improvement of home life. With his brother as partner, he would start his own publishing house, to which he would commit himself for at least two books a year for the next ten years. He would produce a new flute to revolutionize the modern orchestra. He would be Professor of the Physics of Music at Peabody, Professor of Law at Mercer, Professor of Metaphysics at the Johns Hopkins, Professor of English Literature at the proposed new state university at Thomasville, Georgia.

While he sought a livelihood which would allow him to live quietly with his family, his music, and his poetry, Lanier's head teemed with plans—"if the days were forty-eight hours long I would scarcely get through the modicum of work for each." He jumped at each opportunity to write for money so that he could find time to write for fame. He accepted every possible employment as musician. He planned a treatise on metaphysics which would make him famous, a four-volume history of *The First Thousand Years of English Verse*, more books for boys and girls, and on his deathbed listed ten works half-finished or contemplated. We marvel at him—almost six feet tall, weighing sometimes only 113 pounds, and tortured, withal, "with a living egg of pain under my collarbone." Even *The Science of English Verse*, he tells us, "was wrung out of me. I have no desire ever to write anything but poetry, and keenly feel that I go to all else with only half my heart."

This, only a little more than a year before he died, hints at a climax of Lanier's lifetime struggle between his passion for music and his dedication to poetry. It was compromise rather than victory, the result perhaps of failure ever satisfactorily to answer the question he first asked himself in his teens: "What is the province of music in the economy of the world?" In 1861 he was sure that "the prime inclination, that is natural bent . . . of my nature is to music." Three years later he found that "gradually . . . my whole soul is merging itself into the business of writing, especially writing poetry." Just after the war, however, he wrote to Mary Day of music: "Cling to it, it is the only *thing*, the only *reality*"; and by 1873 he could explain to Paul Hamilton Hayne: "Whatever turn I have for art, is purely musical; poetry being, to me, a mere tangent." When knowledge that tuberculosis must inevitably cut short his life made Lanier vow that, in spite of being "born on the wrong side of Mason-and-Dickson's line," he would devote his remaining years to art, he admitted: "Things come to me mostly in one of two forms, —the poetic or the musical. I express myself with most freedom in the former *modus*: with most passionate delight in the latter."

More than fifty years ago H. A. Beers suggested that Lanier's failure as an artist resulted from his wrong choice of the two roads of music and poetry, and many critics since have caught at the hint to explain that he was first and spontaneously a musician, only secondly and more artificially a poet. However this may be, the possibility of Lanier's ever having attained breadth of achievement as a creative musician (one large quarrel with the *Centennial Edition* is that it does not reproduce his songs) must be discounted by his critical attitude toward music. His approach to it was literary.

He expected it to say things. It did say things to him, of cavaliers and fair ladies, of huntsmen and wooded glens, of flirtations and minuets. As Edwin Mims has said, "He saw music as he heard poetry." And he felt music, as "a great, pure, unanalyzable yearning after God." Music was thus the matrix, not only of Lanier's personality and profound religious belief, but of his artistic creed: "Language is a species of music." The poet expressed the inexpressible so that "every poet worthy of that name must in his essential utterance belong to the School of David." He is the "Forlorn Hope that marches ahead of mankind," singing even truths which are belied by appearances.

Music inspired Lanier with vague imaginings, "infinitely sweet and high and lovely." When he played his flute, he watched listeners who "grew solemn and tender, and gazed at me with earnest and half-wondering eyes as at one bringing news from other worlds." Music bore messages, created images, and by means—Lanier learned this in the hardest of ways, as a neophyte in a professional orchestra—of a technique which was greatly exact and scientific. Language, then, as adjunct to music, might through discovery of its own laws more clearly explain the tantalizing "great deeps, the wild heights, the dear, sweet springs, the broad and generous-bosomed rivers, the manifold exquisite flowers, the changeful seasons, the starry skies, the present, the past, the future— of the world of music."

Again Lanier's words ran away with whatever thought had originally called them up, hypnotizing him by the rise and swell of their rhythm, by the "sweet" images they evoked. It was not only, as Lanier said of Poe, that he did not know enough. Lanier recognized his intellectual shortcomings and tried pathetically to cram himself with knowledge that could give meaning to his imaginings. If only he might have one year in the universities of Europe! He applied for a fellowship at Johns Hopkins—to study science, metaphysics, and literature. Oh, for a few weeks more in the laboratory of the physicist friend he found in New York! But life drove him relentlessly on, so that he died at thirty-nine without opportunity ever to mold what he did know into forms which more than suggested his meaning. Harried by poignant assurance that his years were few, handicapped by pain and poverty, overworked and distracted, he was allowed neither time nor tranquillity properly to examine himself or the words to which he intrusted his interpretation of what Virginia Woolf called the "luminous halo" which surrounds existence.

Another way of expressing much the same thing might be to say that Lanier simply never matured, or, better, that amid the febrile business of his life, he never allowed himself opportunity for maturity. His reach so far exceeded his grasp that the present edition may seem, as someone has said, a cumbersomely large pedestal for a very small statue. But Lanier's acknowledgment of literary debts to Emerson, Whitman, Poe, and Hayne, and the ample suggestions offered here and elsewhere that he has spoken in our generation to Vachel Lindsay, Carl Sandburg, Harriet Monroe, perhaps to Robert Frost, place him unequivocally within the main current of American poetry. He knew, as did Walter Pater, that "all art constantly aspires." And he knew, as Milton knew, that only very great men write great poems. It is not difficult to pick him apart, to expose, as he exposed better than any commentator, his grievous deficiencies. He stood for a moment breathlessly on tiptoe to see beyond sectional, beyond national boundaries to a world of spirit, which all men might enter. Though the mysterious regions he dared explore with such meager equipment yielded him few poems which measure to his standards or ours, none need be ashamed of Sidney Lanier, or embarrassed that his was a forlorn hope. He knew, as W. H. Auden said many decades after him, that "we must love one another or die." And he knew, most surely, that "beauty dieth not, and the heart that needs it will find it."

8

❦

Lafcadio Hearn
"One of Our Southern Writers"

WHEN IN MAY, 1887, Charles W. Coleman contributed to *Harper's New Monthly Magazine* an essay on "The Recent Movement in Southern Letters," he included Lafcadio Hearn among "the score or more of . . . writers" who had established "a worthy and characteristic Southern literature." [1] And well he might have, for during the past ten years Hearn had gained a reputation in New Orleans and in Northern magazines as a recorder of the local scene and as a writer who could transform legends of any land to tales at once sensuous and elusive. One month later, he was to leave the American South in continuing search for the exotic and for a way of living compatible with his personal susceptibilities. He was to write better after 1887, with more restraint and controlled artistry. His sketches of island life in *Two Years in the French*

[1] Charles W. Coleman, "The Recent Movement in Southern Letters," *Harper's New Monthly Magazine*, LXXIV (1887), 838. For biographical information throughout this essay I have drawn on Elizabeth Stevenson's *Lafcadio Hearn* (New York, 1961) and, for insight into some of Hearn's ideas, on Beongcheon Yu's *The Ape of the Gods* (Detroit, 1964). For the period of Hearn's life under consideration large debts are owed to Edward Larocque Tinker's *Lafcadio Hearn's American Years* (New York, 1924) and especially to Albert Mordell, who has identified and published in several indispensable volumes many of Hearn's contributions to the newspapers of New Orleans.

West Indies three years later are unmatched for vividness and subtlety of impression, and the vignettes of Japanese life and lore which he produced in the decade preceding his death in 1904 bring continuing joy to readers who admire small things wrought with care. Because of these, Lafcadio Hearn has a secure and permanent place among writers of his time and kind, with Stephen Crane, Oscar Wilde, and Pierre Loti. His years in New Orleans were apprentice years when a young man moved into his thirties toward mastery of a medium, but during those ten years there was not another in the South who dedicated himself more assiduously and successfully to literature as an art.

New Orleans was clearly a way-stop for Lafcadio Hearn. When he arrived there in November, 1877, after experience as a newspaperman in Cincinnati, where his reporting of slum and riverfront life brought local fame but his unconventional personal life brought disrepute, Hearn was admittedly in retreat. "Where shall I go? What shall I do?" he wrote soon after his arrival. "Sometimes I think of Europe, sometimes of the West Indies,—of Florida, France, or the wilderness of London." [2] Even after three years in Louisiana, he confessed, "I fancy that some day, I shall wander down to the levee, and creep on board, and sail away to God knows where." [3] But as a literary man of twenty-seven he was charmed with the old city: "The wealth of the world is here,—unworked gold in the ore, one might say; the paradise of the South is here, deserted and half in ruins. . . . I cannot say how fair and rich and beautiful this dead South is. It has fascinated me. I have resolved to live in it." [4]

Though his first months in New Orleans were starving months, Hearn soon made a satisfactory connection with a

[2] Elizabeth Bisland, *The Life and Letters of Lafcadio Hearn* (2 vols.; Boston and New York, 1906), I, 183.
[3] *Ibid.*, I, 215.
[4] *Letters from the Raven, Being the Correspondence of Lafcadio Hearn with Henry Walkin*, ed. Milton Bronner (London, 1908), 42–43.

struggling four-page daily called the *Item*, which he livened with sketches in prose and with little drawings which pleasantly ridiculed local peculiarities. "I write as I please, go as I please, and quit work when I please," and he had time of his own to do as he pleased. He was full of literary schemes—for the publication of translations from Théophile Gautier which he had brought with him from Cincinnati; for collecting Creole songs and proverbs, which occupation brought him brief friendship with George Washington Cable, six years older than he, and already on the way toward literary fame; and for gathering Indian lore and legends in company with Adrian Rouquette, an eccentric Creole priest who had been educated in France, where in 1841 he had published a romantic poem about Louisiana called *Les Savanes*, which had received praise from Sainte-Beuve and caused Thomas Moore to acclaim its author as "the Lamartine of America." The company was good and the undertakings exhilarating, but literary work went slowly: "Life here is so lazy,—nights are so liquid with tropic moonlight,—days are so splendid with green and gold, . . . that I hardly know whether I am dreaming or awake." [5]

The letters of Lafcadio Hearn, especially the letters written from New Orleans which describe the ups and downs, and ins and outs, of his ambitions and disappointments, his temper and temperament, are among the most lively of his writings. Like the letters of Edgar Allan Poe, who died the year before Hearn was born, and whom Hearn admired, it has been said, as spiritually an older brother in misfortune, they reveal more of the man and his moods, his aspirations and meannesses, than any chronicler has been able to set forth. No complete edition of his letters has been made, and at least a selected edition is certainly an urgent desideratum. They expose him as vain, crotchety, vituperative, and self-seeking, but often tender, and sometimes humble. After five years in

[5] *Ibid.*, 54–59.

New Orleans, and reading which his correspondence discloses as incredibly broad and seriously intensive, he confessed that he was "exceptionally ignorant": "Knowing that I have nothing resembling genius, and that any ordinary talent must be supplemented with some sort of curious study in order to place it above the mediocre life, I am striving to woo the Muse of the Odd, and hope to succeed in attracting some little attention." [6]

Attention was soon attracted, partly because of the subjects about which Hearn chose to write, and partly because of his extraordinary concern, expressed often in his letters, with words and their proper use. He spoke of the "elfish electricity" of words, of "mosaics of word Jewelry," of a poetical prose "fit to satisfy an old Greek ear,—like chants wrought in huge measures, . . . and just a little irregular, like Ocean-rhythm." The dark magic of Baudelaire, the patience of Flaubert, the delicate strokes of Gautier, who painted with words, and the skilled precision of Pierre Loti— these were his early enthusiasms. "It has long been my aim," he explained in 1883, "to create something in English fiction analogous to that warmth and colour and richness of imagery hitherto peculiar to Latin literature. Being of a meridional race myself, a Greek, I *feel* rather with the Latin race than with the Anglo-Saxon; and trust that with time and study I may be able to create something different from the stone-grey and somewhat chilly style of latter-day English or American romance." [7]

"I would give anything," he said, "to be a literary Columbus," to visit strange lands, find new themes, awaken contemporaries to literature as passionate and vibrant as life should be. Unable now to travel, he sought among the streets and saloons, boarding houses and bordellos of New Orleans, and the fishing villages on the Gulf, for the extraordinary,

[6] *Life and Letters*, I, 290–91.
[7] *Ibid.*, I, 275–76.

the sensuous, the common day-to-day happiness and heart-break and passion which seldom found their way into books. "Passion is the mighty electricity which vibrates through all human life and causes all grand vibrations"; writing should be voluptuous, and writers virile.[8] "I am seeking the Orient at home," he said, "among our Lascar and Chinese colonies, and the Prehistoric in the characteristics of strange European settlers." [9] He had no desire to be a realist of surfaces only, like William Dean Howells, whom he was later to identify as the favorite of mediocrities. He disliked the "atmosphere of Puritanism" in American writing, "in which no buds of fancy, no richly tinted flowers of art may live." [10]

As a literary commentator, Hearn is not often arresting or consistent. He had brief good things to say of Henry James, and he later admired Robert Louis Stevenson and Rudyard Kipling, but his estimates could be eccentric: Matthew Arnold was "one of the colossal humbugs of the century"; Longfellow wrote better nature poetry than Wordsworth; Joaquin Miller deserved a place among the greatest of American poets. What Hearn admired were "vapoury luminosities and golden glows, . . . dream tints and transparent shadows," not the thing itself, but what it suggested which was finer or sweeter. He had no patience with Walt Whitman, who was "indecent and ugly, lascivious and gawky, lubricious and coarse." [11] Maupassant also was sometimes coarse, and Zola quite too frequently: "Strictly speaking, he has not written novels, he has only created a pseudo-literary museum." It is

[8] "The Sexual Idea in French Literature," *Item*, June 17, 1881, in *Editorials by Lafcadio Hearn*, ed. Charles W. Hutson (Boston, 1926), 143–44.

[9] *Life and Letters*, I, 291.

[10] "Novels and Novelists," New Orleans *Times-Democrat*, December 31, 1882, in Albert Mordell, *Discoveries: Essays on Lafcadio Hearn* (Tokyo, 1964), 70–71.

[11] Hearn's estimates of native writers are briefly set forth in Ray McKinley Lawless, *Lafcadio Hearn, Critic of American Letters* (Chicago, 1942), and Albert Mordell, "Hearn's Essays on American Literature," in *Discoveries*, 60–77.

the unreality of art, its luminosity, explained Hearn, "that makes its charm." Like Poe, he would reach toward the supernal, to some ideal created in the searching mind of man: "In order to become better, nobler, wiser than we are, we must have a visible goal to strive for, an apparent model to copy, a beautiful incentive to urge to loftier exertion; and only he who is capable of seeing beyond the wretched boundaries of the baser senses, will ever seek consolation by striving to persuade his fellow-beings that they are as worms upon a dung-hill." [12]

So during these apprentice years Hearn steeped himself in the writings of European contemporaries, especially those who probed beyond convention toward controlled description of passionate joys or aspirations. Some of the translations from Gautier and Flaubert which he had made in Cincinnati were later to be published—"sins," he was to call them, "of my literary youth," and several hundred of the translations which appeared in the newspapers of New Orleans have now been identified or collected. [13] Pierre Loti, Jules Le Maître, Gerard de Nerval, Villiers de l'Isle-Adam, Maupassant, Zola, Daudet, Flaubert, and Gautier all attracted him, and many others, including Dostoevski, Tolstoi, and Sienkiewicz. He polished and repolished, and he wished that other writers

[12] *Essays in European and Oriental Literature*, ed. Albert Mordell (New York, 1923), 4, 6, 14.

[13] The Gautier collection was published at Hearn's expense as *One of Cleopatra's Nights, and Other Fantastic Romances* in 1882; the translation of Flaubert's *The Temptation of St. Anthony* was posthumously printed in 1910; a manuscript translation of Gautier's *Avatar*, which Hearn was reported to have destroyed because he could not find a publisher, was in 1959 in the hands of a private collector (see Jacob Blanck, *Bibliography of American Literature* [New Haven and London: Yale University Press, 1955-], IV, 103). After leaving New Orleans, Hearn in 1890 did a hurried translation of Anatole France's *The Crime of Sylvester Bonnard* for Harper's; both it and *One of Cleopatra's Nights* remain today "standard" translations, the first in the Modern Library, the second in several paperback editions. Translations in New Orleans newspapers have been collected by Albert Mordell in *Saint Anthony and Other Stories* (New York, 1924), *Stories from Pierre Loti* (Tokyo, 1933), *Stories from Emile Zola* (Tokyo, 1935), and *Sketches and Tales from the French* (Tokyo, 1935).

would join him in the task— "What a translation of Daudet could not Henry James give us?" It was difficult, demanding work, not to be carelessly attempted:

It is by no means sufficient to reproduce the general meaning of the sentence:—it is equally necessary to obtain a just equivalent for each word in regard to force, colour, and form;—and to preserve, so far as possible, the original construction of the phrase, the peculiarity of the rhetoric, the music of the style. And there is music in every master style,—a measured flow of words in every sentence; . . . there are tints, sonorities, luminosities, resonances. . . . The sense, form, force, sonority, colour of every word must be studied; the shape of every phrase chiseled out, the beauty of every naked sentence polished like statuary marble.[14]

Thousands of Americans first read these foreign writers in the anonymous translations by Lafcadio Hearn. While during the 1880's America was discovering itself in the writings of Mark Twain and Howells, Edward Eggleston and Cable and Parkman, Mary Murfree, James Whitcomb Riley, and many another who dwelt on the local scene, Hearn was more than any native contemporary extending literary horizons toward new themes and bold transatlantic notions of the proper substance of art. His contribution to the cultural expansion of his adopted country has sometimes been made to seem Hearn's whole and sufficient claim to being remembered, and praise has rightly been given New Orleans as the only city in the United States which at that time would have fostered so strange a talent. But New Orleans had more than that to offer, and translating was not in itself an end: "I see beauty here all around me,—a strange tropical, intoxicating beauty. I consider it my artistic duty to let myself be absorbed into this new life, and study its form and colour and passion." [15]

Wandering through the Vieux Carré, listening to street cries and street brawls, "the melancholy, quavering beauty

14 *Times-Democrat*, September 24, 1882, in Tinker, *Lafcadio Hearn's American Years*, 159.
15 *Life and Letters*, I, 217.

and weirdness of Negro chants," absorbing sights and sounds and odors, listening to and reading of strange "traditions, superstitions, legends, fairy tales, goblin stories, impossible romances," blending them, he attempted a new form, based on brief impressions of scene fleetingly glimpsed or conversation overheard, and then painstakingly embellished— "moulded," he said, "and coloured by imagination alone." [16] He called these writings "Fantastics," and some thirty of them appeared through 1881, telling "of wonders and of marvels, of riches and rarities": in "Aphrodite and the King's Prisoners," of a captive kept in luxury, but alone with only an ebony statue of the Goddess of Love for company, until he kills himself at the foot of the statue in "Love which is brother to death"; in "El Vómito," which celebrates beauty and death, and "The Name on the Stone," in which a Ligeia-like maiden returns from the grave to inform her lover that "Love is stronger than death"; or in "The Fountain of God," a parable of eternal youth and love and happiness secured in death and dream.

Many of the Fantastics are slight indeed, like "The Idyl of the French Snuff-Box," from the enameled cover of which a nymph and faun come briefly but charmingly to life, or like "Spring Phantoms," which reminds man of visions of luscious ladies which may come to him as winter wanes. One borrows the semiscientific manner made popular by Oliver Wendell Holmes as a doctor at a boarding-house table holds forth on "Hereditary Memories"—a theme obsessively intriguing to Hearn; another spoke in "A Dream of Kites," of children's windswept toys entangled in a web of telegraph wires, lost and tattered like the dreams of youth. Most of them are too fragile for quick retelling, and Hearn admitted them trivial. But he was right in refusing to be ashamed of them as unworthy of his talents. "I fancy the idea of the

[16] "Some Fancies About Fancy," *Item*, March 28, 1881, in *Editorials*, 135.

fantastics is artistic," he said. "They are my impressions of
the strange life of New Orleans. They are dreams of a tropical
city. There is one idea running through them all—love and
death." [17]

"I live forever in dreams of other centuries and other faiths
and other ethics," he said then, as he gathered from Brah-
manic, Buddhistic, Talmudic, Arabic, Persian, Chinese, and
Polynesian legend a collection of twenty-seven tales which
James R. Osgood in Boston published in the spring of 1884
as *Stray Leaves from Strange Literatures*. Adapted from translations by other men, these fables, Hearn explained, are "re-
constructions of what impressed me as the most fantastically
beautiful in the exotic literature which I was able to obtain."
Though he learnedly discussed sources, he made no claims to
scholarship: he wished simply to share with others the delights which he had experienced among "some very strange
and beautiful literatures."

The tales are brief, and often bold; they speak of passion,
especially the passion of love, and of wisdom which may,
but does not always, bring comfort or calm. Weirdness is
their keynote: spectral lovers and enchantress wives, and love
which leads to death. "The wise," he wrote in introduction
to one tale, "will not attach themselves unto women; for
women sport with the hearts of those who love them," and
women die, even as love dies, so that memories are best, and
sad, strange tales not shrouded in reality. He told of Polynesian lands "where garments are worn by none save the
dead," of youth which might be eternal, and of dreams
despoiled by phantoms, of intelligence greater than wisdom,
and faith superior to truth.

Each tale is carefully chiseled, and meant to be enchanting.
Each is frankly derivative, a retreat to ancient quietness. The

[17] *Life and Letters*, I, 220–21. Ten years after Hearn's death, Charles
W. Hutson collected many of them in *Fantastics and Other Fancies* (Boston,
1914); reprinted in *The Writings of Lafcadio Hearn* (16 vols.; Boston and
New York, 1922), II, 195–386.

language is honeyed with Biblical phrasing, cloyed sometimes with alliterative rhythm, as Hearn strove to attain what Baudelaire had described as "le miracle d'une prose poétic." They were exercises done by a young man who trained for something beyond virtuosity; "veritable poems," Charles W. Coleman thought them, "heavy with the perfume and glamour of the East, delicate, fragrant, graceful." Hearn was, however, to reach closer to an idiom of his own three years later in *Some Chinese Ghosts*, which Roberts Brothers published then in Boston. Having wandered, he said, through "vast and mysterious pleasure-grounds of Chinese fancy," he presented in this, his second volume, "the marvellous flowers there growing, . . . as souvenirs of his curious voyage." He spoke again of spectral lovers, of nocturnal meetings, of passion sublimated to beauty, with no habitation in time or place, only in the questing spirit of man. Myth and legend, and the unlearned yearning of people, contained unchanging essences. He prefaced the book with an epigram from a Chinese poet: "If ye desire to witness prodigies and to behold marvels, / Be not concerned as to whether the mountains are distant or the rivers far away."

But there were marvels also in New Orleans and the bayou country beyond it. Hearn had at one time thought that his first published book would be a "tiny volume of sketches of our creole archipelago at the skirts of the Gulf." The local legends and songs which he had been collecting, and the impressions of the local scene, were printed in the *Item* and the *Times-Democrat*, and in magazines of the North, in the *Century* or in *Harper's Weekly* or *Harper's Bazar*. In 1885 he published *La Cuisine Creole*, an assembly of culinary recipes "from leading chefs and noted Creole housewives who had made New Orleans famous," and *Gombo Zhèbes*, a dictionary of Creole proverbs. And he had begun a collection of "Ephemerae" or "Leaves from the Diary of an Impressionist," which included "Floridian Reveries" written on a journey to that peninsular coast in the summer of 1885. No publisher for this or for the Creole sketches was found during Hearn's lifetime,[18] but they contain his most impressive insights into the life and character of the tropical South, "its contrasts of agreeable color; its streets reëchoing with the tongues of many nations; its general look of somnolent contentment; its verdant antiquity; its venerable memorials and monuments; its eccentricities of architecture; its tropical gardens; its picturesque surprises; its warm atmosphere, drowsy perhaps with the perfume of orange flowers, and thrilled with the fantastic music of mockingbirds." [19]

Even more than George Washington Cable, who Hearn finally decided was handicapped by a Sunday-school compulsion to do something about things, he caught the lush languor of old New Orleans, its Mardi Gras, its Creole girls, its proud but purse-pinching lodging-house keepers, its tales of voodoo and ghostly apparitions, of women tantalizingly lovely, calculating, and bitter. He had a surer ear for words than an eye for exact detail, spoke more confidently of color and shadow than of particularities of place. His people are less often remembered as appearances than as voices, often Hearn's own voice, but often also in dialect which caught nuances of character. People in New Orleans rarely laugh, Hearn said; nor did he, for what he presents is not condescending but human, as when he presented the plaintive, exasperated voice of a Creole housewife explaining to another "Why Crabs Are Boiled Alive":

And for why you have not of crab? Because one must dem boil 'live? It is all vat is of most beast to tell so. How you make dem kill so you not dem boil? You can not cut dem de head off, for dat dey have not of head. You can not break to dem de back, for dat dey not be

---

[18] See, however, *Leaves from the Diary of an Impressionist*, ed. Ferris Greenslet (Boston and New York, 1911), in *Writings*, I, 1–99, and *Creole Sketches*, ed. Charles W. Hutson (Boston and New York, 1922), in *Writings*, I, 107–208.

[19] *Writings*, I, 108.

only all back. You not can dey bleed until they die, for dat dey not have blood. You can not stick to dem troo de brain, for dat dey be same like you—dey not have of brain.[20]

These Hearn did briefly best, renderings of people through what they said and how they sounded. But he did them seldom, preferring instead to turn his ear for tone and modulation to continuing re-creation of tales which came to him at second hand. His writings suggest that he knew few people well, and that what he observed of people was how they talked or what they thought, seldom how they looked or acted—except that he was curiously fascinated by eyes, by sparkling or furtive eyes, Venetian eyes challenging from behind a carnival mask. In telling a story or sketching a street scene, a seascape, or a sunrise, he seems at ease with words, evoking color and movement and sound; but people, unless overheard, eluded him. He was as bookish as he was sensually perceptive, and was finally most comfortable with the rhythm of words skillfully arranged to capture atmosphere or mood.

When Cable told him a sad story of storm and death which years before had visited an island on the Gulf coast, Hearn wove words around it to produce a novelette called *Chita: A Memory of Last Island*, in part a magnificent tour de force, in part briefly evocative character portrayal, and in part pathos shaded toward sentimentality. In attempting a longer story, Hearn did not build well; he could decorate a plot better than he could resolve a situation, and so *Chita*, his single attempt at sustained narrative during his years in New Orleans, fails to please. However clear his intention to present man as part of, but caught relentlessly within, the power of nature, and to demonstrate that simple men who know and respect nature's force live cleaner, more satisfying lives than dwellers in cities to whom nature is hidden "by walls, and by weary avenues of trees with whitewashed trunks," the result is distorted more than Hearn could have

[20] *Ibid.*, I, 133.

meant it to be. As a child of nature, young Chita is never seen as clearly as the sea and sky, whose color may be thought of as in itself a major theme.

For *Chita* is a book of blueness, and blueness is eternity. After mottled rage of storm or sudden glare at birth or death of day, the calmer color returns, inscrutable, insistent. Other colors are stroked boldly through the book: "the golden wealth of orange trees," "clouds brilliantly white and flocculent, like loose new cotton," "the quivering pinkness of waters curled by the breath of morning," the "vaporized sapphire" of cloudless summer days, and the redness of storm and death with which the action opens and closes—black redness like "heated iron when its vermillion dies." Forms are less distinct: "the rounded foliage of evergreen oaks," "beaches speckled with drift and decaying things," girls presented in outline only, "graceful as the palmettoes that sway above them." Occasionally there is a memorable visual image, like that which fleetingly glimpses a passing gull "whirling its sickle wings" against a crimsoning sky. But sounds are everywhere: "the storm-roar of reptile voices chanting in chorus," "the monstrous and appalling chorus of frogs," "sinister, squeaking cries" of gulls, the perpetual rustle of the fiddler crab, and the "moan of the rising surf," the "voice of the sea," which is "never one voice, but a tumult of many voices . . . the muttering of multitudinous dead—the moaning of innumerable ghosts." And the sea, responding to the colors of the sky, implacably eats away at the shore, so that "year by year that rustling strip of green grows narrower; the sand spreads and sinks, shuddering and wrinkling like a living brown skin; and at last standing copses of oaks, ever clinging with naked, dead feet to the sliding beach, lean more and more out of perpendicular. As the sands subside, the stumps seem to crawl, to writhe—like the reaching arms of cephalopods." [21]

[21] *Ibid.*, IV, 153.

Something of what *Chita* is about is suggested by the epigram from Emerson with which Hearn prefaces the book: "But Nature whistled all her winds, / Did as she pleased and went her way." It is the story of a child who is born to the world of nature by a storm in which her mother and, presumably, her father have lost their lives. They had been among lighthearted island vacationers who had not recognized signs of an approaching storm, for "Nature—incomprehensible Sphinx—before her mightiest bursts of rage, ever puts forth her divinest witchery, makes more manifest her awful beauty." All seemed so serene and blue that they failed to realize that there is also "something unutterable in this bright Gulf-air that compels awe—something vital, something holy, something pantheistic: and reverently the mind asks itself if what the eye beholds is not . . . the Infinite Breath, the Divine Ghost, and the great Blue Soul of the Unknown."

All, all is blue in the calm—save the land under your feet, which you almost forget, since it seems only a tiny green flake afloat in the liquid of eternity of day. Then slowly, caressingly, irresistibly, the witchery of the Infinite grows upon you; out of Time and Space you begin to dream with open eyes—to drift into delicious oblivion of facts—to forget the past, the present, the substantial —to comprehend nothing but the existence of the infinite Blue Ghost as something into which you would wish to melt utterly away forever.[22]

Hearn, perhaps inadvertently, is true to his imagery. After the storm had mounted wave after succeeding wave to attack the vacation island, its awful music in horrendous contrast to the waltz to which doomed revelers danced; after the waters had washed away all before it, the child Chita is found afloat "in the liquid of eternity" upon "a tiny green flake," which is a billiard table. The fisherman who rescued her knew and understood the sea, and when he had taught her to know

[22] *Ibid.*, IV, 155.

it also, Chita's "soft, pale flesh became firm and brown, the meagre limbs rounded into robust symmetry . . . ; for the strength of the sea had entered into her." How different the experience of her father, who also somehow miraculously had escaped death in the storm. Amid the "blindness and brutality of cities, where the divine light never purely comes," he practiced medicine, but could not save himself from yellow fever. When he arrives at the gulfside settlement where Chita has lived, he recognizes her because she looks so like her mother, and then, after six pages of delirium, he dies.

The third section of *Chita*, called "The Shadow of the Tide," is crowded and incoherent. It attempts too much— Chita's development over ten years, her discovery of death in a gruesome woodland tomb, her conquering of fear of the sea; and then suddenly a shift in focus, from Chita to her father, his introduction to nature as he journeys to Viosca's Point, his illness, recognition of his daughter, and death. If in *Chita* Hearn was writing the narrative of which he had spoken earlier to friends, "constructed on totally novel principles," grounded in evolutionary philosophy as he had read it in Herbert Spencer and on the kind of benign fatalism he found attractive in Buddhism, such purpose does not come through—certainly not in this third section where he seems, almost frenetically, to be striving toward statement, about rough boatmen who break into beautiful song, about folk memories, and love discovered in death. Nor is the second section, "Out of the Sea's Strength," greatly better, though it is here, as Laroussel, a member of a rescue party which searches the bayou for remnants of the storm, questions the derelict child in Creole patois, that Chita is revealed, albeit briefly, as a person who is heard and known. Laroussel, who speaks and is real, then disappears, later dimly revealed as an enemy, then a friend, of Chita's father, was evidently intended to play a significant part in the development of the plot, though what exactly that part is Hearn never makes clear.

But the first section, "The Legend of L'île Dernière," which has hardly a person in it, but which celebrates calm and storm and blueness, deserves a place beside Mark Twain's "Old Times on the Mississippi" (which Hearn admired) and Thoreau's descriptions of Katahdin and Cape Cod. Hearn was later, he said, ashamed of *Chita* as overworked and overstylized, but he could not have been thinking of the first section, which is heightened surely, but which in tone and substance is almost exactly right. Word and mood and rhythm advance confidently side by side. Hearn's sea is a cradle endlessly rocking, but not by the hand of an elemental cronemother. Mystery and beauty and menace there are one, not to be defined by eyes sharpened for daily use, or ears attuned to pleasing waltzes.

No Southern writer, except perhaps Sidney Lanier, had composed with more exultant fervor. Yet Hearn disliked the localizing of writers, as he might have disliked being remembered as shy, myopic, and irascible. Neither personal defect nor accident of place defines an artist. Writing, he said, "which has no better claim to recognition than the fact that it is Southern, can never maintain its claim to recognition at all." Whatever its substance in locale or dialect, "the art itself must be founded upon catholic principles—upon those touches of nature which make the whole world kin." No work of true merit can be of "merely sectional interest." [23] Magic was needed, of a kind which might be searched out amid the mélange of wildness of the bayou country, or wherever simple people remembered more than they had ever learned, where old songs and customs and superstitions defied corruption, and faith scoffed at learning. "We are nearer God in the South," wrote Lafcadio Hearn in 1887 as he was pre-

23 Mordell, *Discoveries*, 66, 70.

paring to leave it, "just as we are nearer Death in that terrible and splendid heat of the Gulf Coast." By God, he explained, "of course I mean only the World-Soul, the mighty and sweetest life of Nature, the great Blue Ghost which fills planets and hearts with beauty." [24]

Edmund Wilson in *Patriotic Gore* has dismissed Lafcadio Hearn as an impressionist and escapist, without interest in social movements—as if that were the gauge of any artist. Malcolm Cowley, introducing the only easily available collection of Hearn's writing, speaks of him more leniently:

Unlike many authors of broader talents, he had the *métier*, the vocation for writing, the conscience which kept him working over each passage until it had the exact color of what he needed to say; and in most cases the colors have proved fast. Many books written by his famous contemporaries are becoming difficult to read. One can't help seeing that Howells followed the conventions of his day, that Frank Norris was full of romantic bad taste; but Lafcadio Hearn at his best was independent of fashion and was writing for our time as much as his own.[25]

Hearn had almost every minor literary virtue; he succeeded in minor genres, but he is real, as person and artist, and bold enough to stand, however unsteadily, alone. When the critic or literary historian forgets him, something of literary heritage is lost, for he has added, said Paul Elmer More, "a new thrill to our intellectual experience," [26] and people who care for writing as art will not pass him by, even when they are sure that he may finally disappoint them.

[24] *Letters from the Raven*, 86.
[25] *The Selected Writings of Lafcadio Hearn*, ed. Harry Goodman (New York, 1949), 1–2.
[26] Paul Elmer More, "Lafcadio Hearn: The Meeting of Three Ways," *Atlantic Monthly*, XCI (February, 1903), 205.

9

॰ॐ॰

The Awakening of Kate Chopin

As KENNETH EBLE, first modern editor of *The Awakening*, has said, "quite frankly the book is about sex." Larzer Ziff, historian of the 1890's, finds it "the most important piece of fiction about the sexual life of a woman" written in that decades. Edmund Wilson has pronounced it "quite uninhibited and beautifully written, anticipating D. H. Lawrence in its treatment of infidelity." But to present *The Awakening* only because it was first or unique of its kind is to do it disservice, for it is more than a literary curiosity. Van Wyck Brooks, who seems to have known it earlier than any of these others, thought it rare and beautiful in naturalness and grace, a "small perfect book that mattered more than the whole life of many a prolific writer."

The author, Katherine O'Flaherty, who became Kate Chopin, was partly Irish, and partly French also. Her father had come from County Galway by way of New York and Philadelphia, western Pennsylvania and Illinois, to settle finally in St. Louis. There he married, first, the daughter of a Creole family of quiet distinction, and at thirty-five his first wife dead, married again, to sixteen-year-old Eliza Faris, daughter of a Huguenot father, who had migrated from Virginia, and a mother from an old French family, for several generations in Missouri, from Charleville in the Ardennes. Kate, born on February 8, 1851, was the second child and only daughter of the marriage. She lived in St. Louis during the first twenty years of her life.

Captain Thomas O'Flaherty was an active and successful man with a profitable warehouse by the riverside until, when Kate was four, he was killed in the wreck of a train belonging to the Pacific Railroad, of which he was a director. His death was shattering to the family, not least to Kate. She was consoled in part by stories of old St. Louis told by her matriarchal great-grandmother, Madame Victoria Charleville, who spoke French better than English and is said never to have been able to pronounce Kate's outlandish last name. When at nine she entered the local Academy of the Sacred Heart, Kate was bilingual, and seems already to have developed an Irish ear for music and strange tales. She never would forget the terrifying things that happened during the war between the North and the South, especially not the fate of her half-brother who, weakened by life in a Yankee prison camp, died on returning to battle. Not long later, her own and favorite brother was killed by a fall from a runaway horse, so that Kate and her young mother were alone. Her mother did not live long afterward, nor her beloved great-grandmother, who was almost eighty-five. But Kate was a resilient girl, who at fifteen could observe in her copybook, "Mourn not therefore when Death comes into our garden, culling the flowers of Spring, for in their early beauty how far more pleasing an offering are they to God than when sere and drooping."

Knowledge of the mystery of death and acceptance of death thus came early to Kate O'Flaherty, and it remained somberly with her, tempering but never quite dulling the lilt of her tongue or her mimic sense of the way people talked and thought. Self-possessed she was then, and remained, but as a girl, and later, seems to have cared more for broodingly serious things—"her dear reading and writing"—than for thoughtless pleasure. She disdained the "fiddle scraping, flute tooting, and horn blowing" even of the fashionable Philharmonic Society of which St. Louis was proud. Parties, operas, and concerts tired her for she was a lively and self-sufficient young woman who preferred natural things—like the fiddling of the celebrated but untaught Ole Bull, whose music seemed to her to come tenderly from the heart, "displaying," she said, "none of the exaggerated style most usually seen in fine violinists." Brightness she loved, and gaiety and life and sunshine, not dancing through the night "with men whose only talent lies in their feet." Post–Civil War St. Louis must often have seemed cold and cheerless, increasingly bound to convention, and Kate seems often to have thought of exploring more widely, with greater freedom, less caged by the requirements of custom. Among her earliest writings is a fable-sketch called "Emancipation," which tells of an animal that escapes from its cage to explore the world beyond it, "seeing, smelling, touching all things; even stopping to put his lips to a noxious pool, thinking it may be sweet"; living dangerously now, but free, and "ever seeking, finding, joying and suffering."

How much more enlivened, how light and bright and gay must New Orleans have seemed when she first visited it at eighteen. There she met and two years later married Oscar Chopin, to become, she said, "no longer a young lady with nothing to think of but myself and nothing to do," but the bride of an ambitious and warm-hearted Creole, a cotton trader and a commission merchant, who took her on a three-month honeymoon through Germany, Switzerland, and France, and during the next ten years became the father of her six children. People seemed different in Louisiana, and she was intrigued by the social and family life of New Orleans, and the comfortable summer holidays on the islands off the Gulf coast. When the Chopins moved to Cloutierville in the fertile Cane River region of historic Natchitoches Parish, where Harriet Beecher Stowe's Simon Legree was said to have committed fearful deeds among the canebrakes, fields, and woodlands of central Louisiana, she learned to know the country Creole, the Cajun, the half-breed, and the Negro, newly freed and often bewildered. She lived here until Oscar Chopin died of swamp fever in October, 1882. She and the children returned then to St. Louis, where she died twenty-two years later.

That is the familiar outline of Kate Chopin's private years, details of which and observations about which seem so to weave in and out of what she was later to write that some readers have thought her quite too revealingly autobiographical, displaying without realizing it attitudes she would have wished to hide. But to others she is among the least self-disclosing of writers, an artist who used what she had seen and thought and experienced to create avenues of insight into other people who also explore toward freedom and who learn the quickening inevitability of death. "I think," said one of her daughters many years later, "the tragic death of her father early in life, of her much loved brother, the loss of her young husband and her mother, left a stamp of sadness on her that was never lost."

Sadness will not always be found present in what she wrote, though the somber reality of failure or death and its impinging shadow lies behind many stories that on first reading seem to be only lightly perceptive, even gay sketchings of character or theme. Tenderness, compassion, sympathy—these are words that come to mind in attempting to define Mrs. Chopin's attitude, these and an underlying honest questioning which usually avoids irony as deftly as her compassion avoids sentimentality. Both lines were sometimes crossed, for hers was not a new theme, and her problem was to discover new ways of expressing her conviction that life, which was so filled with possibilities for self-expression in freedom, could also be confining as people became willing victims of thoughtless or inherited ways. Nature and natural people were to be admired, wonderingly, for people, too, were animals, caged by custom which is often made to seem comfortably protective. Mrs. Chopin portrays many people who will not or cannot leave the cage, and others who remain within but yearn to be without, and still others who dare, sometimes only for a moment, to break beyond the bars toward experience which is satisfying but perilous also. There are risks, she seems to say, in freedom—dangers and death.

Mrs. Chopin did not begin to write for publication until after her husband's death, and then not immediately. Her children were young and needed care; she was uprooted and perhaps distraught. Tradition says that a family physician suggested that she write about her experiences in Louisiana as therapy for the loneliness she felt as a widow. But not until some five years after Oscar Chopin's death did she begin to experiment with brief tales and a novel, the action of which took place on a plantation much like that of the Chopins near Cloutierville. The tales appeared, one in the St. Louis *Post-Dispatch* and another in the Philadelphia *Musical Journal*, both in 1889; the novel, called *At Fault*, was printed, apparently at Mrs. Chopin's expense, by a local jobbing company. It did not do well, but it showed the way.

At Fault is a story of love and of possibilities for freedom. It speaks of love that restricts and of love that is genuine, of freedom that harms and of freedom that is livening. It suggests questions about the rights of love when convention intervenes as it recounts the story of a man from St. Louis who had been married to an alcoholic wife whom he has come to detest. Having divorced her, he travels southward as representative of a timber company. In Louisiana he applies for and receives permission to cut trees from the woodlands surrounding the plantation of a young Creole widow, with whom he falls in love. On one level it can be thought of as the story of the industrial North invading, conquering, and being conquered by the agrarian South; on another, it speaks of a person's right to freedom, and its cost. Other characters invade the plot, too many of them, for Mrs. Chopin had not yet learned economy, and the novel limps to a completely predictable conclusion: the alcoholic wife dies, the lovers marry.

But crude though it is, *At Fault* does introduce the theme that was to run in and out of much of Mrs. Chopin's later writings. It did not always openly appear in the stories which after 1890 she began to sell to magazines of national circulation, to the *Century*, the *Youth's Companion*, and *Vogue*, though it may be recognized as lying behind many of them. In simplest form, it concerns people's ability to get along with others or within themselves and the handicaps or help contributed by traditional or social forms, and what these do, or can do, to love. "Désirée's Baby," appearing in *Vogue* on January 14, 1893, is among the first and the most popularly lasting of these stories. It presents the theme with pathos, which almost successfully avoids sentimentality, as family pride and traditional attitudes toward race cast out love with false justification. The story owes something of its bold treatment of miscegenation to the example of George Washington Cable, who in New Orleans more than ten years earlier had written on the subject in stories collected in *Old Creole Days* (1879), but Mrs. Chopin approached it more directly, with less sentiment than he, in attitude and manner far in advance of her time. One year later, in 1894, Mark Twain would approach the same subject, though more discursively, in *The Tragedy of Pudd'nhead Wilson*, with hardly greater effect.

Most of Mrs. Chopin's early stories are slight, many hardly more than sketches of people caught in circumstances of their own or of someone else's making. Those that were best received in the more popular periodicals were collected into *Bayou Folk* in 1894 and *A Night in Acadie* in 1897. There were tales of local color, displaying Creoles or Cajuns with sympathetic quiet humor. The themes were not new, nor were the plots. Mrs. Chopin studied other writers who set their stories against quaintness of locale, especially Cable and Sarah Orne Jewett, whose "The White Heron," a story of a New England country girl innocently attracted to a kindly stranger from the city, seems certainly to have provided something of the situation for Mrs. Chopin's "Caline." She studied French writers of short fiction also, learning from Maupassant values of economy and restraint, from Flaubert directness and precision. Throughout her hallmark is honesty; in each story more important than what happens, which is often not difficult to anticipate, is her increasingly skillful portrayal of the inner life of her characters, their yearnings, frustrations, and often futile attempts to escape from restrictions imposed by circumstance.

Her touch was usually light in these stories of Louisiana. She tells of faithfulness of old family servants, of the pride and quick anger but pervasive sense of honor of the Creole, his superstitions but also his quiet humanity, and of the dapper lightheartedness of the Acadian. What they did is often set against backgrounds which seemed to most readers strange and exotic: the countryside of central Louisiana, its swamps and deep woodlands; the bayous at the river mouth; the French market of New Orleans, its bright streets, and the vivacity of its people. "A No-Account Creole," its setting a decaying upland plantation, tells again of the coming to the countryside of a man from the city and of his attraction to a Creole girl who yearns, without realizing it, for freedom from her engagement to a country Creole; but, again, what happens seems less important than why it happens, as a simple story of renunciation which in other hands might have overrun with sentiment is molded by Mrs. Chopin to a subtle revelation of motives and attitudes that seem exactly right. Even more simple, "Madame Célestin's Divorce" presents a young Creole woman who wishes to break with a husband who has left her, but thinks differently of the matter when he returns; yet the story reveals more than only that. For all their starkness of theme or plot, these stories survive because of the insights into character which Mrs. Chopin provides. Her deftness in dialect and skill in suggesting the charm of exotic background can be found to become increasingly ancillary.

Behind many of the stories is a note of subdued and affectionate irony. The Creole dandy in "A Night in Acadie" is in revolt against the traditions of an older generation: because his uncle could not read nor write, he learned to do both; because his uncle liked to hunt and fish, he would do neither; because his uncle "would have walked the length of the parish in a deluge before he would have so much as thought of one," the young man always carried an umbrella. His is a free and dapper spirit, attracted to and attractive to the eligible young women of the parish; he is "a weather-cock for love's fair winds to play with." Unable to make up his mind which of several to choose, he escapes by running away for a carefree weekend in another parish; but on the train he meets a girl as headstrong and as vain as he, and he becomes her champion. Fleeing female entanglement, he runs smack into it again: he meets his match, his independence, if not gone, endangered. Mrs. Chopin allows the reader to wonder whether he will do well thereafter.

For love does not always triumph in Mrs. Chopin's stories. Sometimes it is unselfish love, like that of poor Nég Créol; again it is blind, and holds the threat of destruction, like that of 'Polyte for Azélie, who is wild and pert and beautiful; the cruelty of thwarted love is suggested in "La Belle Zoraïde," and bravery of love in "Beyond the Bayou." "A Visit to Avoyelles" speaks with restrained sentiment of love in poverty. "A Lady of Bayou St. John" presents "that psychological enigma, a woman's heart," as a lonely wife, whose husband is away from home fighting for the Confederacy, is wooed and won by an attractive neighbor, with whom she plans to run away; but when she learns that her husband has been killed in the war, she changes her mind: he "has never," she explains, "been so living to me as he is now."

"A Respectable Woman" is for the 1890's a particularly daring though subtly subdued sketch of a married woman attracted to a man who is not her husband. And the same worldly bachelor, who awakens her to expectations of escape from matrimonial restraint, will appear again briefly in *The Awakening* and appears also, more fully developed, in "Athénaïse," which seems certainly one of Mrs. Chopin's more successful examinations of a young woman's battle against becoming only a useful household possession. It is an examination, more detailed than any she had attempted before, of whether marriage is or is not "a wonderful and powerful agent in the development and formation of a woman's character." Athénaïse, who will not accept the inevitable with patient resignation, breaks from the cage of marriage to explore, though timidly and in innocence, the freedoms of independence. That she returns at last to her husband is proof, not that she has been wrong or right to search, only that the man-managed circumstances into which she has been born require her finally to submit.

However sometimes lightly touched, the submission of women and their struggle against submitting is a theme which pervades much, perhaps all, of Mrs. Chopin's fiction—their shaking off of restraint to become what as women they actually are rather than what a man-managed society expects them to be: beneath the restraint there exists a questing animal. The theme seems to appear more openly in stories which were not collected in *Bayou Folk* or *A Night in Acadie,* probably because in those volumes she was offered to the public as a regionalist writer of local color sketches of a kind that in the 1890's publishers had found most acceptable to readers. Background and characters which seemed strange or quaint, as in "A Night in Acadie," might effectively disguise theme. It may also have been thought, and probably correctly, that fiction which revealed women of any socially accepted class who searched beyond convention for self-fulfillment were somewhat shocking. Readers in the 1890's were not used to public expression of what in private many of them might admit. To them, Mrs. Chopin's collected stories must have seemed to have gone quite as far as could profitably be allowed.

Other stories spoke more freely, often without the palliative disguise of locale. "Wiser Than a God," her first story to appear in a magazine, is headed by the Latin proverb "To love and be wise is scarcely granted to a God." Though crudely put together, it presents a girl who prefers freedom to develop her talent as a musician to marriage to a man she loves. Better done, though clogged with clichés, is "The Maid of Saint Philippe," a historical tale of old St. Louis, in which a pioneer girl, having "breathed the free air of forest and stream," will not exchange these for love which requires her to live in a city under despotic rule. "Mrs. Mobry's Reason" somewhat cumbersomely speaks of love and madness and of marriage that can be cruel. "Miss McEnders" recounts the awakening of a wealthy and prudish young woman of twenty-five. "The Story of an Hour" tells in hardly more than three pages of marriage and death and, again, of the mirage of freedom, as a woman, relieved to be loosed from the shackles of marriage when she hears that her husband has been killed, cannot withstand the shock of discovering that he is not dead after all. "A Shameful Affair" and "The Kiss," each revealing the guile of a girl in attracting a man, are presented with a kind of revelatory freedom not often encountered in print during the 1890's.

No one of these stories is among Mrs. Chopin's most successful; many are slight, but each is bold, and a foretaste of the more sustained and successful boldness of *The Awakening*.

For whatever its excellences otherwise, *The Awakening* is bold, and its title tells exactly what it is about. Edna Pontellier, twenty-eight, married and the mother of two small children, is gradually awakened to "her position in the universe as a human being, and to recognize her relations as an individual to the world within and without her." From girlhood she had "apprehended instinctively the dual life—that outward existence which conforms, the inward life which questions." A Southern girl, born in Mississippi, educated but briefly in Kentucky, she had been married some six years to a prosperous Creole of New Orleans, a man about twelve years older than she. She and her children are vacationing at Grand Isle, where the widowed Madame Lebrun provides board and cabins for summer visitors, and where Mr. Pontellier joins his family on weekends. She is restless, both disturbed and attracted by young Robert Lebrun, two years her junior, who "each summer at Grand Isle had constituted himself the devoted attendant of some fair dame or damsel," and this summer has attached himself playfully though charmingly to her. Edna was fond of her husband, and was fond of her children "in an uneven, impulsive way," but an "indescribable oppression, which seemed to generate in some unfamiliar part of her consciousness, filled her being with a vague anguish."

Through much of the novel like an obbligato refrain runs the voice of the sea—"the everlasting voice of the sea," that "broke like a lullaby" on her consciousness. When Edna is first introduced, returning from bathing in the sea with Robert, her husband's attitude toward her is defined by the remark, "You are burnt beyond recognition"; he looks at his wife "as one looks at a valuable piece of property which has suffered some damage." Four chapters later, when Robert invites her to go bathing again, the sea's "sonorous murmur reached her like a loving but imperative entreaty": the sea is "delicious," her companion tells her; "it will not hurt you." The voice of the sea invites the soul "to lose itself in mazes of inward contemplation. . . . The touch of the sea is sensuous, enfolding the body in its soft, close embrace." These words that appear first in Chapter 6 are repeated almost exactly in the final chapter, as are these also: "The voice of the sea is seductive; never ceasing, clamoring, murmuring, inviting the soul to wander for a spell in the abysses of solitude."

Echoes of the poetry of Whitman can be recognized in these recurrent murmurings of the sea, especially of his "Out of the Cradle Endlessly Rocking," in which the sea whispers the strong and "delicious" word *death*. Mrs. Chopin seems to have known Whitman's poetry well and to have had confidence that her readers did also, as is suggested in her quotation from Whitman's "Song of Myself" in her story "A Respectable Woman," where the quotation depends for its force on the reader's adding to the apparently innocent lines "Night of south winds—night of the large few stars! / Still nodding night—" the sensuous words which Whitman precedes and follows them: "Press close bare-bosom'd night . . ." and "mad naked summer night." Indeed the whole of *The Awakening* is pervaded with the spirit of Whitman's "Song of Myself." Edna Pontellier is awakened to her self, until with Whitman she might finally say, "I exist as I am, that is enough." As she who early in the novel shrinks almost prudishly from physical contact with other people is awakened to the joy of touch, a reader may be reminded of Whitman's "Is this then the touch? quivering me to new identity." And the ending of the novel is suggested in lines from Section 22 of "Song of Myself":

You sea! I resign myself to you also—I guess what you mean,
I behold from the beach your crooked inviting fingers,
I believe you refuse to go back without feeling of me,
We must have a turn together, I undress, I hurry out of sight
    of the land,
Cushion me soft, rock me in billowy drowse.

Not only does the sea sound an anticipatory refrain; incidents and characters early introduced in the novel often seem emblematic or teasingly suggestive of what will happen later.

Some may find it significant that this narrative of self-discovery begins with the voice of an impertinent parrot and with a mockingbird "whistling his notes out upon the breeze with maddening persistence," and that it ends drowsily with "the hum of bees, and the musky odor of pinks." Others may wonder why Edna sleeps so often and so soundly, or whether her appetite for food and her shrugging off of niceness in eating are related, or supposed to be related, to other appetites. The silent woman clothed in black who appears six times in the first fifteen chapters may seem an ominous portent, as may also the pair of anonymous young lovers who roam the seaside, their courtship interrupted by children at play, much as Edna's adventuring toward freedom is disturbed—but how much?—by her concern for children. "I would give my life for my children," she says at one time; "but I wouldn't give myself." The significance of the Spanish girl Mariequita, who appears just before Robert Lebrun flees to Mexico and who appears again just before the final scene of the novel, is worthy of contemplation, as are the implications intended in the carefree and self-indulgent character of Victor Lebrun.

Bird images will be found throughout the novel, sometimes presented with quiet irony, as when Edna, seeking more freedom than her husband's house affords, takes a house of her own and calls it her "pigeon-house," allowing a reader then to recall that the pigeon of the kind she thought of was a domesticated, often a captive bird. The bird with the broken wing which, "reeling, fluttering, circling," is the only witness to Edna's final encounter with the sea may remind a reader that Mademoiselle Reisz had warned Edna earlier that "a bird that would soar above the level plain of tradition and prejudice must have strong wings," and is prefigured also (the ending of the novel may be discovered to be prefigured) in the vision which Edna has in Chapter 9 "of a man standing beside a desolate rock on the seashore. He was naked. His attitude was one of hopeless resignation as he looked toward a distant bird winging his flight away from him."

Things like this do not seem accidental. Almost every incident or reference in *The Awakening* anticipates an incident or reference that follows it or will remind a reader of something that has happened before. Other characters appear only in their relation to Edna Pontellier. Only such elements of background are introduced as contribute to her awakening. The narrative focus remains on her, as "blindly following whatever impulse moved her," she stumbles on finally "as if her thoughts had gone ahead of her. She is timid at first, almost cold: no trace of passion . . . colored her affection for her husband"; she is not accustomed to outward and spoken expression of affection. But as she is aroused by love outside of marriage, and by passion outside of love, she seems finally, not so much an enlightened woman, as "a beautiful, sleek animal waking up in the sun," uncaged and vulnerable.

Everything fits—the imagery and the reasons, gradually revealed, of the awakening. Among Mrs. Chopin's American contemporaries only Henry James and perhaps Sarah Orne Jewett had produced fiction more artfully designed; there is a simpleness and a directness in *The Awakening* which has inevitably reminded readers of Flaubert's *Madame Bovary*, and an economy and mastery of incident and character which seem to forecast the lucid simplicity of Willa Cather's *Death Comes for the Archbishop*, so different in theme, but comparable in technique. Few words are wasted; nothing is incomplete: it is a book about Edna Pontellier, and about her only.

To keep focus sharply on Edna, Mrs. Chopin needed somewhat to blur the supporting characters, revealing just enough about them to enable a reader to recognize their function. Most of them are familiar fictional types, familiarly realized: the kindly family doctor; the husband with a proprietary attitude toward his wife, a vacillating concern for his children, who enjoys weekend card games, and cares greatly for appearances; the irresponsible insolence of Victor Lebrun, which contrasts with the almost storybook concept of gallantry held by his brother; the misanthropy of Mademoiselle Reisz; and the almost professional charm of Alcée Arobin. Conventional characters like Madame Ratignolle, "a mother woman," are described in conventional, romantic terms: "There are no words to describe her," says Mrs. Chopin, "save the old ones that have served so often to picture the bygone heroine of romance and the fair lady of our dreams." Her hair is "spun gold," and her eyes "like nothing but sapphires; two lips that pouted, that were so red that one could only think of cherries or some other delicious fruit in looking at them. . . . Never were hands more exquisite than hers, and it was a joy to look at them when she threaded her needle or adjusted her gold thimble to her middle finger as she sewed on the little night drawers or fashioned a bodice or a bib."

Madame Ratignolle is "a sensuous Madonna," happily pregnant, motherly wise, and mindful of the future: in summer she prepares garments for the winter to come. Edna, obsessively concerned with herself, is careless about the future. Her thoughts are of herself, her concerns are her vague desires. But of all the characters she alone is described with precision, not in clichés but as an individual whose "graceful severity of poise and movement" made her "different from the crowd." She is not another mother woman, like those who "idolized their children, worshipped their husbands, and esteemed it a holy privilege to efface themselves as individuals." Her eyes "were a yellowish brown, the color of her hair . . . . Her eyebrows were a shade darker . . . . They were thick and horizontal, emphasizing the depth of her eyes. . . . The lines of her body were long, clean and symmetrical; it was a body which occasionally fell into splendid poses; there was no suggestion of the trim stereotyped fashion plate about it."

Surrounded by other characters, most of whom are typical,

Edna Pontellier gradually emerges as an understandable, though perhaps not completely admirable, individual reality. Whether she is weak and willful, a woman wronged by the requirements of society, or a self-indulgent sensualist, finally and fundamentally romantic, who gets exactly what she deserves—these are not considerations that seem to have concerned Mrs. Chopin. *The Awakening* is not a problem novel. If it seems inevitably to invite questions, these are subsidiary to its purpose, which is to describe what might really happen to a person like Edna Pontellier, being what she was, living when she did, and where.

Mrs. Chopin has presented a compelling portrait of a trapped and finally desperate woman, a drama of self-discovery, of awakening and doom, a tragedy perhaps of self-deceit. No questions are required, no verdict is given. Here is Edna Pontellier, a woman. She is awakened to possibilities for self-expression which, because she is what she is or because circumstances are what they are or because society is what it is, cannot be realized. Her awakening, only vaguely intellectual, is disturbingly physical. But wronged or erring, she is a valiant woman, worthy of place beside other fictional heroines who have tested emancipation and failed—Nathaniel Hawthorne's Hester Prynne, Gustave Flaubert's Emma Bovary, or Henry James's Isabel Archer. Readers are likely to find something of themselves in her.

That may have been one reason why *The Awakening* was so roundly condemned when it appeared on April 22, 1899. It was "too strong drink for moral babes," said the St. Louis *Republic*, "and should be labeled poison." The *Nation* in New York praised its style, but wondered how either "literature or the criticism of life can be helped by the detailed history of the . . . love affairs of a wife and mother." The St. Louis *Post-Dispatch* found it able and intelligent, but "disturbing—even indelicate" in daring "to mention . . . something which, perhaps, does play a part in the life behind the mask." It has recently been translated in France, where it has been said to anticipate the writings of Simone de Beauvoir. "How strange and awful it seemed" to the awakened Edna Pontellier "to stand naked under the sky! how delicious!"

10

❧

Kate Chopin's Other Novel

INTEREST RECENTLY SHOWN in Kate Chopin's *The Awakening* of 1899 makes it seem profitable briefly to examine her other novel, *At Fault*, which nine years earlier anticipated some of the directions which Mrs. Chopin's talent would take. It appeared at the outset of her career, before her tales of Creole life had begun to receive wide attention: only two brief sketches preceded it (one in the St. Louis *Post-Dispatch*, the other in the *Musical Journal* of Philadelphia) and one short poem (in an iconoclastic Chicago publication called *America, a Journal for Americans*). Her biographer records that Mrs. Chopin began to write *At Fault* in July, 1889, that it was completed in the following April, and that in September, 1890, she paid the Nixon-Jones Printing Company of St. Louis an unspecified amount for printing one thousand copies, bound in paper covers. Bibliographical guides list only two surviving copies in institutional collections, one at Yale University, the other at the Library of Congress, where it was deposited on October 3, 1890.

Rare and unread, it deserves some attention, for what it says as well as for what it promises. Like *The Awakening*, it speaks of marital unhappiness and of dangers which lie in wait for people who do as they want to do without concern for other people. It is more cluttered than the later novel, with characters and with convolutions of plot; its thesis is more overtly but less expertly enforced; Dickens and the American local colorists seem more of an influence now than Flaubert or Madame de Staël. But Mrs. Chopin's ear for dialect is already developed. Her Creoles and Negroes and her Northern vulgarians are made to talk as they would talk: "Mine out fur that ba'el, . . . it's got molasses in"; "I reckon you're all plumb wore out"; he is a "feller without any more feeling than a stick"—and enough more to make a study of her colloquialisms worthy itself of an essay.

The setting of *At Fault* is a plantation in Natchitoches Parish of central Louisiana, modeled on the one which Mrs. Chopin's husband's father had purchased in 1854 from the estate of Robert McAlpin, supposedly the original of Simon Legree in Harriet Beecher Stowe's *Uncle Tom's Cabin*. Her husband's younger brother lived on the plantation when in 1880, Oscar Chopin having failed as a commission merchant in New Orleans, he and she and their five young sons moved to nearby Cloutierville. There she lived until her husband's death in 1882, after which, in her early thirties, she returned with her children (now six) to St. Louis, where she had been born. The action of *At Fault* begins in that year, when the Texas and Pacific Railroad thrust its way through the plantation, driving resident Chopins some miles westward to a new home in the comparative quiet of Derry, Louisiana.

That is one of the things that *At Fault* is about, how the railroad came and made available forests of uncut timber, bringing noise and disruption to the placid plantation land, and how "this intrusive industry" fired "the souls of indolent fathers with greedy ambition for gain, at the sore expense of revolting youth." But little is made of this theme though the owner of the plantation did feel herself to be "one upon whom partly rested the fault"; nor is much made of the crueler faults of its former owner, here named Robert McFarlane ("They say he's the person that Mrs. W'at's her name wrote about in Uncle Tom's Cabin," and "they's folks round yere says he walks about o'nights; can't res' in his grave for the niggers he's killed") except to provide an ominous, somber obbligato to the ill-starred courtship of a young couple who visit his grave.

The fault which dominates and gives title to the novel is less obvious and less confidently designated: it concerns love and morality and obstacles which can be thought to stand in the way of happiness in marriage between a person from a place like St. Louis and a person from a place like Louisiana. The fault may be interpreted as that of an agrarian, land-preserving South, lulled by traditions of ease and morality and religion, as it fails to respond to the industrial, land-destroying North, whose morality is modern and utilitarian. Or it may be the other way around. Mrs. Chopin is not aggressively, nor even, I think, inadvertently autobiographical, and is pleasantly not explicit in finding fault. Nor need she be.

Instead she tells a story about young and impulsive loves which do not work out well and love which is mature and, presumably, lasting. At its center is Thérèse Lafirme, a widow in her early thirties, who lived in Place-du-Bois, a plantation of four thousand acres which stretched along the banks of the Cane River. When the railroad had come, with its clamor and efficiency, driving her back from the river to a new home, she had in building it resisted "temptations offered by modern architectural innovations," preferring "the simplicity of large rooms and broad verandas: a style that had withstood the test of easy-going and comfort-loving generations." A "perfect lawn . . . encircled the house for an acre"; Negro quarters "were scattered at wide intervals over the land, breaking with picturesque irregularity into the systematic division of field to field" and gleaming in their springtime "coat of whitewash against the tender green of sprouting corn."

Mrs. Lafirme shares placid Creole characteristics with Madame Ratignolle in *The Awakening*, who is described as "the embodiment of every womanly grace and charm. . . . the bygone heroine of romance and the fair lady of our dreams." She managed her acres well, and without loss of femininity or languid poise. Like Madame Ratignolle's, the "roundness of her figure" suggests "a future of excessive fullness if not judiciously guarded; and she was fair, with a warm whiteness that a passing thought could deepen into color. The waving blond hair, gathered into an abundant coil on the top of her head, grew away with a pretty sweep from the temples, the low forehead and the nape of the white neck that showed above the frill of soft lace. Her eyes were blue, as certain gems are [Madame Ratignolle had "blue eyes that were like nothing but sapphires"]; that deep blue that lights and glows, and tells things of the soul." She takes pride in her land, and enjoys walking "the length of the wide verandas, armed with her field-glass, and to view her surrounding possessions with comfortable satisfaction"; her eyes move "from cabin to cabin; from patch to patch; up to the pine-capped hills," then down to the new railroad station which now "squatted a brown and ugly intruder into her broad domain."

But industry intrudes also, in the person of David Hosmer, "a tall individual of perhaps forty, thin and sallow," a man of little seeming charm, who seldom smiles. His hair is streaked with gray, and his face is "marked with premature lines, left there by care, no doubt, and by a too close attention to what men are pleased to call the main chances of life." He has come from St. Louis, to offer money for the privilege of cutting timber from Thérèse's land for a given number of years. He would erect a sawmill in her woods, close beside the bayou. He is brusque and grasping, but his gruff tenacity attracts the handsome Creole widow: a color comes to her cheek, "like the blush in a shell," as they discuss the turning of her forest lands to cash. And then she goes alone "to her beloved woods, and at the hush of mid-day, bade a tearful farewell to silence."

The first chapter is pastoral and prelude, an introduction to an unlikely pair of lovers. With Chapter 2, the story strides smartly forward: Hosmer is settled into work at the sawmill— "Orders come in from North and West more rapidly than they can be filled"; he works quite too hard, thinks Thérèse, and is in danger of allowing his "fondness for money-getting" to deprive her and others of the "charm which any man's society loses, when pursuing one object in life, he proves insensible to any other." Her nephew, Grégoire Santien (a type and a person whom Mrs. Chopin would sketch again in her short stories [1]), lives on the plantation also (he had been "goin' to the devil" in Texas when his Aunt Thérèse had sent for him); he also works at the mill, but not very hard: he prefers to spend his time with Hosmer's younger sister Melicent, who at twenty-four had been five times betrothed, who is a "new woman," emancipated and opinionated but rootless, and who leads poor Grégoire mercilessly on, attracted by his casual resourcefulness, the quiet strength of his hands as he guides his pirogue through the bayous, and their quickness as, with no break in bantering talk, he draws his pistol to fire from his seat in the little boat a single, effective shot at a menacing alligator:

His hands were not so refinedly white as those of certain office bred young men of her acquaintance, yet they were not coarsened by undue toil: it being somewhat of an axiom with him to do nothing that an available "nigger" might not do for him.

Close-fitting high-heeled boots of fine quality encased his feet, in whose shapeliness he felt a pardonable pride. . . . A peculiar grace in the dance and a talent for bold repartee were further characteristics. . . . His features were handsome, of sharp and refined cast; and his eyes black and brilliant as eyes of an alert animal are. Melicent could not reconcile his voice to her liking;

[1] Grégoire's older brother, Placide, is the title character in "A No Account Creole," his oldest brother, Hector, is a central character in "In and Out of Old Natchitoches," and Grégoire is gallantly the hero of "In Sabine," the first three stories in Mrs. Chopin's Bayou Folk (New York, 1894).

it was too softly low and feminine, and carried a note of pleading
or pathos, unless he argued with his horse, his dog, or a "nigger,"
at which times, though not unduly raised, it acquired a biting
quality that served the purpose of relieving him from further form
of insistence.

Mrs. Chopin's portraits of and allusions to the Negro, here
or elsewhere, will not endear her to all modern readers; she
sketches most of them briefly, often with what in 1890 must
have seemed realistic exactness. Something of her attitude is
suggested when a visitor from the North attempts to engage
one of Thérèse's Creole neighbors in a discussion of the Negro
problem, "rather bewildering that good lady, who could not
bring herself to view the Negro as an interesting or suitable
theme to be introduced into polite conversation." Most of
the house servants at Place-du-Bois are indolent but loyal:
the scene in which they refuse to work for Melicent, who as a
Yankee does not understand them, seems true to character,
and the Negro boy, Sampson, who lights the morning fire and
performs surreptitious errands for a fee, is a believable, though
familiar, young scamp. The old retainer who navigates a
flatboat across the river is self-important and obdurate, at
the same time sassy and subservient. Better drawn is Joçint,
half-Indian, who is ominously sullen, a "bad son" to his
Negro father and a source of concern to Thérèse: his "straight
black hair hung in a heavy mop over his low retreating forehead, almost meeting the ill-defined line of eyebrow that
straggled above small dusky black eyes." Wrenched from his
natural habitat in field and forest, he submitted unwillingly
to monotonous labor at the sawmill, where he was a troublesome, careless worker, a danger to life and to profits: "his
heart was in the pine woods, . . . knowing that his little
Creole pony was roaming the woods in vicious idleness and
his rifle gathering an unsightly rust on the cabin wall at
home."

Characters introduced, the plot moves steadily forward

through the twelve chapters of Part I, Mrs. Chopin in poised control of scene and action. Hosmer increasingly depends on the strong, warm sympathy of Thérèse. If she were to leave Place-du-Bois, "Oh," he says, "it would take the soul out of my life." But no sooner has he told her of his love than his meddlesome sister tells her also that her brother has had a wife, whom he had divorced two years before. Confronted by Thérèse, Hosmer admits that he had married ten years ago, that a year later a son had been born to his wife but had died at the age of three, and that then the marriage had fallen apart: "I saw little of my wife, being often away from home." He had disapproved of her friends, who seemed shallow and vulgar; work had engrossed him; his wife, left too much alone, had taken a drink; encouraged by Melicent, he had for that reason divorced her.

To a person of Thérèse's Catholic background, divorce is repugnant. She explains to Hosmer that he had been at fault: "You married a woman of weak character. You furnished her with every means to increase that weakness, and shut her absolutely from your life and yourself from hers. You left her there as practically without a moral support, as you have certainly done now in deserting her." Hosmer counters in words which briefly underline the theme of self-fulfillment which threads uncertainly through the novel: "Do you think a man owes nothing to himself?" And Thérèse: "A man owes it to his manhood to face the consequences of his own actions." And he: "What would you have me do?" To which, "eagerly approaching him," she replies: "I would have you do what is right." And he: "Whatever I do must be because you want it; because I love you. . . . To do a thing out of love for you would be the only comfort and strength left me." "Don't say that," she entreats. "Love isn't everything in life; there is something higher."

Obedient to her request, Hosmer goes unhappily to St. Louis, to find and remarry his former wife. He has some

quarrel about what he is doing with an intrusive, cynical
friend named Homeyer, whom Thérèse, and the reader also,
becomes convinced does not really exist but is an alter ego
with whom Hosmer converses in moments of crisis. Homeyer
"railed of course as usual, at the submission of human destiny
to the exacting and ignorant rule of what he termed the
moral conventionalities." He scoffs at the notion that Hosmer's former wife could be redeemed, "pooh-poohed the notion as untenable with certain views which he called the rights
of existence: the existence of wrongs—sorrows—diseases—
death—let them all go to make up the conglomerate whole—
and let the individual man hold to his individuality." But
there was "an element of the bull-dog in Hosmer. Having
made up his mind he indulged in no doubts. . . . Love was
his god now, and Thérèse was Love's prophet."

In St. Louis he found his former wife, Fanny, still pretty,
though her once "merry blue eyes" are now "faded and sunken
into deep, dark round sockets," a "net-work of little lines all
traced about the mouth and eyes"; her "once rounded cheeks
. . . now hollow and evidently pale and sallow, beneath a
layer of rouge which had been laid on with unsparing hand."
Hosmer also becomes acquanted again with Fanny's friends,
characters who are well drawn but, so far as movement of plot
is concerned, are diversionary. Belle Worthington is large,
soft, and vulgar: "her broad and expressionless face and meaningless blue eyes were set to a good-natured readiness for
laughter, which would be wholesome if not musical." Her husband, Lorenzo, is an unobtrusive, bookish custom-house clerk,
secretly a freethinker who reads Ruskin, Schopenhauer, and
Emerson, and who thinks of "all women as being of peculiar
and unsuitable conformation to the various conditions of life
in which they . . . [are] placed; with strong moral proclivi-
ties, for the most part subservient to a weak and inadequate
mentality." Their twelve-year-old daughter, devotedly a student at the Sacred Heart Convent (which Mrs. Chopin had

attended as a girl), is a sanctimonious prig. Another friend, Lou Dawson, is a fast woman who when her traveling salesman husband, Jack, is away, accepts favors from other men. Mrs. Chopin must have enjoyed presenting these not unfamiliar characters, and a reader may enjoy them briefly, however they clutter the plot.

After Hosmer and Fanny are remarried, in the library of their Unitarian clergyman, the bridegroom ponders at some length the moral problem which now confronts him:

> How hard to him was this unaccustomed task of dealing with moral difficulties, which all through his life before, however lightly they had come, he had shirked and avoided! He realized now, that there was to be no more of that. If he did not wish his life to end in disgraceful shipwreck, he must take command and direction of it upon himself.
>
> He had felt himself capable of stolid endurance since love had declared itself his guide and helper. But now—only to-day— something besides had crept into his heart. Not something to be endured, but a thing to be strangled and put away. It was the demon of hate; so new, so awful, so loathsome, he doubted that he could look it in the face and live.
>
> Here was the problem of his new existence.
>
> The woman who had formerly made his life colorless and empty he had quietly turned his back upon, carrying with him a pity that was not untender. But the woman who had unwittingly robbed him of all possibility for earthly happiness—he hated her. The woman of whom he must be careful, to whom he must be tender, and loyal and generous. And to give no sign or word but of kindness: to do no action that was not considerate, was the task which destiny had thrust upon his honor.

Part I ends with Hosmer again musing on the kind of morality which has led him to his present unhappy situation: "Homeyer would have me think that all religions are but mythical creations invented to satisfy a species of sentimentality—a morbid craving in man for the unknown and undemonstrable."

Part II moves through fifteen chapters resourcefully but

with lessening control toward climax. Fanny, brought now to Place-du-Bois, is lonesome for the city and her city friends; but she responds finally to the kindness of Thérèse and the doggedly simulated attentions of Hosmer: "if David'd always been like he is now, I don't know but things'd been different. . . . He's a true, honest man." Meanwhile Melicent, who had been shocked at her brother's remarriage, continues her flirtations with Grégoire, her sophistication only a light covering for a kind of storybook sentimentality: "Our love," she tells the young Creole, "must be something like a sacred memory —a sweet recollection to help us through life when we are apart."

But then Thérèse begins to wonder whether she had not been at fault in her requirement that Hosmer remarry; she finds herself becoming jealous now of the love for him which she sees reflected in the reclaimed Fanny's face; she imagines what greater "capabilities lay within her of arousing the man to new interests in life"; she "pictured the dawn of unsuspected happiness coming to him: broadening; illuminating; growing in him to answer to her own big-heartedness." To calm herself, she rides off alone and crosses the river to visit her old nurse, who lives alone in a cottage perilously close to the river waters that every year eat farther and farther into the bank on which the cottage stands. Mrs. Chopin must have expected readers to recall George Washington Cable's "Belles Demoiselles Plantation," and what happened there when the river rose.

On the next afternoon, which preceded All Saints' Eve, when spirits are abroad, the people at Place-du-Bois set out on an excursion on horseback. Hosmer and Fanny are outdistanced by the rest; unused to riding, she is saddle-sore and weary, and can go no farther; so Hosmer leaves her at the cabin of Joçint's Negro father, while he returns to the plantation for a buggy. Her Negro host, seeing her fatigue, offers Fanny a drink of whiskey; she takes one, then another, and finally steals the bottle. At just the time when she thus slips, Hosmer slips also. Meeting Thérèse, with whom he had not been alone since his return from St. Louis, he again avows his love, explaining of his remarriage: "I didn't do it because I thought it was right, but because you thought it was right." He wonders that she, of all people, "shouldn't have a suspicion of the torture of it, the loathsomeness of it." He rebukes her because of the "sweet complacency with which women accept situations, or inflict situations that it takes the utmost of a man's strength to endure"—that fault was "one of the things which drive a man mad."

That evening—Fanny drunk, Hosmer pacing the veranda at Place-du-Bois, a lovelorn Grégoire riding unhappily through the spirit-haunted woodland—Joçint creeps stealthily toward the mill and sets it afire. Grégoire, his pistol always in readiness, shoots the arsonist, an act for which Melicent does not forgive him. She leaves the plantation without allowing him a word of farewell, as a result of which Grégoire goes on a rampage, drinking and whooping and shooting through one town after another, until he is also shot and killed in a bar brawl in Texas. These chapters are resourcefully done, with atmosphere, suspense, and some restraint: Joçint's approach in darkness toward the mill is described in ominous, dark phrases; Grégoire's destructive visit to a local saloon is re-counted through the words of a Negro servant who had been reluctantly a witness; Grégoire's death is reported by a laconic Texan who happens to be passing through.

Action is then slowed, as the Worthington family breaks a journey from St. Louis to the Mardi Gras in New Orleans a visit at Place-du-Bois. Urbane Nell teaches the country folk to play euchre; her priggish daughter dicusses the rightness of absolute faith with the daughter of a visiting neighbor; her bookish husband roams Thérèse's fine library—Balzac, Scott, Racine, Molière, Bulwer—engrossed finally by a *Lives of the Saints* which recounts the sad fate of Saint Monica, whose life was so closely guarded that in recompense she took to drink. Mrs. Chopin must have meant these visitors and this brief visit to point up in miniature some of the themes woven through the novel: the contrast between Northern (and vulgar) sophistication with the more natural and wholesome Creole customs, the lack of true rapport between husband and wife (Belle and Lorenzo) when their union is not bound by mutual understanding, and the questionable place of conventional religious mores, even in a child; but these analogues do not come clear, however effective the interlude of comparative quiet is in preparing for the rush of events which concludes the action.

The interlude is extended through a long passage of moralizing, in which Mrs. Chopin for almost the first time intrudes herself into the narrative, with thoughts which must be suspected again to underscore a theme:

> Who of us has not known the presence of Misery? . . . It may be that we see but a promise of him as we look into the prophetic faces of children; into the eyes of those we love, and the awfulness of life's possibilities presses into our souls. Do we fly him? hearing him gain upon us panting close at our heels, till we turn from the desperation of uncertainty to grapple with him? Fleeing, we may elude him. But what if he creeps into the sanctuary of our lives, with his subtle omnipresence, that we do not see in all its horror till we are disarmed; thrusting the burden of his companionship to the end! However we turn he is there. However we shrink he is there. However we come or go, or sleep or wake he is before us. Till the keen sense grows dull with apathy at looking on him, and he becomes like the familiar presence of sin. . . .
>
> My friend, your trouble I know weighs. That you should be driven by earthy needs to drag the pinioned spirit of your days through rut and mire. But think of the millions who are doing the like. . . . What are they to me. My hurt is greater than all, because it is my own.

By this time Fanny is hopelessly in the power of drink. She bribes the Negro boy who makes her morning fire to bring her a daily bottle. When one day he fails to appear and she is driven to desperation by discovery that honest David is really in love with Thérèse, she crosses the river to find her bottle, and takes refuge with it in the periously perched house of Thérèse's old nurse. Hosmer seeks her out, and pleads with her to return to Place-du-Bois; when she refuses, he leaves, hoping that she will follow. As he starts across the turbulent river, he sees the cottage swept into the waters, and she with it. He tries to save her as she clings in drunken bewilderment to the doorway, and he almost does, but is hit over the head by a floating beam and loses consciousness. The next thing he knows he is lying on the ferry which will take him back to Place-du-Bois, his wife dead beside him, and Thérèse bending above to give him comfort.

A year later, after Thérèse has spent months in Paris and Hosmer has recuperated with his sister at the seashore, the two lovers, middle-aged indeed in the lexicon of romance, marry—he to continue to manage the intrusive sawmill, she to carry on old traditions in working the plantation, reconciled each to life as it must be: "the truth in all its entirety isn't given for man to know—such knowledge would be beyond human endurance. But we do make a step toward it," says Hosmer, "when we learn that there is rottenness and evil in the world, masquerading as right and morality." The action sputters to a close as a letter from Melicent in St. Louis discloses that the traveling salesman Jack Dalton (who has not been heard of for more than a hundred pages) has shot and killed one of the suitors of his errant wife.

True love is sanctuary from the meanness of the world—this certainly is suggested; but Mrs. Chopin was not finally able to turn her tune, to make whatever point she had to make come effectively through. Manifestly something or someone was at fault. Perhaps it was everyone, for one distinguishing mark of this first attempt at long fiction is that no one is free from fault, and that the world is indeed spoiled with "rut and mire" for every "pinioned spirit" who submits to "earthy needs." Something lurks behind these words which Mrs. Chopin in 1890 could not or dared not express. Sexual overtones are sensed rather than heard.

For Mrs. Chopin evidently had something which she wanted to say about self-fulfillment, its possibilities and its cost, which she would say better and more simply, with deeper psychological insight, in *The Awakening*. Melicent's imperious selfishness, her desire to be free from restraint of convention, and her dabbling in "culture" may be recognized as foreshadowings of the more intense fumblings toward freedom of Edna Pontellier in the later novel, and Hosmer in some sense can be supposed to anticipate Edna's businessman husband, who leaves his wife too much alone, but neither is fully nor consistently realized—in fact, no character in *At Fault* (except perhaps Grégoire) is presented convincingly in depth. Throughout much of the action focus is unsteady, plot is choked with incident, contrivance usurps the place of motivation, and themes so jostle one another than none is ultimately articulated.

But for all its faults of occasional melodrama or shrillness, *At Fault* need not be dismissed as simply another bad novel. There is too much good in it, for an artist can be seen at work, learning her trade, to be sure, and often fumbling, but with a touch which is sometimes sure. She was to do greatly better, in a few short stories and in her second novel, but this other novel also deserves something more than casual remembrance.

By the time she had come to the writing of *The Awakening*, Mrs. Chopin had utilized many of the insights into local character which brighten at the same time that they confuse the action of *At Fault*. Her short tales, collected in *Bayou Folk* (1894) and *A Night in Acadie* (1897) played on just such lovable eccentricities as those exhibited by Grégoire in the early novel, and by the Negroes (though she may never have sketched them so well again), and in plantation life such as that over which Thérèse presided. These tales depend, as *At Fault* often depends, upon background which is lush and spectacular, within which characters who are somewhat unusual move and have adventures. They are sketched in, most of these characters, without excessive shading. A reader watches them and chuckles or feels sad because of what they do, but he seldom discovers why they do it. They are more than cardboard figures, painted and costumed, for the sketching is effective and usually individualized. They are made to speak well, though strangely sometimes, for that is what they are supposed to do—to attract as curiosities who, however different, have feelings and misadventures much like other people. But they remain sketches, effective because they reveal a character in an attractive pose. But why he is in that pose or what he will do as a result of having been in it is not often revealed. Motivation, when present, seems superimposed rather than an inevitable precursor of action.

Mrs. Chopin's superb mimic skill stood in her way in these early writings. She sketched well, and her sketches revealed attitudes which were fresh and sometimes by implication in advance of her time. Grégoire in *At Fault* is three times described as an animal, lithe and sinuous and attractive, to be sure, but an animal nonetheless, ruled by instinct, at the mercy of emotion. Hosmer is a freethinker (at least when his alter ego, Homeyer, speaks) and Lorenzo Worthington is a freethinker also, and Melicent is an emancipated "new woman"; but these things are revealed by statement or by action which often seems its own excuse for being, or by authorial asides which explain better than they convince. No character really develops—progresses or retrogresses. Hosmer, after weathering his ordeal of duty, is much the same stylized money-grubber that he was at the beginning. His sister, for all her façade of modernity, is frightened and attracted to the end by the animality of Grégoire: when he is dead, she imagines that she loves him more. Thérèse's capacity for sensuous satisfaction is never revealed as fulfilled.

Yet the elements are all there: the freshness of perception, the acknowledgment that flesh demands its share from living, the eye for scene, the ear for dialect. What is lacking is a sense of timing, of economy, of focus. Contrivance is imperfectly masked. Superfluous characters come and go. Reasons for resolution are harshly improvised—arson, murder, drunkenness, drowning. The richness of Mrs. Chopin's mimic imagination is dissipated through scenes which are often more pictorial than necessary. But the principal fault, and one so magnificently overcome in the portrayal of Edna Pontellier in *The Awakening*, is that of not being able effectively to present any convincing reason why any character acts as he does. In her second novel, Mrs. Chopin displays the gradual awakening of a woman to the gratification and the peril of extramarital sexual satisfaction. Edna Pontellier's fumbling toward freedom elicits sympathy, disapproval perhaps, but understanding certainly. Given what she is and where she is and how she reacts, she could not have done otherwise. In *The Awakening* a master handles her tools with expert skill in analysis of a single character—nothing is wasted, the focus remains sharp; in *At Fault* she is experimenting, producing rough first designs of what later would be fashioned to art.

11

H. L. Mencken and the Reluctant Human Race

TIME HAS NOT been kind to H. L. Mencken. The terror of the twenties has become something of a period piece, embarrassingly a reminder of rejected taste, like an old sofa on which we wonder how we could ever have been comfortable. Its curious curls and furbelows are outrageously disproportioned. Even the lines which pleased us once as svelte and debonair are bumpy now with prejudice and wrongheadedness. The springs are sagging and the stuffing shows, so that we put it aside, no longer useful except as lumber stored for keepsake.

Yet hardly more than a quarter of a century ago and during the two decades of his ascendancy as editor of the *Smart Set* and then the *American Mercury*, Mencken provided a rallying point for the literature of protest in the United States. Every young man read him as surrogate for his own father, who was not so wise, and thrilled to what the Sage of Baltimore had to say of venality in the United States. With the sybaritic George Jean Nathan at his right hand and, finally, with Alfred A. Knopf substantially at his left, he dedicated himself, he said, to "the most noble and sublime task possible to mere human beings: the overthrow of superstition and unreasoning faith."

Like Bernard Shaw, whom he admired, he pampered the masochism of young America by beating it about the head until the ringing in its ears was interpreted as cerebration. So wanton were his strokes and so responsive his victims that the New York *Times* was soon to describe him as "the most powerful private citizen" in the United States. "If I had the power," said Sinclair Lewis, "I'd make Henry Mencken the Pope of America. He spreads the message of sophistication that we need so badly."

Sophistication was then a favorite word, and Mencken was fond of recalling evidences of it in his own family history. His forebears in Germany had included learned and iconoclastic professors at the University of Leipzig and sophisticated professional men, even one who had employed Johann Sebastian Bach as choirmaster. But Mencken's grandfather, who left the homeland in the turbulent 1840's, and then his father had become prosperous in the tobacco business in Baltimore, their sophistication diluted by baseball and beer. And young Henry was a bookworm who returned, he thought, to an older and better tradition, which would have none of trade. His appetite for books was large, and he wrote poetry. When he later recalled the days of his youth in autobiographical volumes, he called them *Happy Days, Newspaper Days,* and then *Heathen Days.* For books were finally to be no more satisfying than cigar-making. In his late teens he abandoned them, he said, "in favour of life itself." He became, that is, a newspaperman, then an editor, and finally an editorial commentator, and these he remained the rest of his days.

His comment was brisk, witty, and devastating. He was bumptious and unfair, and he stung even pious men to intemperate reply. In the verbal warfare which resulted Mencken was castigated as a wild-eyed, wide-mouthed jackass, a maggot, a ghoul, a bilious buffoon, a British toady, a super-Boche of German *Kultur*. But he gave as good as he received, and his barbs stuck. He was shockingly improper and vulgar, raucous and unrepentant, and the tempo of intellectual life in America sccmed quickened by his verbal pyrotechnics. No idol was safe, neither religion nor manners, and particularly not the idols of pretension.

During the years just before and just after the First World War the United States needed someone like H. L. Mencken to sting it from complacency, just as it needed Ezra Pound, Theodore Dreiser, and others among its rebels. "America," Robinson Jeffers was to write,

> settles in the mold of its vulgarity,
> heavily thickening to empire,
>
> And protest, only a bubble in the molten mass,
> pops and sighs out, and the mass hardens.

Mencken's protest against America's perverse wrongheadedness, his championship of intellectual unrest, if even for its own sake, was something more than a bubble. His bellicose and pretentious extravagance was peculiarly American, and met an American need.

For the United States was settling in the mold of vulgarity during the early decades of the twentieth century. She had grown too fast and had not caught up with herself. The resources of the continent had been explored and exploited. The robber barons of the Gilded Age fattened on oil and coal and steel and corruption. Railroads spread their octopus arms throughout the land. Titles and castles and works of art were imported to reinforce the pretensions of the *nouveau riche*. Literature had become platitude. And hand in hand with the vulgarity of display went the not lesser vulgarity of reform, of provincial morality which found release in censorship, the prohibition of alcoholic beverages, and the eccentric notion that each man was in fact his brother's keeper.

Things of this kind inevitably breed revolt, and men like Mencken inevitably arise to lead the charge. What it is difficult for those of us who grew toward maturity under his spell to remember is that it was not really the bellicose Mr. Mencken who pulled the United States from the quagmire of self-satisfaction in which it then wallowed. His emergence as an intellectual force coincided almost exactly with the appearance during the second decade of the century of poetry by Pound and Eliot, Robert Frost, Carl Sandburg, Vachel Lindsay, and Wallace Stevens, and during the third decade of the century with the resurgence in fiction which brought forth Scott Fitzgerald, Ernest Hemingway, John Dos Passos, Thomas Wolfe, and finally William Faulkner. It was people like these who created the real image, the abiding criticism, of contemporary America. Mencken was a cheerleader, an energetic man who bounds boisterously up and down on the sidelines, shouting encouragement, and inciting an almost mindless mob of spectators to roars of properly placed approval.

He was of an older generation than most of these others. Unable or too self-conscious seriously to create, he encouraged; criticism, he said, is the beating of a big drum, and that he did, and loudly. "What ails the beautiful letters of the Republic," said Mencken, "is what ails the general culture of the Republic—the lack of a body of sophistictated and civilised public opinion, independent of plutocratic control and superior to the infantile philosophies of the mob—a body of opinion showing the eager curiosity, the educated scepticism and hospitality of ideas of a true aristocracy." This was good and right, we thought, and better said than when Henry James or Fenimore Cooper or Brockden Brown had said it many years before. We responded to it without recognizing that it brought us little farther than we had been. And Mencken, to whom we looked for guidance, stopped right there.

For behind his mask of pert ingenuousness, Mencken, bred

in an age of pretension, was himself a pretentious man, proud in display of his mind or person. His weapon was the cudgel, and he practiced its devastating, strong strokes before the mirror of contemporary approval. Superficially educated and writing faster than he learned, he was a man of few basic ideas, and even those who admired him most admit that many of them were absurd, others cheap or factitiously false. His was a simple Manichean universe of light and darkness, and the torch which he held in his pudgy hand was the light of the world. Like the Puritans whom he affected to despise, he was upheld by assurance of grace, and weighted with the burden of shaping an unregenerate people to his pattern.

His most effective writing has been described as a single, continuing harangue directed against things of which most of his countrymen were most proud: the efficacy of education, the sanctity of the home, the purity of marriage, love, religion, and the United States Supreme Court, children and obnoxious women without the "decency to keep quiet when their menfolk talk," and clergymen, because, he said, "the man of the cloth is *ipso facto* a fraud and to be watched especially when there are young girls or young boys around." His heavy club swept through a wide circle: "From the Boy Scouts, and from home cooking, from Odd Fellows' funerals, from Socialists and Christians—Good Lord, deliver us!" The harangue was smart and cheap, vulgar and invigorating. We were too young in rebellion to remember that the same things had been better said before.

"Blow the froth off Mencken," it has been suggested, "and you get Shaw; skim the scum off Shaw and you get Nietzsche; drain the lees and settlings of Nietzsche's melancholy brain and you get Schopenhauer." As a journalist and free-lance writer of fiction at the turn of the century, Mencken had been attracted to the Irish iconoclast, on whom in 1905 he wrote what is said to be the first critical volume. From Shaw he was inevitably led to Nietzsche. "After that," he said, "I was a critic of ideas, and I have remained so ever since." But what kind of a critic? And of what ideas?

His book *The Philosophy of Friedrich Nietzsche* in 1908 sketched the ground plan on which most of Mencken's subsequent notions were to be erected. The world was divided, we were there told, into two kinds of people, those who were congenitally superior and those who were congenitally inferior—those who were supermen and those who were slaves, those who were elect and those who were unregenerate. There they were, and there they remained. Mass education was a waste of money because the inferior could not be taught and the superior needed no teaching beyond what their superior, and inevitably wealthy, parents could provide. Public charity was to be avoided because the congenitally inferior mass was not worth saving. They were mongrel and mediocre people, incapable of spiritual aspiration. Religion was a ruse by which the weak attempted to reduce the strong to their level. Politics was a game for charlatans, and democracy was the worst possible form of government, the tool of "poltroons and mob masters": "All government, in its essence," he said, "is a conspiracy against the superior man; its one permanent object is to oppress and cripple him."

The climate of political opinion of another day once tempted commentators to bow towards Mencken as one who was almost alone among his generation in resisting lip service to the Marxist way, for socialism was to him simply democracy advanced from lunacy to madness. They spoke of his "somewhat battered optimisms," as if he were a piquant and perverse Carl Sandburg whose secret insistence was on "The People, Yes." Whatever his private sentiment, his public image of America was of "a horde of peasants incredibly enriched, and with almost infinite power thrust into their hands." It was a mindless mob, motivated by self-admiration and controlled by fear. It was on these that superior men could play.

Ideas like Mencken's have become distressingly familiar. They disturb us because they remind us of times, even of temporary commitments, which we are uncomfortable in remembering. We are continuingly disturbed because people like the late senator Joseph McCarthy have championed ideas not greatly unsimilar. Mencken's espousal of them explains why he was called the Mussolini of American letters, why during both world wars he was avoided as pro-German because, at the same time that he ridiculed the goose step or the Nazi salute, he spoke quizzically of the Kaiser or in sympathy with Hitler's program for European conquest, and why, finally, he was embarrassed to meet Ezra Pound in St. Elizabeth's Hospital in Washington, where the poet was incarcerated because he had spoken openly of matters about which Mencken during the 1940's was studiously silent.

Something of a similar embarrassment confuses us who admired him in the 1920's and who find the aftertaste of Mencken unpleasant today. We remind ourselves that he was a poseur, that his tongue was more blunt than his mind, that his heart, we say, was in the right place. We recall that his genius was for hyperbole, that his method was that of shock, that he was a gadfly who stung us toward thinking. He ridiculed our fathers' gods, he pointed derisively at our own inherited deficiencies, and in his often simulated and pretentious wrath seemed genuinely funny in the tradition he had learned from Mark Twain and the exaggerations of frontier humor. And we laughed.

But the fun was of the surface, and the surface was kaleidoscope. He posed as an irascible and ribald Teutonic god. The world of ideas, we have been told, was his bowling alley, and he toppled the props of our innocence with his chattering verbiage. His seemed so refreshing, so necessary a voice. The targets of his rage were progressives, prim novelists who made the desert of American fiction at once so populated and so dreary, vice crusaders, patriots, osteopaths, Methodists and

Baptists and Christian Scientists (and, not always for the same reasons, Jews), the Anti-Saloon League, and American women "who were full of Peruna and as fecund as the shad." He derided Woodrow Wilson's League of Nations and Franklin Roosevelt's New Deal. He considered the Library of Congress under the direction of Archibald MacLeish a Communist propaganda agency. Social reform of any kind was repulsive to him, or any of "the bilge of idealism" which runs in American veins: "A good politician," he said, "is quite as unthinkable as an honest burglar." H. G. Wells should have stuck to fiction rather than attempt to remake the world. Even Shaw, once admired, was finally dismissed as the "Ulster Polonius," a windbag blown large with platitudes: "it was his life work to announce the obvious in terms of the scandalous."

The temptation is to dismiss Mencken with the same glib aphorism. But Mencken is not easily dismissed, and we hold tentatively to our admiration for him, not because of his view of the world or his estimate of its literature, but for two things besides: his championship of the right of any author to freedom of honest expression and his vitalizing effect, as writer and as lexicographer, on the American language.

His part in the great American battle of the books, when he defended Dreiser, Sinclair Lewis, Sherwood Anderson, and others who would write realistically of the world as they saw it, places us with only few reservations greatly in his debt. He was on the right side, whatever his reasons, and his impudent diatribes against genteel critics, some of them ultimately more right but less vigorous than he, undoubtedly did smooth the way for better novelists, like Hemingway and Faulkner. But even in this he was a man of his time, effectively expressing convictions which many of his less articulate or strategically less well placed contemporaries held as strongly. It is difficult from this distance to assess the situation clearly, but it seems reasonable to suppose that we should have proceeded quite as far without him. One is even tempted by the notion that his bluntness may have done us harm, for it forced us to assumptions about the relation of realism to literature which quieter thinking has tempted us to put aside.

In our present perhaps equally perverse but more analytical mood, we suspect that Mencken was in no genuine sense a critic of literature at all. He was a moralist, a sociologist with a blistering vocabulary. The function of criticism, he said, was to lunge about right and left in vigorous strokes which knock the reigning idols off their perches. As editor, his measure for acceptance was often the inability of an author to find publication elsewhere. He never really admired or understood James Joyce, but he printed him when few else would: it was a symbol of his protest. Dreiser was "flaccid, elephantine, doltish, coarse, dismal, flatulent," but Dreiser was worth championing because, like Sinclair Lewis and Ben Hecht, he exposed the scandalous shortcomings of the "boobs, dupes, and lackies" of America. People like James Branch Cabell and Joseph Hergesheimer were excellent because they wrote with "the artless and superabundant energy of little children" in producing "a faithful reflection of national life . . . more faithful in its defects . . . than in its merits." He liked the early Willa Cather for the same reasons, but he virtually ignored Henry James, Edith Wharton, Ellen Glasgow, Stephen Crane, and (strangely) Frank Norris. He responded with little enthusiasm to the postwar fiction of Hemingway, Dos Passos, or Faulkner. George Ade was a great humorist, Ring Lardner was not. "The purpose of novel writing, as that crime is committed in the United States," he said, "is not to interpret life but to varnish, veil and perfume life—to make it a merry round of automobiling, country-clubbing, seduction, money-making and honeymooning, with music by Victor Herbert."

One does not prove a man no critic by this touchstone method in reverse. Mencken had standards. We are reminded that he introduced a whole generation to Hermann Sudermann, Maeterlinck, Sainte-Beuve, and, at one remove, Ibsen. He flaunted his standards: "I am by nature a vulgar fellow. I prefer *Tom Jones* to *The Rosary*, Rabelais to the Elsie books. . . . I delight in beef stews, limericks, and burlesque shows. When the mercury is above ninety-five I dine in my shirt sleeves and write poetry naked." He did not necessarily mean a compliment to Lizette Reese when he said that she wrote more genuine poetry than all the new poets put together, and he said something teasingly acute when he called Robert Frost a Whittier without whiskers. But his standards were not literary standards, nor were they moral in the sense that Lionel Trilling has used the term. They were derivative, stubbornly partisan, and more than often wrong. He struck about him with demonic glee, as enraptured as we by the fresh vigor of his vocabulary, and how the heads did roll.

Whether he wrote it naked or not, Mencken had no patience with poetry, even his own, which was of the self-consciously humorous kind which approaches a subject seriously but then backs off with an embarrassed quip at what it was about to say. "Women, damaged men, and others who are ill at ease in the world of sound ideas," he said, "write poetry." It was a little un-American, unless written as Sandburg or Lindsay wrote it. He relegated the Nashville Fugitives to "the Fringes of Lovely Letters," because they "tried to detach themselves from the ordinary flow of American ideas and convert themselves into an intellectual artistocracy" —by which he meant an intellectual aristocracy other than his own. Eliot and Pound were fetal poets, perversely un-American. Exceptions were made for Poe and Whitman because they dared swim against the tide, but he found even Poe sometimes ridiculous, and sponsored an article on Whitman as a rhymer of not even the second class, but only a word-monger and general phony—a judgment to which he did not subscribe but which he was eager to present because, he explained, "I think we ought to get the professors sore. For years they said Whitman was a bum, now they say he's an angel. Let's keep them hopping and squirming."

If Mencken was neither an original thinker nor a critic, he was an excellent journalist, with an eye on circulation, and he became also a sociologist who amused himself with collecting material on the folkways of the United States. Not the least of these were idiosyncrasies of American speech, curious examples of which he had filed away for many years. When during the First World War he found it good sense to be quiet, he turned to his notes and put together the first edition of his giant study *The American Language* which pointed to "salient differences between the English of England and the English of America as practically written and spoken—differences in vocabulary, in syntax, in grammar."

The impact of the book was immediate and large. "Never," said the reviewers, "has the flourishing personality of H. L. Mencken been so happily exercised." His biographer tells us that "with one powerful stroke he hewed in half the umbilical cord which philologically bound the nation to England." There were protests, of course, that Mencken, an Anglophobe and no patriot, attempted to "split asunder the two great English-speaking peoples," but the book, conceived as an innocuous avocation during troubled times and described by its compiler as "a heavy indigestible piece of cottage cheese," sold amazingly well.

And it is probably this book, which has gone through four editions and to which two large supplements have been added, for which Mencken, even against his protest, will be remembered. "I have never been a scholar and have never pretended to be one," he scolded. "I am just a scout for scholars. I accumulated the material and tried to put it in readable form, so people could understand it, and dug out of it whatever human juices there were, and there were plenty, and my hope and idea was that the material I had accumulated would be used by actual philologists." It has been used, and with gratitude, even by philologists who dismiss it as "an elephantine newspaper story."

It is a catchall and it does sprawl, but here finally was a sedate and serious, even a humble, Mencken, different indeed from the man who during these same war years wrote a pert volume, *In Defense of Women*, which put forward the not incredible theory that wives are more competent than their husbands, who, beneath a noisy play at efficiency, are really nincompoops with shoddy souls: "A man's women folk, whatever their outward show of respect for his merit and authority, always regard him secretly as an ass, and with something akin to pity." But women should remain women, and stay out of trousers. How ridiculous they looked in uniform: "like a dumbbell run over by an express train. Below the neck by the bow and below the waist astern there are two masses that simply refuse to fit into a balanced composition."

We are tempted to believe that behind Mencken's bellicose exterior lurked a gentler soul, easily shocked. The postwar freedom of America, especially of American women, saddened him. The most virtuous of lady novelists wrote things which would make a bartender blush: "When I began reviewing," he said, "I used to send my review copies, after I had sweated through them, to the Y.M.C.A. Now I send them to the medical college." Nightclubs saddened him also. They were filled with "middle-aged couples bumping and grunting over the dance floor like dying hogs in a miasmic pen." He detested the radio, Hollywood, and literary cocktail parties. Yet he found himself and enjoyed himself as spokesman for just the people who created and patronized these things. He ridiculed scoutmasters and clergymen as delayed adolescents, their brains so flooded with poisons of piety that there was no room for thinking. But Mencken was really the most adolescent of them all. It was wonderful sport, he thought, to steal Gideon Bibles from hotels and send them to his friends inscribed as from the author. When a neighbor complained that Mencken's woodpile was unsightly, Mencken soberly painted it in gaudy colors. Nothing was more fun than to borrow a friend's distinctively styled automobile and park it conspicuously in front of some notorious bordello.

How then is it possible to take a man of this kind seriously? Yet we did, and we do. His principal vocation was supplying sharp new teeth to old saws, like the one which describes love as the illusion that one woman differs from another. His technique was of shock and surprise. His protest was for protest's sake, and he could not resist a quip even when directed against something which he had formerly defended, when the words sounded better that way. It has been said in his defense that he spoke always in a state of frenzy, and that the "frenzy was generally the frenzy of love, love of America and of its history and traditions, people and customs, heroes and rogues, saints and sinners and clowns . . . glories and aberrations, and dreams and hopes and regrets and miseries and—all that is America."

He loved life, that is to say, and had an avid appetite for it. He wished, he said, that he might attain the "worldly wisdom of a police lieutenant, a bartender, a shyster lawyer, and a midwife." And this he may be supposed to have done— he policed his constituents with ruthless power; he intoxicated with attractive strong words; as shyster, he befuddled us with half-truths; and sometimes he presided over the birth of an idea, not the less precious because he had not fathered it but only held it by its heels and slapped it hard so that other men could hear its voice.

Love of life and love of ideas are admirable things, and love which reacts in angry protest against unnecessary deficiencies in life as it is lived in one's country is admirable also. But to say that Mencken served a purpose is not to say that he was a great or admirable man. He has been compared, with what justice I do not know, with Malcolm Muggeridge. He has been compared also with Juvenal, Dryden, Swift, Voltaire, Ambrose Bierce, and Philip Wylie, but the favorite comparison among his admirers today is with Dr. Johnson. His biographer invites us to consider the obvious parallels:

They were both periodical essayists, both popular critics. Each became famous as a literary dictator, though neither was in fact any such thing. Both were lexicographers who worked under immense handicaps, yet neither of them had more than scant regard for his lexicography. Each professed Toryism loudly yet preferred the residue of humanity to its froth. . . . They were boyhood prodigies who all their lives looked back upon their schooldays as the happiest of their lives. Each was the eldest son of a tradesman who impressed him into the family business against his will. Each received a limited formal education, educated himself irregularly, and had small regard for the lecture platform. . . . Each believed mankind happier in a state of subordination and endeavored to put all men who entered his company in that situation. Each was a lover of good food and drink, of earnest conversation with men and playful banter with women, and neither could talk unless he could dominate the conversation. Neither believed that there were two sides to any question; both served as parlor conservatives in periods when the left was advancing; each could be outrageously sophistic; each could be terribly wrong. Both admired the city extravagantly and despised the provinces. For Johnson it was Scotland; for Mencken the plains of "sunbaked, unwashed Kansas." Johnson, an Englishman, hated America; Mencken, an American, hated England. They were gargantuans both, wits both, neurotics both—the one a feeler of lamp-posts; the other an inveterate scrubber of hands. . . . Each was hard on incompetence, stern with cant, brutal with dishonesty.[1]

The capacity of each for work and anger seems to have been unlimited, and each mirrored some of the virtues and many of the shortcomings of his age. If such a comparison

[1] William Manchester, "H. L. Mencken at Seventy-five: America's Sam Johnson," *Saturday Review*, XXXVII (September 10, 1955), 11.

as I have quoted in outline seems meretricious, perhaps that
speaks also of shortcomings which we who admired him
have inherited. In Mencken, these included lack of candor,
limitation of intellectual equipment or, at best, its misuse, and
an inability to respond to the aspiring spirit of man with
anything more than embarrassment which retreats to derision.
Victimized by journalism, which Henry James once described
as "so pervasive, so ubiquitous, so unprecedentedly prosperous,
so wonderful for outward agility, but so unfavorable, even so
fatal, to development from within," Mencken made shoddy
use of his talent for language. He was not as wise, nor was he
as perverse, as Ezra Pound. He had some of the traits but
few of the submissive virtues of Henry Thoreau. It is not his
vulgarity that we resent, his writing in shirt-sleeves or his
great belly laughs—we are used to those. We admire something much like them in Mark Twain and Walt Whitman,
whom Mencken admired also.

It comes, then, with something of a shock that no better
words are found for summing up this restrospective view
of Mencken than those which Henry James used almost a
hundred years ago in talking about Walt Whitman. "We
look in vain . . . for a single idea. We find nothing but
flashy imitations of ideas." Things which we have learned to
look upon as faulty because man is faulty, but which are
human and therefore good, are "sneered at on every page,
and nothing positive given us in their place." We still admire
the sparks which Mencken gave off and wish some of them
had quickened to fire. There was grit in him and resonance.
He could have been a good reflector, making magic with
words like Whitman and Pound, and that might have been
enough. What destroyed him was pretension. "To be positive," Henry James continues, "one must have something to
say; to be positive requires reason, labor and art; and art
requires, above all things, a suppression of one's self, a subordination of one's self to an idea."

This Mencken could not do. That is one of the reasons why, as he pointed like an irascible schoolmaster to the iniquitous shortcomings of the "ordinary, dreary, sweating, struggling people," and the mountebanks, sharpers, and coney-catchers of his generation, there was something distinctively American about H. L. Mencken. Not in his ideas, which were from the ragbag of European thought, but in his use of them as sticking plasters to mend the mind and manners of men. As a moralist, he was an opportunist, striking at the manifestation rather than at the root, at the form rather than the substance. He led us, we can say, toward the brink with no sure knowledge of what lay beyond. Like Sinclair Lewis and Scott Fitzgerald, whom he admired or disliked for the wrong reasons, he was finally as much a symptom as a corrective of the maladies he would mend. We stomped and we snorted to the rhythms which he beat, so busily engaged that we had no time to notice that the mirror he held up to his time was so steamed over by the force of his breath upon it that it concealed as much as it reflected.

Perhaps we are wrong to expect more than titillation from those who inspire us toward rebellion: they the drummers, we to march beyond. Mencken was an expert pitchman, a crowd-pleaser, insistently prodding. But he was a journeyman content with patchwork repairs. He never dived deeply like Melville; he had not the quirky consistency of a Thoreau or an Ezra Pound, nor the deep abiding insights of an Emerson or a Santayana who dared tentativeness and profundity. He recognized the idiosyncrasies but not the abiding spirit of man, and so he failed us, as Mark Twain finally did, by representing us too well.

But when we are tired, daring no further flight, Mencken sometimes reassures us still. One of the last things that he wrote before he was incapacitated by illness was a credo which said in part: "Today no decent value in all the scale of human values is safe, and neither is any decent man," yet "intelligence is at work all the while, though from time to time it must go underground. Let us hope that it will emerge more anon, and pull the reluctant human race along another peg." In this hope, even today, we join him.

12

※

William Faulkner
and the Grace of Comedy

MOST PEOPLE WHO care about literature agree that William Faulkner has taken a place beside Nathaniel Hawthorne, Herman Melville, and Henry James as one of the rare artists in fiction produced in the United States. Yet, perhaps more than any of these others, he has become also an international novelist, admired, honored, and imitated in many lands. His reputation, large in his own country, grows even larger abroad, where his books are found in translation in most of the major literary centers of the world. Throughout much of Europe, especially in France, he has been named among the first of novelists, with Dostoevski, Tolstoi, Proust, or Sartre, nor is he less admired in Tokyo or New Delhi, Cairo or Rio de Janeiro, where readers have long responded to his way of regarding people and his way of using words which seem extraordinarily his own, yet catch and hold the imagination of readers everywhere.

Faulkner's reputation outside the United States is different from that of many other native writers who have become popular abroad. He is not read, as Theodore Dreiser or Sinclair Lewis, for examples, are read, because he reveals or satirizes the faults of his countrymen; nor is his appeal that of Ernest Hemingway, whose brittle, brilliant, but restricted style, and whose stoic passivity, are much admired. Many readers abroad do not think of Faulkner as a foreign writer at all—he certainly does not seem to them simply an American who reveals shortcomings of life in the United States or who uncovers idiosyncrasies of native provincial character. Faulkner strikes them rather as a world-embracing writer, because he speaks to them of the plight of man everywhere, with compassion and outrage, even with insinuations of tragedy in an old and understandable sense of that word, but conditioned by his humanity to an indomitable, comic, and sorrowful quest toward values necessary for survival.

Blinded by what they must be, the people whom Faulkner presents in his fiction do not always discover these values, and the mistakes they make as they search for them are often hideously grotesque. They stumble toward death, as Joe Christmas does, or toward success, like Flem Snopes, or toward brief, almost illusionary understanding, like Ike McCaslin, never without the uncomfortable necessity of overcoming difficulties which they or other men place in their way, and seldom without the heretical and never quite plausible belief that each man may somehow work his way toward happiness or security or salvation. Theirs is not in the strictest sense a tragic plight, for though each is pitted against natural forces, implacable but inherently beneficent, his principal antagonist is himself and what his obedience to the demands of other men has made him. As much as Emerson's, Faulkner's age, he might have said, is retrospective, dwelling within sepulchers of its fathers, giving lip service to creeds which stultify and misdirect.

1

For all his universality, Faulkner can be discovered to have been shaped by several native traditions, so that he appeared among us, not as a new man entirely, but as a talented successor to others. His allegiance to the spirit of Nathaniel Hawthorne, for one, rests on more than the circumstance that each man was, almost apologetically, descended from a family once prominently a part of the history of its region; that each on becoming a writer changed the spelling of his name—Falkner to Faulkner, Hathorne to Hawthorne; that each tacitly encouraged other people to think of him as an isolated man, removed from conversation with other writers; or that Faulkner titled his first book *The Marble Faun*. Each may be remembered as a romancer, less interested in the rational and realistic than in the nebulous and inexpressible reachings of the human heart, so that his characters expand into psychological archetypes, more recognizable for what they suggest of people everywhere than as exactly defined individuals.

Faulkner spoke much as Hawthorne might have spoken when he told a class of young writers at the University of Virginia that "it's the heart that has the desire to be better than man is; the up here can know the distinction between good and evil, but it's the heart that makes you want to be better than you are. That's what I mean by to write from the heart. That it's the heart that makes you want to be brave when you are afraid you might be a coward, that wants you to be generous, or wants you to be compassionate when you think that maybe you won't. I think that the intellect, it might say, 'Well, which is the more profitable—shall I be compassionate or shall I be uncompassionate? Which is most profitable? Which is most profitable—shall I be brave or not?' But the heart wants to be better than man is."

Right or wrong, and anti-intellectual as they may be, statements such as that are familiar to any reader of older American writings. They underline and rephrase distinctions on which Emerson insisted, between Understanding, which is man-devised and very likely to be wrong, and Reason, which is intuitive and which can be divine. They explain again what

Melville had Plotinus Plinlimmon explain in *Pierre* about differences between chronometrical and horological time— the one, man-made and useful, but incorrect; the other, eternal, often inconvenient, but everlastingly true. They say again, with less economy of words, almost exactly what Hawthorne often said about the superiority of heart over head, or what Whittier said, or even Longfellow when he had anything to say. They represent an adaptation and extension of what Coleridge said in England, and Goethe in Germany, about man's allegiance beyond all knowledge to what he recognizes without thought as good. They have been found to echo Jonathan Edwards' earlier certainty that people are better when they place love, which is intuitive understanding, and compassion and admiration of those things which are by divine right true, above the presumptions of creeds invented by man.

And they are far older than that, reflecting Biblical injunction and a humanistic tradition seldom without advocates in Europe or the East, but which became in the United States in the nineteenth century a view of knowledge and a way of thinking about facts that lie beneath appearances, which has given to much American writing since certain identifiable characteristics. Most of us agree that Richard Chase was correct in saying that the tradition of fiction among us is the tradition of romance, and that Northrop Frye is correct in explaining that the romance "radiates a glow of subjective intensity that the novel lacks," so that "a suggestion of allegory is constantly creeping about its fringes." We have become accustomed to agreement with D. H. Lawrence, who many years ago instructed us that fiction in the United States is characterized by an unwillingness to take off its clothes in order to show what is underneath, with the result that many American writers often seem to mean something quite different from what they say.

We are likely to call such writers symbolists, though perhaps they might be more truly designated as allegorists manqué, and to present Faulkner as chief among them. Like the Melville whom Lawrance Thompson once disclosed as having so intense a "quarrel with God" that he dared not express it directly, like the Hawthorne whose *The Scarlet Letter* has been interpreted in a dozen ways, like the Henry James whom Quentin Anderson has discovered to be a devious deviser of parables, or like Katherine Anne Porter who delights with indirection, Faulkner also suggests more than he ever says. He once described himself as a "failed poet," forced against his will to prose, much as Emerson once spoke of himself as a poet maimed. Robert Penn Warren, also a poet, first reminded us, I think, that if we read Faulkner as if he were a poet, many difficulties would disappear.

For, more than most writers of his time, Faulkner tempts readers toward discovering something like allegorical meanings in his fiction. But one suggestion of allegory tumbles so fast after another which seems to hint at something quite different from the first that even many of his most devoted readers have difficulty in determining what Faulkner in that sense really intends. If he says this, they are likely to ask, how can he say that? The truth may be that Faulkner intends few of the meanings ascribed to him. In social matters he seems the least programmatic of writers, and that has been supposed to be one of the reasons why in the 1930's he was unpraised by many contemporary critics, most of whom during that decade were sure that an important responsibility of literature was to help people recognize improvements in the way they might assist one another. Hardly anything that Faulkner has written seems to inspire reform in a social sense. It is even unlikely that many people have been led to wanting to be better people as a result of reading him. To those who require of literature what it is not always capable of producing, this lack of what used to be called social consciousness has sometimes made Faulkner difficult to understand. How can a person have such fun or relate such horrors without serious civic purpose?

But to those who cherish literature as a pinwheel throwing off a profusion of sparks, Faulkner has provided luxurious opportunities for adventures in interpretation. Catching at one spark or another, enchanted by its single glowing brightness, readers have pursued Faulkner to gloomy or luminous areas where he may never have intended to be found. He has tempted with symbols which dart toward meaning and then fall short, to be replaced by other symbols, equally undefining, until the attentive reader's mind, teased from one intimation to another, becomes a kaleidoscope of impressions, as chaotic as the fables which Faulkner has set before him. Without attention, any reader can become lost in any Faulkner book.

He can become confused by Faulkner's manner of talking and the way he tells a story. First things do not always come first. Events do not progress in simple chronological order. Late in any narrative, the reader may discover something about a character which, if he had known it earlier, would have quite changed his former estimate of that character. Many of Faulkner's sentences seem interminably long, with one parenthetical aside dangling from another, and others dangling from that, until the weight of digression may seem to submerge what grammatically the sentence is about. Faulkner may frequently seem compulsively a talker, so fond of his flow of words that he forgets what he had set out to say. He may seem to become, as someone has said, hopelessly involved in his own technical virtuosity. He speaks so profusely that he does not always speak carefully.

Some have supposed that Faulkner insists on experimenting with new ways of saying things because old ways have been so smudged by use that they no longer reflect what is meant to be said. Others have supposed him to be an incorrigible tease who plays games with his readers and sets traps for them. Time is often snapped quite out of joint, so that it becomes difficult to determine, not only when a thing happens, but whether it really has happened at all or is only a hallucination in the mind of some character. Nor is it always possible to understand what his characters are up to. They are treated, it has been said, "in such a way that while their motives are apparently crystal to each other, the reader has to work like the very devil to find out why they do what they do." Most of them seem motivated, observes Wilbur Frohock, "by obsessive neuroses, and tortured by anxieties which the reader does not share and which lead to actions which take place outside the normal order of events at abnormal speed."

But in spite of these difficulties, and perhaps in recognition of the universality of these obscure anxieties, thoughtful readers have responded to the challenge of Faulkner's writings. They have agreed with Robert Penn Warren that the evaluation of these writings presents "the most challenging single task in contemporary American literature for criticism to undertake," because "in mass of work, in scope of material, in range of effect, in reportorial accuracy and symbolic subtlety, in philosophical weight," Faulkner proves himself worthy of testing beside any master of the past.

Among the more popular early interpretations were those which found Faulkner an apologist for problems unique to the American South. The familiar lore or local gossip which he had heard recounted in kitchen or country store or beside the evening fire on hunting trips had been "elaborated, transformed, given compulsive life by his emotions," explained Malcolm Cowley, "until by the simple intensity of feeling, the figures in it became a little more than human, became heroic or diabolical, became symbols of the old South, of war and reconstruction, of commerce and machinery destroying the standards of the past." In doing this, Cowley continued, "Faulkner performed a labor of imagination that has not been equalled in our time, and a double labor: first, to invent a

Mississippi county that was like a mythical kingdom, but was complete and living in all its details; second, to make his story of Yoknapatawpha County stand as a parable or legend of the Deep South."

Others, recognizing Faulkner as a writer who speaks best of what he knows most intimately in scene and character, so that his stories are of course Southern and his people inhabitants of that legend-filled region, find him nonetheless in theme and situation quite transcending locality, to speak of kinds of people who might be found anywhere, and of motives and tensions which are shared by all. Yoknapatawpha County is often explained as a microcosm of the modern world, a Spenglerian nightmare filled with violence and greed, without an ethical center, and driving fast toward disaster. It is seen as a cheap, tawdry, and soulless world, a wasted land in which the Snopeses and their kind, little men of niggling morality, inspired by no standards except those set by ambition and self-admiration, scheme and cheat and fawn their way toward success. It has been called a weaseling world, dominated by hollow men who stamp on every human decency as they climb. But it is also a world in which love and honor and pity and pride and compassion and sacrifice—these are Faulkner's words—still quietly prevail as man's bulwarks against disaster.

"It took us a long time," says one of the characters in *The Wild Palms*, "but man is resourceful and limitless in inventing too, and so we have got rid of love at last just as we have got rid of Christ. We have the radio in place of God's voice, and instead of having to save emotional currency for months and years to deserve to spend it all for love we can now spread it out thin into coppers and titillate ourselves at any newsstand, two to a block like sticks of chewing gum or chocolate from the automatic machines. If Jesus returned today we would have to crucify him quick in our own defense, to justify and preserve the civilization we have worked and suffered and died shrieking and cursing in rage and impotence and terror for two thousand years to create and perfect in man's own image; if Venus returned she would be a soiled man in a subway with a palm full of French postcards."

It is not only of Mississippi, nor the American South, nor even the United States, of which Faulkner writes, though it is of these also; it is the whole of Western civilization which he sees in dreadful vision as "paying the price for having erected its economic edifice not on the rock of stern morality but on the shifting sands of opportunism and moral brigandage." So perhaps it is with the poets, with T. S. Eliot and Ezra Pound, Wallace Stevens and E. E. Cummings, that Faulkner is to be remembered, and in the climate of whose opinions he must be read. His iconoclastic vision of the world is filled, like theirs, with bitterly nostalgic reminders of what could have been, of what can be, and of what must be, if the world is not to torment itself to physical as well as moral destruction. When Faulkner is violent in action or rhetoric, he portrays a world in which violence seems to lead man toward what he most desires. But it never does, nor does despair.

2

Again, Faulkner is discovered to be within a familiar American literary tradition, which insists that particulars rightly seen become universals, so that any man is the microcosm of all men. In this view, which Emerson and Thoreau and many of their nineteenth-century compatriots inherited from and shared with other men in other lands, nature is recognized as symbol of spirit. When Faulkner has Doc Peabody in *As I Lay Dying* speak of "our land: opaque, slow, violent; shaping and creating the life of man in its implacable and brooding image," he is approaching an attitude similar to that of earlier Americans. Only when Ike McCaslin, after initiation and trial, gives himself wholly to nature by divesting himself of man-devised, distracting instruments—like watch and gun and compass—does he glimpse truth, which is all truth, and which he can experience but never explain.

Nature is more than a backdrop for the drama which Faulkner's fiction reveals. It looms, never completely personified, as an irrational, primal force, at once beautiful and ominous. "God created man," Ike McCaslin explains in "Delta Autumn," "and He created the world for him to live in and I reckon he created the kind of world He would have wanted to live in if He had been man—the ground to walk on, the big woods, the trees and water, and the game to live in it." Nature is lush, amoral, fecund, implacably competent, "with woods for game and streams for fish and deep rich soil for seed and lush springs to sprout it and long summers to mature it and serene falls to harvest it." But the land also contains people who make it a "doomed wilderness . . . constantly and punily gnawed at by men with plows and axes." Bright meadows become golf courses, cities encourage corruption.

For man disfigures nature—no conservationist could be more explicit on this than Faulkner. As the wilderness vanishes under macadam and steel, it becomes part of a native adaptation of the Christian myth of a vanished paradise which Fenimore Cooper recognized and struggled to explain. Hacked at and mutilated, nature continues to menace the ambitions of men. Eden is lost because man is man, impatient and ruthless, falsely ambitious, and without the wisdom to know his ordered place. Nature is despoiled, yet uncorrupted and timeless, she ultimately takes her revenge, as she does in *Moby Dick* and less violently in *Huckleberry Finn*. But once, long ago, so the fable familiarly begins, there had been a time when people lived in truer relationship with nature—until mortal sin brought death into the world, with all its woe.

That perhaps is every poet's theme—the relationship of man to forces which cripple or exalt him. As an American, Faulkner shared old certainties with earlier native writers about beauty and truth in essential unity, though he preferred to quote Keats's familiar formulation, which spoke of them more satisfyingly. He shared immensely with Thoreau in recognition of the awful loveliness of nature and its inscrutable demands. With Emerson and Henry James, he shared a brooding sense of history—how past infiltrates present until time becomes at once eternal and contemporary, so that man's contentment where he is depends on knowledge of where he has been. Apprehension of the past cannot be reached out for, nor can it be limited to that which is convenient or pleasant or prideful to recall. To passive and receptive people, like the boy in "The Bear" or Dilsey in *The Sound and the Fury*, it comes all at once as an informing vision which needs no explanation. To Hightower in *Light in August*, it is hallucination of which he must talk incessantly.

Recognition of Faulkner's attitude toward time is often thought to be central to an understanding of his work. But this central area is where Faulkner is usually least explicit. He cannot be said to have an articulated theory of history, only a brooding sense of the importance of the past. It impinges on the present, distorting or clarifying. As tradition or recorded fact, as legend or myth, it weaves a web in which all men are entangled. Sometimes beneficial, sometimes harmful, it relentlessly molds man's opinions and actions. If Faulkner is to be found to any degree a tragic writer, it is in his attitude toward man's absorption in the continuum of time.

"Faulkner's vision of the world," Jean-Paul Sartre has said, "can be compared to that of a man sitting in a convertible looking backward. At every moment shadows emerge on his right, and on his left flickering and quavering points of light, which become trees, men, and cars only when they are seen in perspective. The past here gains a surrealistic quality; its outline is hard, clear, and immutable. The indefinable and elusive present is helpless before it; it is full of holes through which past things, fixed, motionless, and silent, invade it." All that exists is a pattern, that web which the past has woven. A sense of present time can only be expressed in terms of the past, in concept and images which the past has provided. Thus Sartre speaks of the feeling of suspension in Faulkner's writing, as if man was poised now as the cumulation of a series of events which had all been in the past— poised momentarily, waiting for the past to thrust him, willy-nilly, into a future of which his imperfect knowledge of the past allows him no foreknowledge.

In thus presenting historical fictions which treat of the past as story, anecdote, fable, and myth, none completely told, but each shaping some part of the web which is the present, not flowing but intertwined, sometimes grotesquely, Faulkner draws on a remarkable and apparently uncontrolled flow of rhetoric. It is not unusual to find—as, for example, in some of those unforgettable interchapters in *Requiem for a Nun*—single sentences which speak all in one breath of historical or actual past, traditional or commonly accepted past, and legendary or mythic past, piling suggestions of meaning layer on layer, until the sentence seems to catch up and hold suspended the whole of time. Conrad Aiken has described Faulkner's style as fluid, slippery, and heavily mannered, over-elaborated and involuted, as if the writer, "in a sort of hurried despair, had decided to tell us everything, absolutely everything, every last origin or source of quality or qualification, and every future permutation as well, in one terrifically concentrated effort: each sentence to be, as it were, a microcosm."

The extravagance of William Faulkner, who fills sentences so abundantly, is related also to the extravagance of the American tall tale. It presents the view of an alert but ruminative countryman on whom events and memories impinge with such rapidity that he has no time to sort them to simplicity. He must talk, and endlessly talk, about what he knows and sees and remembers, because he is sure that if he stops talking to order them to system, other sights and memories will pass him by. Faulkner is the talkingest man in modern literature. He can talk simply and well, can tell an exciting story with casual directness, as he does in the slapstick tale of the spotted horses, or in recounting Senator Snopes's curious adventures in Memphis. He often sounds as if he were speaking from the depths of a great chair set before an open fire, with glass in hand and friends around him, all comfortable and a little sleepy, oblivious of time and the necessity for hurry. His voice drones on, lavishly and discursively, as he elaborates on familiar twice-told tales.

Faulkner's voice inevitably reminds us then of that native oral tradition which Mark Twain once spoke of as "a high and delicate art," in which the narrative flows "as flows the brook down through the hills and leafy woodlands, its course changed by every boulder it comes across and by every grass-clad gravelly spur that projects into its path, its surface broken but its course not stayed by rocks and gravel on the bottom in shoal places." Rambling and disjointed, these slowly voiced excursions do however have a destination, "a nub, point, snapper, or whatever you like to call it." To recognize this, "the listener must be alert," Mark Twain warns, "for in many cases the teller will divert attention from the nub by dropping it in a careful casual and indifferent way, with the pretence that he does not know it is a nub."

Faulkner's leisurely voice may not always seem attractive. It moves on in circles, slowly, obtusely, delaying expectations. Little is ever simplified for the convenience of fast reading. Time is made to stand still for page after page, while past time crowds up on it, disfiguring and obscuring as often as it clarifies. Faulkner requires of each reader a willingness to sit with him a long time, until from the mesmeric rhythms of his speaking something emerges of understanding of the complicated meshing of humor and pathos and misdirected good intentions which make up the substance of most men's lives.

He is an American writer certainly, in tone, in themes, in attitude. His native origins are certified by his insistence on the preeminence of the human spirit, even when that spirit is crippled or deformed; by his attitude toward nature as a balm, a corrective, and a kaleidoscope of elusive symbols; by his sense of the past; by his sophisticated development of native lore and his drawling, laconic or tensely excited, manner of telling a story. He is in the line of frontier humorists, as extravagant as Sut Lovingood or Mark Twain, as "extra-vagant" as Thoreau. No section other than the American South could have produced him.

3

Yet in none of his characteristics is Faulkner more native than in his refusal to be limited by section or nationality. From the first raising of voices in the wilderness of the Western world, Americans have insisted on their right to speak for all men. Their experience was not exclusive, but provided a mirror in which all mankind might see its own. One man's sin became humanity's burden, and one man's glory a beacon for all. When they sang to celebrate themselves, they welcomed universal recognition that what belonged to them or was discovered by them, belonged as well to others. America opened its arms wide to strangers, and then often did not treat them well. The way they acted and their reasons for it were determined by local situations and contemporary events, complicated by each man's inevitable entanglement with what his people had been. As a result, they sometimes had some explaining to do.

But to read Faulkner as a social or political or explanatory novelist in a regional or sectional sense is to read him incompletely. As a man of his time, living where he did, he had opinions and attitudes, with some of which not all of his contemporaries could agree. His characters more than once speak with disrespect or lack of understanding about other characters who differ from them in race or religion or education or social class. It may even be true that Faulkner is condescending toward Negroes, just as he is condescending toward women and bankers and lawyers. If the faithful family retainer, Dilsey, is a stereotype, so also is Jason Compson or Colonel Sartoris. Joe Christmas' problem, that he could not determine who he was, quite transcends the terms of black and white in which Faulkner presented it. The swarming, grasping people of Yoknapatawpha County, whether morally deteriorated or spiritually uplifted, are real people, in a real locality, in the United States, because Faulkner has placed them there; but they are other people also, who live or have lived anywhere in a world disrupted. These things never happened and these people never lived, except as Faulkner created them.

"As one reads about them," says Steven Marcus, "one gets a renewed sense of how one of the primal powers of literature is to raise mythology to the level of history, to treat the material of the imagination as if it were indistinguishable from the actuality it invades and transcribes."

Faulkner is the only contemporary American writer who has a facility for this; perhaps he is the only modern writer who has it at all. The stories he wrote over twenty-five years have become part of the given; he takes a past which he has created himself and deals with it as recorded reality. It is "out there," independent of his ministrations, waiting for him to record and recreate rather than invent. And as the degree of Faulkner's conviction about the historicity of his imagination seems positive, so, too, does the degree to which he seems able to represent concretely the deterioration in American life of those institutions and values which allow for the cultivation of the imagination and the spirit.

It is not necessary to stop there, nor have Faulkner's readers over the world so limited their interpretation of Faulkner's vision. By an incredibly complex series of creative acts Faulkner has transformed the particular to the universal, so wrenching geography from moorings that Yoknapatawpha County becomes the place where any reader lives; and Joe Christmas and Dilsey and Jason Compson and Flem Snopes become, not distorted representations of people who are known and disliked or admired, but recognizable fragments of every reader's opportunity or doom.

This transformation has little to do with what Faulkner intended or with the burdens which critics have placed upon him. Perhaps because he has until recently been actively with us, his own statements so greatly a part of our estimation, Faulkner has not yet been seen in his complex entirety by any single commentator. Olga Vickery may come closest, for she puts aside more successfully than most the temptation to make Faulkner an apologist for some favorite view. For Faulkner does tease readers to find meanings of their own in what he has written, to the point where Irving Howe, in intelligent exasperation, has accused him of "failure of intellect" because he failed to supply a "high order of comment and observation *within* the structure of his work," and because of his inability "to handle general ideas with a dramatic cogency equal to his ability to render images or conduct."

Others, however, suppose that Faulkner's success derives precisely from his refusal to give allegiance to any but the simplest of meanings. To them, his writing, at its best, presents a series of dialogues in which this view is presented, then that, and then another, leaving resolution to each reader. People who hold this view do not say there is no center in Faulkner, only that there is no ideological center. No more than most of his literary contemporaries, or his American literary antecedents, was Faulkner, they would say, a thoughtful, idea-expanding man. He flew, as old-time aviators used to express it, by the seat of his pants, observant, resourceful, quick at maneuvering, skilled at balance, looping or diving just for the sport of it, or to thrill spectators, but never quite able to explain his movements on charts, although he did know, in a general way, and with confidence no charts could challenge, what he was about and where he was going. If other people did not care to follow, so much the less fun for them.

Most commentators pull Faulkner up short by dividing his career into three, sometimes four, carefully charted segments: the first, a period of trial and error, when as a young man he learned his trade; the second and most significant, beginning in 1929 and extending into the later 1930's, when Faulkner in his thirties did not quite know what he was about, but produced in quick succession *Sartoris, The Sound and the Fury, Sanctuary, As I Lay Dying, Light in August, Pylon,* and *Absalom, Absalom!*; the third, beginning in 1938 with *The Unvanquished* (some would begin this period with *The Hamlet* in 1940, and slip in a brief catchall period between), when for the rest of his life Faulkner, as if disappointed that his earlier books had been misunderstood, attempted through patient and simplified restatement, especially in "The Bear" and *The Fable,* and in iterative public comments at Stockholm, Nagano, and Charlottesville, to put forward an explanation of what all the time he had intended. However convenient such a division may be, it can be thought of as representing exactly the kind of orderly commentary which Faulkner particularly distrusted. He never really admitted what he was up to.

But he never had to, for critics from the first have been eager to provide that service to Faulkner which D. H. Lawrence once explained that every critic owed to each author—to rescue the author from himself, by explaining to him what he must have meant. At first, Faulkner was explained as a salesman of vice, a deliberate and scandalous exploiter of sensational, often erotic, devices, whose perverts, degenerates, and introverts identified him as one of those writers who "set themselves up in a literary business, with unmitigated cruelties and abnormalities as their stock in trade," a forerunner of Mickey Spillane in the novel of violence, a deftly elusive John O'Hara. His apocalyptic vision—in Faulkner's case the paradise lost in the American South—placed him beside Brockden Brown and Poe and, as if in afterthought, Melville. People like Clifton Fadiman spoke of his antinarrative techniques, as if Faulkner, like a perverse child, had gone to work with a pair of scissors to cut a good yarn to shreds. Sociological writers, Marxist or worse, found him a master of aristocratic mores, with the Southern gentleman's no longer elegantly concealed hatred of all women and all Negroes. He became a man of perverse, exasperating suggestiveness, who "crowds symbols in" until "There is a hidden meaning / In every glass of gin."

At other extremes, he has become known as a kind of redeemer, who borrows religious imagery and symbolic suggestions of the continuing efficacy of the Christian mythos, set forth through phrases reminiscent of the Sermon on the Mount, to suggest that man may become better than he has been. Sometimes salvation is explained as willingness humbly to submit one's self as an innocent companion to other creatures who inhabit and do not mutilate the good land which has been given as gift to all. Again, with compulsive modernity, Faulkner's gift to a reader's enthusiasm for the explicit is explained, most recently by Cleanth Brooks, as a subtle reinforcement of an American yearning toward community. We are all in this together. Let us then take hands and have compassion one for another.

All of these things may be in Faulkner, and more besides, but a statement of them does not exhaust his curious multiplicity. "I wish I could have managed him," Ernest Hemingway is once said to have said, thinking of Faulkner as if he were a prize fighter who could be taught feints and jabs and delicately controlled footwork. Faulkner was a wild swinger who missed many marks, and sometimes, it has been supposed, fell flat on his face. He admired, or pretended to admire, the even wilder swinging of Thomas Wolfe, because Wolfe dared to put all of himself into everything he ever wrote, in a tremendous effort, said Faulkner, "to put all of the history of the human heart on the head of a pin." When Faulkner's characters are careful contrivers, proud of the effectiveness of their footwork, they become wealthy, like Flem Snopes, but impotent.

Searching for meaning in Faulkner's writing probably results in each searcher's finding meaning in himself, and that is usually a good thing, if it is not taken too seriously. For meanings slither and swerve and turn about on themselves, especially when suggested by so thoughtless but so thought-provoking a writer as Faulkner. If he does often seem uncertain of ideas, he is observant and insightful and honest, fundamentally simple. The simplicity is not of surface, because the surface which Faulkner presents is an uncertain surface, roughened by people who act strangely, compulsively, and self-consciously, or with so much lack of self-consciousness that they fail in humanity, restrained by being what they have to be from becoming what they could.

His fools and knaves and retrospective people, his tin men (like Popeye), his hollow men (like Jason Compson), his scarecrows (like Horace Benbow—headpiece stuffed with straw, alas!); his popinjays, his sacrificial Lee Goodwin and his self-righteously avenging Percy Grimm, his virtuous and self-congratulatory virgins and his lush, fecund female destroyers who consume as they create; his proud Snopeses and his humble Snopeses, his idiots and lawyers, sewing-machine salesmen, farmers, and woodsmen—Melville might have noticed that there is not a poet among them—are all caught and held, not in logical association one to another, but in a net of language which reaches out, with many a breathtaking swerving, finally to bind them in a series of relationships greatly more human than tragic.

4

To understand living, Faulkner may seem to say, one must live. Only then, when errors have been made, can experience be examined to discover, perhaps too late, what life intended. The words in which other men have wrapped creed or tradition can be misleading: "words go straight up in a thin line, quick and harmless," Faulkner has one character explain, so that "sin and love and fear are just sounds that people who never sinned nor loved nor feared have for what they never had and cannot have until they forget the words." Hot-blooded, rash, ambitious man rushes through time, pursued or pursuing, with his mouth open wide, shouting explanations for what he must do: to "people to whom sin is just a matter of words, to them salvation is just words too." Even the best of words are caught and marred by time: when most explicit, they are likely to be most wrong. They have been used as spurious counters, as counterfeits of spirit.

Yet Faulkner's large achievement as an artist has been in the manipulation of words. Weaving them to massively intricate patterns in which one element counterbalances another, so that meaning in any usual sense becomes confused, he evoked suggestions of meanings which no words express. Any attempt to explain him, explains him only in part; for what Faulkner wrote is not meant to be explained, only experienced. Each tale is complete, yet each comments on every other, until the whole becomes an intricate reflection of men and women entangled in living. Whether with conscious aesthetic purpose or as a brooding, questioning, haphazard recorder of what he has seen and heard, Faulkner thus has created a montage of people stumbling and constantly talking, a world disordered within which most readers inevitably discover themselves.

By some it is cherished as a tragic world, meaningless and

damned, and Faulkner more than once, perhaps teasingly, seems to encourage this view, even to giving dark characters such tragedy-suggesting names as Clytemnestra or Christmas. Sad things happen in many of the tales, and people die, sometimes violently and unnecessarily, as people do. Yet, unless living itself is tragic because it must end without fulfillment of all it has desired, Faulkner's view may be recognized as comic, as he speaks with affectionate compassion of people who are human enough to make their own mistakes. Tragedy, he may seem to say, is devised by man as a simple explanation —such as Quentin Compson devises in *Absalom, Absalom!*— of why he does not do better than he does. It is neither necessary nor final, only an expedient, comforting because it eases a burden. The comic view, more difficult to sustain, requires recognition of the "old verities and truths of the heart, the old universal truths lacking which any story is ephemeral or doomed"—the love and honor and pity and pride and compassion and sacrifice which guarantee that "man will not merely endure, he will prevail."

Unlike many of his contemporaries, Faulkner seems to have withstood the dour Central European invasion of Western culture by men like Conrad and the Russian novelists, to hold fast to an older, perhaps ultimately more realistic, and not at all simple, but optimistic, view of man. In this also he reveals the influence of native predecessors who gave allegiance to attitudes borrowed from abroad, which Faulkner now returns in generous measure.

Southern Excursions is a rich collection of essays by a distinguished literary critic whose writings are widely read both here and abroad. While the primary focus of the book is on Mark Twain, a transplanted southerner, it ranges from Sidney Lanier and Kate Chopin, whose work most reflects what Leary calls "the spirit of the South," to H. L. Mencken, who growled at what he considered the excesses of that spirit. The volume also includes essays on William Faulkner, George Washington Harris, and Lafcadio Hearn.

In an analysis of Mark Twain and the comic spirit, Professor Leary discusses the literary achievement of the perceptive humorist who saw "beyond locality to qualities which men universally, sometimes shamefully, share." In other essays Leary examines the critical opinion of Samuel Clemens and his creation Mark Twain; Clemens' financial and moral bankruptcy; the degree to which he was a "wounded man"; and *The Adventures of Tom Sawyer* as a fable of "innocence on trial."